The Canadian Defence Industry
in the New Global Environment

The defence industry in Canada is facing serious challenges. Declining defence expenditures, protectionism in Canada's principal markets, political resistance, and escalating costs of weapons technology all threaten it. *The Canadian Defence Industry in the New Global Environment* is a thorough examination and assessment of the problems and prospects of the industry given the recent dramatic changes that have transformed the international security environment.

Alistair Edgar and David Haglund examine changes in the international demand for defence products in the post–Cold War era, review the reorganization and rationalization of the supply side of the international defence market through various government policy initiatives and corporate strategies, and discuss the ways in which the Canadian government and defence producers have attempted to cope with this new and uncertain international environment. They also explore the international and domestic contexts – military, economic, and political – within which defence industries operate.

Edgar and Haglund's analysis draws on extensive interviews with political and industry leaders, military personnel, and government officials from Canada, the United States, the United Kingdom, France, Belgium, the Netherlands, Norway, Denmark, Spain, and Germany. This timely study of the domestic, American, and other NATO defence markets will interest scholars and students of Canadian defence policy, Canadian foreign policy, and Canadian external relations, and public servants, politicians, and personnel in the industry.

ALISTAIR D. EDGAR is assistant professor of political science, Wilfrid Laurier University.
DAVID G. HAGLUND is director of the Centre for International Relations and head of the Department of Political Studies, Queen's University.

The Canadian Defence Industry in the New Global Environment

ALISTAIR D. EDGAR

and

DAVID G. HAGLUND

McGill-Queen's University Press
Montreal & Kingston • London • Buffalo

© McGill-Queen's University Press 1995
ISBN 0-7735-1272-1 (cloth)
ISBN 0-7735-1273-X (paper)

Legal deposit second quarter 1995
Bibliothèque nationale du Québec

Printed in Canada on acid-free paper

This book has been published
with the help of a grant from the
Social Science Federation of Canada,
using funds provided by the
Social Sciences and Humanities
Research Council of Canada.

McGill-Queen's University Press is grateful to the
Canada Council for support of its publishing program.

Canadian Cataloguing in Publication Data

Edgar, Alistair D., 1962–
    The Canadian defence industry in the new global
    environment
    Includes bibliographical references and index.
    ISBN 0-7735-1272-1 (bound) –
    ISBN 0-7735-1273-X (pbk.)
    1. Defence industries – Canada. I. Haglund, David G.
    II. Title.
    HD9743.C22E33 1995 338.4′76233′0971 C95-900177-8

Typeset in New Baskerville 10/12
by Caractéra production graphique, Quebec City

Contents

Tables

Acronyms

ACE	Allied Command Europe
ACV	armoured combat vehicle
ADATS	air defence/anti-tank system
ASW	anti-submarine warfare
CAPS	Conventional Armaments Planning System
CDI	Conventional Defence Improvements Initiative
CFE	Conventional Forces in Europe Treaty
CIS	Commonwealth of Independent States
CNAD	Conference of National Armaments Directors
CPF	Canadian Patrol Frigate
CSCE	Conference on Security and Cooperation in Europe
DARPA	Defence Advanced Research Projects Agency
DDI	developing defence industrial (countries)
DDSA	Defence Development Sharing Arrangements
DEAIT	Department of External Affairs and International Trade (now DFAIT)
DFAIT	Department of Foreign Affairs and International Trade
DGS	Department of Government Services
DIB	defence industrial base
DIPP	Defence Industry Productivity Program
DND	Department of National Defence (Canada)
DoD	Department of Defense (U.S.)
DPSA	Defence Production Sharing Arrangements
DSP	Defence Services Program

EAITC	External Affairs and International Trade Canada
EC	European Community (now European Union, or EU)
EC92	EC 1992 program
ECSC	European Coal and Steel Community
EDEM	European Defence Equipment Market
EEC	European Economic Community
EFA	European Fighter Aircraft
EIG	economic interest group
ESDI	European security and defence identity
ESPRIT	European Strategic Program for Research in Information Technology
EU	European Union
EUCLID	European Cooperative Long-term Initiative in Defence
EURATOM	European Atomic Energy Community
EUREKA	European Research Coordination Agency
FF	French francs
FSX	Fighter Support Experimental
FTA	Canada–U.S. Free Trade Agreement
FY	fiscal year
GATT	General Agreement on Tariffs and Trade
GDP	gross domestic product
IEPG	Independent European Program Group (now WEAG)
IJDP	international joint development project
INF	Intermediate-range Nuclear Forces agreement
IRB	industrial and regional benefit
IRI	Istituto per la Ricostruzione Industriale
ISTC	Industry, Science and Technology Canada (now Industry Canada and Science Canada)
LAV	light armoured vehicle
LLAD	low-level air defence
LRPA	long-range patrol aircraft
LSVW	light support vehicle, wheeled
MBT	main battle tank
MCP	major crown project
NADIBO	North American Defence Industrial Base Organization
NAFTA	North American Free Trade Agreement
NATO	North Atlantic Treaty Organization

NSA	new shipborne aircraft
OTA	Office of Technology Assessment (U.S.)
PAD	Preliminary Analysis Document
PAPS	Phased Armaments Programming System
POM	personnel, operations, and maintenance
R&D	research and development
RDP	research, development, and production (agreement)
SEA	Single European Act
SIPRI	Stockholm International Peace Research Institute
TRUMP	Tribal-class update and modernization program
U.N.	United Nations
UTTH	utility tactical transport helicopter
WEAG	West European Armaments Group
WEU	Western European Union

Preface

The furor triggered by the federal budget of February 1994 demonstrated once again that defence spending can stir passions in Canada. This has to do, in part, with the lingering suspicion held by many Canadians that there is something inherently dubious about military expenditures in a country that, in their eyes, has no interests that could effectively and ethically be safeguarded by the use of force. It also has to do with a long-standing tendency, in certain regions and certain segments of society, to regard defence spending as one more form of transfer payment to which they are entitled – and which can only be withdrawn at some pain, as shown by the recent controversy over the decision to close the Collège militaire royal de Saint-Jean. And finally it has to do with the sheer size of the defence budget: although the Department of National Defence is by no means the money pit that its harshest critics imagine it to be, in 1993–94 it still ranks as a relatively well-funded arm of the federal government, with $12 billion of authorized expenditure, or slightly more than 7 percent of total federal disbursements for the year. But while defence expenditures may represent only a small percentage of overall federal spending and an even less conspicuous (less than 2 percent) share of gross domestic product, they do account for a significant share (36 percent) of "discretionary" federal spending in 1993–94 – that is, of spending that is tied neither to debt servicing nor to transfer payments to individuals.

Yet despite, or perhaps because of, all the attention focused on defence spending in Canada, there has been surprisingly little public discussion of that sector of the economy known as the "defence industrial base" – the subject of this book. Apart from a few vested interests – on the one hand, defence producers and preparedness advocates; on the other, disarmament groups – few seem to know much about how and from whom Canada procures its military hardware in an environment marked by declining defence budgets, ever more diffuse threats, and increasingly fierce competition for what little defence business remains.

Our purpose here is to shed some light on these issues in the context of what is likely to be a period of great uncertainty for the Canadian defence industry. One of the most striking characteristics of the defence industrial base in Canada since at least the early 1960s has been its dependence on exports. Not only does this dependence affect the general economic well-being of much of the industry (shipbuilding and repair being exceptions), but it is essential to its basic economic viability. Export dependence has been long recognized as a necessity in order to foster a reasonably broad-based and advanced defence manufacturing capability. Moreover, for some years government defence procurement policies have been used in the pursuit of non-defence objectives, such as regional development and technology transfer.[1]

A necessary consequence of this level of export dependence is that the medium- to long-term prospects of much of the Canadian defence industrial base are strongly influenced – and even determined, at times – by the impact of changes in the international demand and supply for defence equipment and not just by decisions made by the federal government or in corporate head offices elsewhere in the country. Canadian government officials and industry executives must therefore consider carefully legislative initiatives and other policy issues that are discussed in Washington, at the headquarters of the North Atlantic Treaty Organization (NATO) in Brussels, and at the European Union, as well as corporate strategies that are crafted by global (but mainly Western) producers of defence equipment. Even those foreign-owned companies initially established in Canada purely to service Department of National Defence (DND) contracts are today buffeted by the changing climate of the international defence market, whether as a result of corporate restructuring strategies pursued by their parent organizations, of changes in ownership, or of the almost inevitable need to seek new business once a contract has been completed.

This exposure to external influences is a determining factor in our analysis in Part One, where we examine the major events and trends in areas of the international defence market that have a direct or indirect impact on the economic viability of Canadian defence companies. In chapter 1, we seek to illustrate the impact of the international political-security context on the demand for defence, and hence for the material wherewithal to pursue defence policies. Three broad groupings of issues are examined. First, we explore those factors associated with the disintegration of the Soviet Union, the declining (or nonexistent) threat of large-scale conventional military conflict in much of Europe, and the ability of the Soviet Union's successor states to abide by existing arms-control or -reduction agreements. The second set of demand-side factors, also related to the end of the Cold War, includes the reformulation of strategy and structure in NATO, and efforts to rationalize and coordinate national armaments-procurement planning through the Conventional Armaments Planning System (CAPS). Finally, we turn our attention briefly to new (or re-emerging) security concerns that may require greater attention in the post-Cold War era, ranging from regional or "out-of-area" conflicts or crises to calls for concerted action regarding the international trade in narcotics or international environmental problems.

In chapters 2 and 3, we review the evolution of transatlantic defence economic relations and other intergovernmental political or economic activities affecting the demand for, or supply of, defence-related products, as well as trends or pressures operating within the international defence market itself, especially the various corporate strategies emerging as businesses navigate their path through a period of great uncertainty. These chapters provide background analysis for the consideration, in Part Two, of potential corporate and governmental responses in Canada to the phenomenon that we label "defence industrial Darwinism." Throughout, our principal concern will be to demonstrate the constraints and opportunities facing the Canadian defence industrial base in conditions of increasing interdependence and declining defence budgets.

Naturally, we do not have ready answers to the questions facing policy makers as they seek to determine how – or even whether – Canada's defence industry can remain viable in this era of what we term "Darwinian struggle." We believe, nevertheless, that our study can be of use to those wishing to learn more about the international and domestic challenges confronting Canada's defence industry. Inasmuch as it does so, it will be so largely as a result of the cooperation that we received from numerous individuals in the course of our research and of the financial assistance that we secured from some institutions. Among the latter, we are happy to acknowledge the Centre for Studies in Defence Resources Management, of the National Defence College of Canada, which provided the major source of funding for this project. We wish to cite, in this regard, Pat McDonnell and Serge Caron for the sympathy and understanding they demonstrated over the course of the research and writing. As well, the Military and Strategic Studies Program of the Department of National Defence, through its ongoing contributions to the Queen's Centre for

International Relations, played its usual invaluable role in enabling the Centre's researchers to turn an idea into a finished product. We are also grateful to the Aid to Scholarly Publications Programme of the Social Science Federation of Canada for providing a grant towards the publication of this work, and to Wilfrid Laurier University for having awarded us a Book Preparation grant.

We are also pleased to acknowledge the following persons who kindly shared with us some of their time and expertise in Washington, Brussels, London, Ottawa, and a few other locales over the past several years: Gerald Abbott, Panayotis Andreakos, John Barrett, Justin Battle, Jim Bishop, Mario Bonomo, Erik Brühn, Glenn Brown, Robert Brown, Thomas A. Callaghan, Jr., Don Chambers, Elizabeth Cherrett, Bill Claggett, David Collins, Gordon Coombe, David Cooper, Vic Coroy, John Day, Nicolas de Chezelles, Michael D. Delia, Terrence J. Dooner, John E. Dubreuil, Ken Epps, Gabby Ferenczy, D. J. Field, Keith Gardner, Tim Garrard, Bill Gerard, Francis Gevers, Cynthia Gonsalves, Robert Hawkins, Cal Hegge, William Hinks, Theresa Hitchens, David Hobbs, Sharon Hobson, Caroline Holmes-Higgins, James Holt, Fred Jardine, Richard Jones, Robert Kemerer, G.H. Kimbell, Lucien Klein, Robert Lancashire, Marcel Leroy, David Lightburn, E. Mark Linton, Brian Lowe, Geoff Magnus, Paul Manson, Alan Martel, Dave McAnich, Martin McCusker, Simon McInnis, Bob McKendry, Thomas M. Meagher, Alastair Merrill, William S. Meyer, C.J. Mialkowski, Michael Moodie, Thomas Niles, Louis Parai, Bill Pettipas, Erik Poole, James Pugh, Max Reid, William Reid, Borden Ronald, Michael Rühle, Diego Ruiz Palmer, Rainer W. Rupp, Robert Sandor, Raymond Schaus, Derek Schofield, Tony Scott, Friedhart Sellschopp, Graham Sharp, Arcangelo Simi, General N. Skarland, Michael Slack, Herman Stakler, Donald Stein, Simon Street, William B. Taylor, Jr., Beth Thomas, Rick Thomas, Peter Trau, David Vadas, Anton van de Grampel, Luc van der Laan, Cent van Vliet, Jean Velon, Dirk de Vos, Philip Wall, Stein Weber, Scott Whiley, Nicholas Williams, Marvin Winklemann, Simon White, and Bill Yost.

Finally, to Mary Kerr, Kay Ladouceur, and Marilyn Banting goes our appreciation for so efficiently and good-naturedly typing this manuscript and steering it through a series of ever more refined technical stages. Michel Forand acted as editorial consultant and made a number of helpful suggestions.

Alistair D. Edgar and David G. Haglund

PART ONE

The International Context

CHAPTER ONE

The International Security Structure and the Demand for Defence

The signing of the Intermediate-Range Nuclear Forces (INF) Treaty on 8 December 1987 by Presidents Ronald Reagan and Mikhail Gorbachev in Washington marked a watershed in East-West relations. For the first time, the two superpowers agreed to the elimination, under the terms of the treaty, of an entire category of weapons from their respective nuclear arsenals. The INF agreement, ratified in Moscow in May 1988, gave a clear and highly visible signal of a more positive and cooperative U.S.-Soviet relationship.[1]

The following year, the pace of change in the external relations of the Soviet Union gathered speed in a manner that few could have expected. Not only did Soviet troops finally withdraw from Afghanistan after a decade-long political and military debacle, but the physical division of Germany – and of Europe – ended dramatically with the opening of the Berlin Wall. Despite the much-publicized, albeit unwarranted, fears of some commentators, especially in Britain and France, and the potentially more difficult obstacle of Soviet resistance, the reunification of Germany became a reality on 3 October 1990. East Germany left the Soviet orbit, thus following in the footsteps of Poland, Hungary, and Czechoslovakia.[2]

Inside the Soviet Union, the pace of subsequent change was even more dramatic. The Supreme Soviet reacted to the failed coup of 19–21 August 1991 by banning indefinitely all Communist Party activities in the government or the military. Despite his rescue from the hands of the coup leaders, President Gorbachev's influence dwindled rapidly, while that of Boris Yeltsin, the president of the Russian Federation, grew, especially after he concluded an agreement with the leaders of Ukraine and Belarus that established the Commonwealth of Independent States (CIS). Their declaration effectively undermined President Gorbachev's proposed new union treaty, and he resigned on 25 December 1991, four days after eleven of the newly independent republics had declared themselves to be members of a revised version of the CIS.[3]

SECURITY AND STABILITY
IN POST-SOVIET EUROPE

These rapid and mostly unanticipated changes in the domestic- and foreign-policy circumstances of the former Soviet Union raise a number of questions regarding security and political stability that have profound, though still indeterminate, implications for those demand-side factors operating on the international defence market. How could such a redistribution of power between the major actors in the international system – the United States and the Soviet Union (or, more broadly, the North Atlantic Treaty Organization [NATO] and the Warsaw Treaty Organization) – have been accomplished without conflict? Although that issue has been debated mainly among academic observers, it is worth touching upon here since it also addresses the concerns of those who caution that the transformation of the Soviet Union and the end of the Cold War are not irreversible. At the very least, these analysts argue, there is wisdom in waiting to see the true nature of whatever new political entity emerges in the East before proceeding too far in the West with disarmament and conversion schemes.[4]

The management of peaceful change in the international system, which rests on the relative status and strength of Great Powers, has long been a central concern in international relations theory. The principal reason for this concern is clear: what Robert Gilpin calls "systemic change," or change in the distribution of power between the Great Powers, has historically been associated with large-scale "hegemonic" war.[5] Thus one might have expected the decline and disintegration of the Soviet Union to be accompanied by military conflict in Europe, where the opposing blocs' military forces remained in close proximity. Or one might at least have anticipated a potentially dangerous crackdown by the Kremlin authorities as their former East European satellites, especially East Germany, began to replace the defunct Brezhnev Doctrine with what some have referred to as the "Sinatra Doctrine," each state deciding to "do it my way."[6]

Despite such fears, however, the most important characteristic of the disintegration of the Soviet Union has been its essentially peaceful nature: not only at the international level, but also (if only for a short time) at the domestic level, the Soviet empire collapsed without triggering a cataclysmic system-wide war.[7] As a result, commentators who in earlier times were engaged in prolonged disputes over the origins and basis of the Cold War have now turned their attention to debating the causes of its sudden ending and assessing the frequency of ethnic conflict and its meaning for European security in the post-Cold War era.[8]

Although the experts disagree on many aspects of the post-Soviet era, there does seem to be consensus on one point that is critical to the defence industries in Canada and other Western countries: while future "significant lurches in political developments" such as the August 1991 coup attempt remain a possibility, it is highly unlikely that a reconstituted Soviet Union or even just a reinvigorated Russia could again, at least over the short to medium term, present the West with a conventional military threat comparable to that of the Cold War period.[9] As the notion of "threat" encompasses both the capability and the intention to carry out a threat, it is also important to note that the latter element largely disappeared with the collapse of the ideological basis of the former Soviet Union.[10]

The control and disposition of the nuclear weapons of the former Soviet Union will undoubtedly remain a matter for close attention in the West. This concern is warranted for a variety of reasons, including the safeguarding of nuclear facilities against accidents or terrorism, the safe dismantling or transfer of existing warheads (possibly to become part of the fuel cycle for civilian nuclear reactors in the United States and other Western countries, as well as in Russia itself), and the threat of transfer of weapons or related technologies to other states.[11] As with the conventional military threat, however, no one doubts that profound changes have also taken place in the "intentions" component of the full-threat calculus. While their existence does constitute a risk, Russian nuclear weapons do not appear to pose any immediate threat to Western security in the coming years.[12]

The events that have taken place since August 1991 in the former Soviet Union should not obscure another demand-side factor already in place – namely, the implementation of conventional arms-control or -reduction agreements that had been reached previously. In particular, NATO officials have continued to seek assurances from the members of the CIS regarding their adherence to the terms of the Conventional Forces in Europe (CFE) Treaty, signed in Paris on 19 November 1990. The goal of that treaty is "to strengthen stability and security in Europe through the establishment of a stable and secure balance of conventional armed forces ... at lower levels."[13] These "lower levels" concern seven carefully defined categories of "Treaty Limited Items," including aircraft, helicopters, tanks, armoured personnel carriers, armoured infantry fighting vehicles, heavy armoured combat vehicles, and artillery. The successful completion of the treaty in 1990 was especially noteworthy as it followed fifteen years of frustration and failure at the previous Mutual and Balanced Force Reduction talks in Vienna. In contrast to the earlier negotiations, the CFE meetings began in 1989 against a background of unilateral Soviet force reductions (which were later subsumed within the CFE limits) and, most importantly, with Soviet negotiators expressing their willingness to accept intrusive verification techniques, asymmetrical force reductions, and the adoption of the concept of "defensive sufficiency" into their military doctrine.[14]

Although the CFE negotiations were to provide for a balance of forces "at lower levels," the equipment ceilings eventually agreed to would have had only a comparatively limited impact on NATO equipment levels as they stood in late 1990. As Table 1.1 indicates, by far the greatest reductions would have been borne by the Soviet forces, which had traditionally been numerically superior to NATO forces. Under the terms of the treaty, any required reductions were to be completed forty months after the treaty had entered into force, with special procedures to be established both for the equipment reductions and for the ratification process. The latter involved the depositing of instruments of ratification by all CFE signatories, with the date of the last deposit also establishing the date (ten days later) at which the treaty would come into force. When this complex process was completed, reductions would then take place, in three stages, over the forty-month period.[15]

Following this agreement, and prior to the August 1991 coup attempt in Moscow, a number of potential difficulties regarding Soviet compliance with NATO interpretations of the treaty had already been addressed and overcome.[16] In the aftermath of the dissolution of the Soviet Union, additional concerns were raised regarding the treaty's future. The ratification process was further delayed, as it required approval by all of the eight republics within the CFE Treaty's geographical scope – Armenia, Azerbaijan, Belarus, Georgia, Moldova, Russia, Ukraine, and Kazakhstan. At the time of writing, representatives from these republics, with the exception of the last-named, had met with NATO officials and agreed to ratify the treaty without renegotiation.

An issue that poses a potentially more serious obstacle to the full implementation of the accord is whether the republics can agree on a division of the military assets of the former Soviet Union that is compatible with the geographical limits and other terms written into the treaty. Some of the republics harbour the ambition to develop their own armed forces, and this raises questions about what equipment they should or could retain from the conventional arsenal of the

Table 1.1

CFE[1] Treaty Limits on NATO and Warsaw Treaty Organization Equipment: Estimated
Holdings and Required Reductions, February 1991[2]

	CFE Limits	NATO	German Democratic Republic[3]	Canada	Warsaw Treaty[4]
Tanks	20,000	24,325	2,274	77	31,713
Armoured combat vehicles	30,000	34,230	5,817	277	41,832
Artillery	20,000	20,443	2,140	38	24,754
Aircraft	6,800	5,708	392	45	8,368
Helicopters	2,000	1,719	51	12	1,662

Source: Canadian Institute of International Peace and Security, *Guide to Canadian Defence Policies.*

1 CFE = Conventional Forces in Europe [Treaty].
2 Based on final data exchange by the parties to the Treaty.
3 Equipment from the former German Democratic Republic was counted as part of NATO holdings.
  Their inclusion here in a separate category is to give an indication of NATO holdings just prior to
  German unification (3 October 1990) and the signing of the CFE Treaty (19 November 1990).
4 The Warsaw Treaty Organization no longer exists, but its former members are treated as a group
  for the purposes of the reductions required by the CFE Treaty.

predecessor of the CIS. In addition, a number of technical and financial difficulties have arisen with respect to the declarations of current
equipment holdings made by individual republics and to the verification of their compliance with treaty-defined limits and reduction
procedures.[17]

Dividing the conventional forces of the former Soviet Union may
ultimately prove far more difficult than dividing the nuclear arsenal.
Once the turmoil and euphoria of independence have abated, a
recognition of the financial and organizational burdens caused by the
creation of separate, large republican armies may provide greater
impetus for a compromise solution in this area.[18]

It would not be proper to conclude our discussion of the Soviet
"contribution" to the demand for defence without brief mention of
the growing concern about ethnic tension among and between the
republics of the former union. With the new republics dashing "madly
off in all directions,"is it so far-fetched to think that the West might
even come to regret the passing of the Cold War?[19]

As the bitter fighting in Moldova, Georgia, Tajikistan, and Azerbaijan
indicates, there are certainly good reasons to be concerned about
ethnic violence and nationalist aspirations among the former members
of the Soviet empire. The geographical boundaries established under
Lenin and Stalin often deliberately cut across ethnic and national
groups; however these might be redrawn under new agreements, large

ethnic minorities will remain in many of the republics.[20] It would be unrealistic to expect dramatic and rapid shifts such as those taking place in the internal political and power relations of the territories of the former Soviet Union to occur without generating instability, uncertainty, and even bloody violence. Indeed it may well be that, in a Mearsheimer-like scenario, the post-Cold War world will eventually be viewed as the "Era of the War(s) of the Soviet Succession."[21]

But what is really at issue here is the extent to which events in the former Soviet Union, however significant they may prove for the long-term stability of Europe, will have short-term effects on the West, especially given the regnant mood favouring the downsizing of militaries and the reaping of "peace dividends." The disappearance of the Soviet threat has led to a loss of credibility of any new "preparedness" appeal made to Western publics, who are now convinced that domestic programs must take priority over foreign (including defence) policy. Not even the emergence of a Vladimir Zhirinovsky has been able to deflect Western countries, especially in North America, from their focus on domestic agendas. Nothing illustrates this inward focus as clearly as the West's response to the civil wars in former Yugoslavia, which betrays a deep-seated reluctance on the part of many Allies to intervene unless a clear threat to "vital interests" could be discerned in the midst of spreading instability. As the following section illustrates, NATO analysts are far from having identified such a threat.

NATO IN THE 1990S: STRATEGY, STRUCTURE, AND ARMAMENTS PLANNING

At the May 1989 Summit marking its fortieth anniversary, the Alliance began a review of its role and its relations with other organizations in Europe and a reexamination of its strategy and force structure in the light of momentous changes in the European security order. The major phases of this review were the 1989 summit itself, the meeting of the Defence Planning Committee on 22–23 May 1990, the discussions of the North Atlantic Council at Turnberry on 7–8 June 1990, the London Summit in that same year, and the Rome Summit in November 1991.[22]

Notwithstanding the rhetoric about the merits of "interlocking institutions," the relationships between NATO and other political, security, and economic institutions – in particular the European Union (EU),[23] the Western European Union (WEU), and the Conference on Security and Cooperation in Europe (CSCE) – have yet to be fully determined. NATO has expressed its strong support of CSCE, while the Brussels

Summit in January 1994 gave the Alliance's seal of approval to a European "pillar of defence" as constituted by the WEU.[24] As Michel Fortmann notes, so long as this institutional confusion persists, "a basic question still remains unanswered, namely, who will lead Europe's new security policy: NATO itself? The Twelve? Or a combination of both?"[25] Recent ambiguities attending the future of the Maastricht Treaty, especially given the narrow "*oui*" of the French electorate in September 1992, have simply exacerbated this situation. As we write this, it remains far from clear whether the European Union will succeed in accomplishing monetary unification, to say nothing of the equally problematical foreign and defence policy unity.[26]

Despite the continued uncertainty over the future of this European security "architecture," NATO's strategy review began in earnest in 1990 at the London Summit, where Alliance leaders announced their intention to "profoundly alter the way we think about defence" – a statement borne out in the subsequent London Declaration on a Transformed North Atlantic Alliance, which signalled their intention to transcend forward defence in favour of a minimized forward presence and reduced reliance upon nuclear weapons.

Following the London Declaration, the strategy review was divided into three related fields. The first set out general principles and evaluations of the security environment, to serve as guidelines for the strategy. The second part of the process was the strategy review itself, with the formulation of related operational concepts and force structure recommendations. Finally, the third, on-going, element is a modification of the strategy and the formulation of associated recommendations in light of current or predicted shifts in the European security environment.[27]

The first part of the review process, which establishes basic guidelines, assumes that the likelihood of a return to Cold War levels of threat is negligible, though the analysts do warn against discounting the continuing dangers of political instability. As NATO Secretary General Manfred Wörner stated in October 1991, "conflict, albeit limited in scope, will be our travel companion on the road to a new European order. Hence, the primary role of our forces will be to prevent (or manage) crises as part of a more political concept of security."[28]

At the same time, while disagreements emerged at the Rome Summit in November 1991 over the possibility of expanding the Alliance's ability to respond to crises outside its borders, there appeared to be a consensus that the new strategy and structure would allow sufficient flexibility to adjust to changing circumstances. Thus the third part of the review process should not lead to significant changes, at least over the short- to medium-term future. In assessing the impact of NATO's responses to the evolving security environment in Europe on the international demand for defence, therefore, it is the *second* element of the review process that is most pertinent – the new Alliance strategy and, especially, the new force structure required to fulfill its objectives.

The critical difference in NATO's strategy for the 1990s, of course, is that it is no longer assumed that there is a direct military threat from the CIS or from its larger republics (Russia, in particular). Instead of potential conflict, the relationship is seen as one of "incipient cooperation," with the political keynote of the Rome meeting being the consolidation of East-West liaison in the form of the North Atlantic Cooperation Council – a consolidation that remains the stated goal of the "Partnership for Peace" developed in the autumn of 1993 and officially approved at the Brussels Summit in January 1994.[29] In place of the central Cold War assumption, the concepts of crisis prevention, management, and resolution have emerged. These might usefully be understood to correspond to situations of peacetime, growing tensions, and conflict, respectively, with a geographical referent that includes mainly the Alliance's northern and southern regions.[30]

In order to fulfill these missions, a fundamental NATO force restructuring is required – and, in fact, has been approved. The standing ground forces will be smaller since they are no longer designed to withstand a massive frontal assault; the indeterminate nature both of the threats to which they might have to respond and of the locus of such threats will call for greater flexibility, higher levels of mobility, and more sophisticated command, control, communications, and intelligence ("C^3I") capabilities. For a variety of political, military, and financial reasons, the ground forces will be composed of multinational, as well as national, formations. Because of the requirements for flexibility and mobility, and of the emphasis on reinforcement, air and maritime forces will remain very important components of the newly emerging strategy, which will also feature an emphasis (yet to be refined) on "Combined Joint Task Forces." Finally, nuclear weapons will still be valued for their deterring function, although NATO now views them more emphatically as weapons of last resort, whatever that may mean.[31]

The new force structure will be made up of four principal components: the Immediate Reaction Force, the Rapid Reaction Force, the Main Defence Forces, and the Reinforcement (or Augmentation) Forces.

The first of these, the Immediate Reaction Force, is based on the existing ACE Mobile Force Land and ACE Mobile Force Air. Along with standing naval forces, it will be employed, as its name suggests, to fulfill peacetime, crisis, and incipient-conflict missions. It is intended to be a multinational force in order to demonstrate Alliance-wide commitment. The second component, the Rapid Reaction Force, will also be a permanent force but will be composed of home-based national units designed to respond in support of Immediate Reaction Force activities.[32] The Main Defence Forces will provide the bulk of the military forces but will be maintained at a lower level of readiness than the two preceding bodies and will thus require a longer mobilization period, while the Reinforcement (or Augmentation) Forces, at yet lower levels of readiness, will ensure a sustainable combat capability during a period of protracted conflict. Finally, to coordinate these reduced and reorganized forces, the command structure will be altered by the elimination of one of the three major military commands – Allied Command Channel – while the regional commands (northern, central, and southern) will remain essentially unchanged, except for some smaller readjustments.[33]

Before turning to consider how NATO's armaments planning process has also been adjusted to meet the new military, political, and (perhaps most especially) financial realities of the last half-decade, it may be helpful to highlight some of the difficulties that may yet face the strategy review process over the longer term as members rush to implement and "operationalize" the new strategy.

One of these difficulties, alluded to above, is the continuing uncertainty over the shape of the emerging European security "architecture."[34] The unsettled future of the agenda set out in the Maastricht Treaty makes it impossible to predict what form of European leadership will develop on security-related matters. At least for the medium-term future, it seems safe, therefore, to assume that NATO will retain its pride of place in coordinating the national defence policies of the Western European states. The weakness of the European Union and of the Commission was apparent both in the inability to obtain a settlement in the Yugoslav civil war and in the internal disarray over how to respond to the Gulf crisis. The second potentially critical actor – the Conference on Security and Cooperation in Europe – remains hamstrung by financial weakness, lack of enforcement capabilities, and, to a great extent, its own internal political processes.[35]

The new roles envisaged for NATO – the prevention, management, control, or resolution of crises – may offer attractive options for the moment, but they raise new problems for Alliance members as they try to determine just what the organization's new functions should be without the spectre of massive military conflict. In particular, since the first two sets of tasks are essentially diplomatic and political in nature, is a military alliance the best forum in which to deal with such goals?

Again, at least in the short term, few viable organizational or institutional alternatives have emerged, but this does not provide a satisfactory long-term solution. The possible reemergence of the United Nations in enforcement as well as peacekeeping roles is one alternative, which we shall discuss below.

Finally, a critical issue in the implementation of the strategy and the establishment of the proposed force structure is financial support. To be credible, the strategy requires a well-equipped, highly trained standing force (the Immediate and Rapid Reaction Forces). It also requires careful planning and long-term government support for the development and maintainance of industrial mobilization capabilities for the Main Defence and Augmentation Forces. These are expensive undertakings, and it is unclear whether taxpayers will be willing to pay for either of them. The pressures for "peace dividends" in Western Europe and in the United States – especially, in the latter instance, from a government increasingly concerned with finding solutions to the domestic societal malaise – suggest that taxpayer resistance may well prove to be very limiting.[36] In that case, the strategy and force structure proposals currently being advanced in NATO may turn out to be largely symbolic.

Given these hurdles, one mooted, albeit partial, solution for the operationalization of the NATO strategy review is in the form of the Conventional Armaments Planning System (CAPS). As its name suggests, the CAPS was intended to help set out in a coherent manner the Alliance-wide "demand for defence" currently expressed in terms of national armaments plans and equipment requirements: "The basic intent of the system is not to align replacement schedules and funding plans, or even identify early collaborative projects. Rather, CAPS has the more fundamental aim of ensuring that national armaments plans take fully into account NATO's new long term force goals."[37]

Successful armaments planning cooperation through the CAPS would serve to address some of the problems facing the new "reconstitution strategy." In particular, it would demonstrate the Allies' political resolve to work together; improve the standardization and interoperability of equipment essential to a smaller, multinational, and highly flexible force structure; and reduce costs by minimizing the duplication of R&D and production, and allowing increased economies of scale.[38]

The CAPS is not the first attempt by NATO to coordinate the armaments planning or procurement policies of member states. Previous initiatives have included the establishment, as early as 1949, of the Military Production and Supply Board, the NATO Basic Military Requirement procedure in the late 1950s, and more recently the

Conceptual Military Framework, part of the Conventional Defence Improvements initiative. In each case, however, "the collective will necessary to raise the needs of the Alliance over national interests, of both the armed services and the defence industries, was absent."[39] Only one initiative, the Phased Armaments Programming System, met with measurable success, but as the system was simply a programming methodology for bureaucracies managing individual NATO projects rather than an overall strategy, its goals were rather limited.[40]

Developed in two-year cycles, each CAPS begins with the receipt and analysis of national responses to an Armaments Planning Question-naire, collated initially as the first volume of a Preliminary Analysis Document (PAD). The second volume, "PAD2," presents the analysis of this data and is then distributed to national delegations for their information and further comments. This process takes up the first year of the cycle, with the second year being used to produce the CAPS document itself, based on PAD2 and the various national responses. The initial CAPS cycle was 1988–90, but the 1992–93 planning year saw the first full test involving efforts to implement the 1990–91 CAPS while undertaking the planning of the 1992–93 exercise.[41]

The politics surrounding the CAPS, however, amply confirms the adage that "there is no altruism in defence manufacturing," notwith-standing governments' rhetoric to the contrary.[42] NATO members gen-erally see some basic philosophical merit in the project's long-term objectives, and initially they worked within it as a politically visible expression of support for cooperation. However, the CAPS is also capable of making individual NATO governments and defence minis-tries very uncomfortable by clearly pointing out areas of wasteful duplication in planning and in expensive R&D or production. Though governments may be ready to make a relatively painless "positive" commitment to the concept of cooperative armaments planning, they have proven far less willing (or able) to accept the idea of an interna-tional body that could pressure them towards such "negative" commit-ments as actually cancelling major national programs shown to be duplicative. As a consequence, it appears unlikely that national dele-gations will ever allow the CAPS to become anything more than a valuable multinational information-exchange mechanism and a forum for relatively limited consensus-building.[43]

NEW SECURITY ISSUES IN THE POST-COLD WAR ERA

Until now, we have argued that two broad sets of influences are helping to shape the international demand for defence in the 1990s

– the problems posed by the dissolution of the Soviet Union, and the challenges confronting NATO as it responds to those problems. Our analysis of the range of global security issues that could have a bearing on the Western (and Canadian) defence industries would be incomplete without the inclusion of a third set of possible influences – the emergence of new security "threats" or the re-emergence of older ones heretofore viewed as secondary relative to the core Cold War concerns. For the sake of simplicity, these threats are divided into two categories – regional and "out-of-area" conflicts involving states or "non-state actors"; and less traditional topics that have recently gained some notoriety, especially the international drug trade and environmental problems. Our focus, again, is not so much on the particulars of these issues themselves, about which a considerable analytical literature already exists, as on whether they will have an impact on, or create "demands" for, defence.[44]

The possibility that NATO forces, as well as logistics, infrastructure, and intelligence capabilities, might be called upon by the United Nations to engage in military activities outside NATO territory (i.e., "out-of-area") is growing, even though the idea seemed to have been rejected at the Rome Summit in November 1991. As long as France, in particular, continued to oppose any such expansion of NATO's carefully defined geographical mandate, it was unlikely that the Alliance's strategy and force structure would be applied to the resolution of "out-of-area" regional conflicts. The Allies' reluctance to offer definite commitments to the territorial security and sovereignty of those central European states – particularly Poland and Hungary – which have expressed an interest in joining the Alliance, and their cautious avoidance of more extensive involvement in the Yugoslav civil war suggest that over the short term NATO will likely remain a defensive alliance focusing on its members' territorial boundaries. Nevertheless, as the decision to impose an ultimatum on Bosnian Serbs besieging Sarajevo illustrates, there are limits even to NATO's ability to remain aloof from the war in Bosnia, and it cannot be excluded that NATO will assume a peacekeeping role in the Balkans, should a partition formula acceptable to Muslims, Serbs, and Croats battling in Bosnia be discovered. Over the longer term, it is difficult to see how NATO could retain its credibility – and thus its relevance – if it shows itself consistently incapable of taking action in those parts of Europe that are beset by the continent's most urgent security problems.[45]

Even though the Alliance itself may be reluctant to assume additional responsibilities, the involvement of forces from individual NATO states in regional conflicts cannot be precluded. In 1991, six international missions of this type were conducted, five of them either directly or indirectly related to the Gulf War.[46] In 1994, three NATO members – France, Britain, and Canada – were prominent among the U.N. peacekeeping forces operating in Croatia and Bosnia-Herzegovina.[47]

The example of successful international action in the Persian Gulf under the auspices of the United Nations has stirred debate over the possible resurrection of chapter VII of the U.N. Charter, which deals with "Action with Respect to Threats to the Peace, Breaches of the Peace, and Acts of Aggression." In particular, attention has been centred on Articles 43 to 47, which call on U.N. members to provide to the Security Council, upon its request, armed forces, facilities, and other assistance to carry out the restoration of peace and security. Since the signing of the U.N. Charter, the Security Council has never tried to implement these articles, but the end of the Cold War, in the view of some commentators, now provides the United Nations with an opportunity to fulfil the function of peace enforcement required by a collective-security organization in addition to being the "half-way house" of peacekeeping.[48]

Any move to revitalize the enforcement function of the Security Council may be fraught with problems, however, as the difficult intervention in Somalia shows. The success in the Gulf still may prove to be the exception rather than the rule, as one Egyptian diplomat explains: "When you move from the Gulf to any other issue, the Palestinian issue for example, or any other that the United States does not believe is urgent, you will find the Security Council returning to the very poor performance of the last few years."[49]

Whether or not such criticism accurately reflects the U.S. government's interest in the resolution of the Palestinian issue, it is safe to assume that for an international mobilization on a scale comparable to that of the Persian Gulf crisis to be successful, the direct interests of the United States must be involved and there must be a clearly unacceptable breach of international norms. Otherwise, U.N. activities are most likely to continue to be limited to what has been termed "chapter VI½" – the peacekeeping function. As even the most cursory comparison of the Persian Gulf War and the recent peacekeeping operation in Yugoslavia indicates, the "demand for defence" implications of enforcement and peacekeeping are quite simply of different orders of magnitude altogether.

And what of such new security threats as the international trade in narcotics or of environmental and resource-protection issues? Should or could these offer viable roles for the armed forces of Western countries?[50] Despite such well-known instances as U.S. military aid packages designed to support and assist the efforts of some South American governments to fight powerful drug cartels or the older example of the infamous "cod war" between Iceland and Great Britain, these problems are unlikely to have a significant impact upon the international demand for defence, for various reasons. First, where military actions are useful or appropriate, as perhaps in the drug-trafficking case, U.S. activities have been carefully limited to financial support or the provision of equipment, in either case taken from existing resources. Second, in many instances there are other more appropriate bodies, such as drug-enforcement agencies or coast guards, to perform the tasks required. And third, the military is understandably averse to the dilution of its core task and function through the diversion of increasingly limited financial resources to such novel ends. These new concerns may well offer specialized opportunities to equipment suppliers, but they are unlikely to have a noticeable impact on the overall demand for defence.[51]

THE EVOLVING POLITICAL-SECURITY CONTEXT AND THE DEMAND FOR DEFENCE

As our discussion of the CAPS showed, while the member-states of NATO look to the Alliance for assistance in coordinating their defence plans and while they regard it as an instrument for demonstrating collective resolve, the changing demand for defence ultimately finds expression not through Alliance-wide policy choices but through those of *individual* governments and defence ministries. The end of the Cold War, the disintegration of the Warsaw Pact, the achievement of independence by the Eastern European states and the reunification of Germany, unilateral and multilateral arms reductions and troop withdrawals, and finally the collapse of the Soviet Union itself – all have created vociferous demands in every NATO country for the collection of a "peace dividend" that will give governments additional resources with which to tackle more pressing domestic economic and social problems. A brief survey of the budget debates in recent years in three major countries of the Alliance – the United States, Great Britain, and Germany – amply illustrates the growing pressure for reductions in defence spending.[52]

In the United States, the Five-Year Defense Plan announced by the Pentagon in February 1991, which covered the period 1992–97, included proposals for drastic cuts to be made in the Army, Navy, and Air Force. Following the announcement of the FY1992 budget request of US $278.3 billion, defence spending was predicted to fall at an annual rate of 3 percent after adjustment for inflation.[53] Even before the year was over, however, pressure from both Democratic and Republican members of Congress led to a review of these estimates and to proposals for additional reductions of between 5 and 9.5 percent below the "base force" level.[54] In February 1992, the Pentagon announced a proposed defence budget for the following year of US $267.6 billion – a decrease of 7 percent from what had been proposed in 1991 (again, after adjustment for inflation).

Overall, the proposed FY1993 budget was 29 percent below the 1985 peak in defence spending that occurred during the Reagan administration; it represented 4.5 percent of gross national product (GNP), compared with the post-Vietnam War low of 4.7 percent. Defense Department figures indicate that the ratio will continue downward – to 4.0 percent in 1995 and 3.4 percent in 1997, each percentage in turn marking the lowest level since the late 1940s.[55] And it is by no means certain that even this revised spending level will remain untouched. When President Bush stated resolutely, in his 1992 State of the Union address, that "these cuts are deep, and you must know my resolve: this deep, and no deeper," Congressional opponents labelled the proposed cuts as "token," adding that, in the ironic words of one Democratic senator, "this will not stand."[56] The election of Bill Clinton later that year certainly has done nothing to arrest the long-term downward trend in U.S. defence spending, even though the $263.7 million defence budget that he has presented to Congress for 1995 is nearly $3 billion higher than that approved by Congress the previous year.[57]

The cuts in the U.S. defence budget have been echoed elsewhere among the larger states of the Alliance. In the United Kingdom, following on the heels of the controversial 1990 "Options for Change" review, the Defence White Paper released in mid-July 1991 announced plans to reduce force levels by 20 percent and defence spending by 6 percent (after inflation) over the next three years.[58] In Germany, after discarding a proposal in July 1991 to lower defence spending by 3 percent annually and setting the budget at 52.9 billion Deutsche marks (some US $29 billion at 1991 values), Defence Minister Gerhard Stoltenberg on 11 January 1992 announced a new spending plan that would represent the largest defence budget decline in postwar German experience. The Bundeswehr Plan 1993, which covers the period 1993–2005, caps defence spending at DM50 billion a year – a figure that has already been criticized as being too high by the opposition Social Democratic Party and that Chancellor Helmut Kohl himself hinted in February 1993 could no longer be afforded.[59]

As national defence budgets decline, increasing emphasis is now being placed by defence departments and ministries on the creation of flexible, highly mobile forces. The new NATO strategy review both reflects and reinforces this budgetary and force-restructuring trend.[60] All members of the Alliance, it goes without saying, will be procuring fewer major combat systems (e.g., main battle tanks, fighter aircraft, and warships), and those procurements that do take place will be accompanied by program stretch-outs, deferments, and reductions. In this regard, it is worth recalling that the CFE Treaty did *not* require large-scale cuts in NATO equipment levels; factors other than recent reformulations of defence policies have been largely responsible for the emerging pattern of lower procurement levels and fewer numbers of platforms. (We allude here to the phenomenon of "structural disarmament," to which we shall return in chapter 3.)

The new force structures currently being proposed should, on the other hand, create some new requirements associated with the focus on flexibility and mobility – that is, better sea- and air-lift capabilities, fully mobile land forces, and improved command, control, communications and intelligence (C^3I) capabilities.[61] However, such equipment tends to be costly, and it is by no means certain that governments will be either able or willing to explain these costs to an electorate more concerned with other policy issues, above all those in the domestic arena. As the downward pressure on defence budgets continues, even the reduced requirements that are being discussed now may turn out to be too high.

As they face an increasingly Darwinian marketing environment, the producers of defence goods may take solace from one trend that runs counter to the current pattern – namely, that the relative (and even the absolute) value of electronic systems and components is likely to increase, for various reasons.[62] As aging weapon platforms are kept in service for longer periods, life-cycle extensions and upgrade packages will be used more frequently. Improved realism in training simulators will increase the usage of this cheaper, more "environmentally friendly," and less intrusive alternative to field exercises. Last but not least, one initial lesson of the Gulf War appears to have been that many types of advanced-technology weapons can be used to prevail in an armed conflict while seeking minimal human casualties.[63]

Admittedly, the trends that we have discerned in the international security structure, and their impact on the general demand for defence by national governments, remain only one aspect of the broader set of issues that affect changing external market conditions, with all the implications of the latter for the Canadian defence industrial base. In the next chapter, we shift the emphasis from demand- to supply-side issues and examine closely the evolution of transatlantic defence economic relations.

CHAPTER TWO

The Evolution of Transatlantic Defence Economic Relations

Changes in the international demand for defence, however momentous they are likely to be, have only slowly begun to take clearer form,
as the case of the NATO strategy review shows. As with the international
economy, so too with the international (or at least Western) defence
industrial base: *evolution* rather than rapid transformation seems to be
the guiding principle – a somewhat paradoxical one, given the truly
revolutionary transformation that has occurred in the field of international security from the period of the Cold War to the present.
While the end of bipolar conflict has further sharpened those stresses
previously evident in defence economic relations within the Alliance
(and, say, between the United States and Japan), one should not
overlook the importance of that prior evolution, paralleling as it did
developments and trends in the broader international economy.[1]

We employ the term evolution here not only to suggest that the
pace of change in the broader international economy (including
defence economic relations) over the past several years has been
relatively measured, but also because evolution is such a suggestive
concept, connoting a more competitive, indeed Darwinian, struggle
among the "fittest" of the defence companies. Our focus in this
chapter is on the supply side of the international defence market and,
in particular, on how the initiatives and policy choices of governments
and international organizations may be pushing international defence
economic relations towards either end of a spectrum of possible
outcomes ranging from cooperation to conflict. We will argue that
defence-economic relations between the United States and its Japanese and European allies have definitely moved from the cooperative
pole since the mid-1980s and, by the early 1990s, had become sus-
pended between the two intermediate positions of "competitive interdependence" and "divisive competition."[2]

After taking a brief look at the structural issues associated with the consequences of change and uncertainty in the international economy, we examine the policies of various governments on either side of the Atlantic as they seek to come to grips with the progress of commercial market integration within the European Union (until recently, the European Community) and with the defence market integration undertaken through the Independent European Program Group. We also explore a subject of critical significance for export-dependent defence industries – namely, the debate within the United States over the "defence industrial base" and evolving trade policies and practices as defence budgets continue to adjust downwards. Our focus here will be on assessing the prospects of the chief remaining attempt to pursue multilateral defence economic cooperation – the U.S.-sponsored idea of negotiating a NATO-wide, GATT-like defence trade agreement.[3]

STRUCTURAL CHANGE IN THE INTERNATIONAL ECONOMY

Structural change, viewed here as a set of alterations in the relative economic standings of the major countries that make up the international economy,[4] has been mostly overlooked in analyses of the defence-procurement, industrial-base, and trade policies of NATO members. Instead, attention has usually focused on matters regarded as being of more direct military relevance to those countries – the need for rationalization, standardization, the interoperability of equipment and supplies, and so on. Even debates over questions of burden-sharing and the "free rider" phenomenon have been slanted more towards issues of individual members' financial contributions to NATO (in the form of their defence budgets) than to the logically prior contextual issue of international economic change.[5]

Why does structural change matter? It matters because the dissolution of the Warsaw Pact, and that of the Soviet Union itself, have served to reemphasize the more general economic policy concerns that animated the framers of NATO's founding agreement in 1949 when they included in the North Atlantic Treaty the requirement that Alliance members work to coordinate their economic policies and thus seek to avoid the potential for conflict in that important area of their relations. Just as earlier observers clearly recognized the close relationship between "power and plenty" – between national security and economic vitality – analysts have recently sought to incorporate more explicitly into their work the premise that "the defence economy is not a 'closed,' national system, but it is an integral part of the world economy."[6]

The decline and ultimate collapse of the postwar Bretton Woods system of international trade and payments – which, most observers agree, occurred when President Richard Nixon announced his "New Economic Policy" on 15 August 1971 – ushered in an extended period of uncertainty in the world economy. Inflation and recession in the advanced industrial countries and the absence of stable international regimes for trade, monetary, and energy policies were the dominant aspects of this period of structural instability.[7]

A principal feature of this period, and arguably the cause of much of this general malaise, was the relative economic decline of the United States. Nixon's 1971 initiatives signalled that Washington would no longer be willing to act as the "system stabilizer" (to use Charles Kindleberger's famous description).[8] With production increasingly becoming a global activity and with the economies of Japan and Germany reaching maturity and those of newly industrializing countries (Taiwan, Singapore, Hong Kong, and South Korea) expanding dramatically, a new international division of labour has evolved, and fundamental changes have occurred in the competitive positions of both the developed industrialized countries and the less developed ones. Even a cursory glance at changes in relative factor endowments between the mid-1960s and the early 1980s will suffice to illustrate these trends.[9] For example, while in 1963 the United States boasted 41.9 percent of the world's capital and 62.5 percent of its R&D scientists, by 1980 these figures had fallen to 33.6 percent and 50.7 percent, respectively. During the same period, Japan's shares of capital and of R&D scientists rose from 7.1 to 15.5 percent and from 6.2 to 23.0 percent, respectively. For six newly industrializing countries (Argentina, Brazil, Mexico, India, Hong Kong, and South Korea), the combined share of global capital rose from 6.2 to 10.1 percent; and while figures for R&D scientists are not available, their share of skilled workers by 1980 was 22.0 percent compared with 27.7 percent for the United States.

Although such figures signal trends that have alarmed Americans concerned about the prospects for their country's economic renewal – a theme encountered frequently in the 1992 presidential campaign – they may be less important than the actions or reactions that occur as governments in the advanced industrial countries seek to reduce or pass on the pain associated with domestic economic adjustment. During the 1980s, many of these countries increasingly resorted to such nontariff barriers as voluntary export restraints, orderly marketing arrangements, and countervailing and antidumping duties – instruments that were designed primarily to protect domestic industries from competitors in Japan and among the newly industrializing countries, and thus instruments whose rationale was not founded upon disputes over transatlantic economic relations.[10]

But while in the early 1980s these measures were primarily aimed at keeping out-of-area competitors at bay, the latter part of that decade saw a greater emphasis on "in-area" regional and bilateral economic arrangements – e.g., the Single European Act (SEA) and the Canada-United States Free Trade Agreement. This has led some commentators to predict the collapse of the multilateral trading system, or at the very least its fragmentation into a number of economic blocs. In the rest of this chapter, we analyze this concern – first, by briefly examining the impetus behind European market integration in the form of the "EC92" program, as well as the concurrent effort to establish a "European defence equipment market"; and second, by probing contemporary policy debates and initiatives in the United States, in both the wider context of commercial activities and the more specific area of defence economic matters.

"EUROPE 1992" AND TRANSATLANTIC TRADE

Since the endorsement of Lord Cockfield's proposed 279 measures for the reduction or elimination of physical, technical, and fiscal barriers by the European Council in 1985 and the passage of the Single European Act in December of that year, the movement towards the establishment of an integrated European market has gathered speed and made substantial progress, notwithstanding the difficulties encountered by the Maastricht Treaty following the Danish referendum of 1992. The success of the so-called "Europe 1992" (EC92) program took by surprise many observers who initially paid only limited attention to what they regarded as another in the long history of integrative initiatives and proposals made by the Community.[11]

As EC92 gathered momentum in the late 1980s and as its "deadline" of 1 January 1993 drew nearer, a wide variety of views emerged concerning the potential implications of European market integration both for the EC members themselves and for those who would remain outside the Community. Although our focus here is on the likely impact of the 1992 process on transatlantic relations, the internal aspect must also be addressed, at least to the extent of noting that there seems to have been, until recession struck the European economies in 1992, a psychological quickening, a shift from "Eurosclerosis" to "Europhoria," fuelled by an expectation of somewhat undetermined material advantages.

While the debate over the *external* context managed to escape resolution, it did not escape polarization, with contrasting visions of
"Fortress Europe" and "Opportunity Europe" being championed by
participants on opposite sides of the debate. For American and Canadian companies and investors, as well as their EC-based subsidiaries,
there are at least four major concerns with respect to the interpretation and implementation of the general principles contained in the
market integration project: 1) emerging EC regulations on "rules of
origin"; 2) the criteria determining which companies qualify for
"national treatment"; 3) the European Commission's interpretation of
reciprocity for market access; and 4) the prospect of additional costs
resulting from Commission President Jacques Delors' proposed new
European social programs.

By contrast, the more optimistic (but perhaps ultimately more simplistic) camp argues that the fear that external protectionism will
expand in Europe as a consequence of market integration is unwarranted and reflects nothing more than a failure to grasp the impetus
behind the European Commission's efforts. As one proponent of this
view puts it, "EC92 is intended to be a supply-side revolution … To be
successful, it presupposes free and open trade between the EC and
North America."[12] Since a major objective of the internal EC program
is to stimulate more open and vigorous competition, and thus to foster
more internationally competitive European companies, the optimists
believe it would be counterproductive for the Commission to create
new trade barriers or enhance existing ones in order to exclude
external sources of competition. The European marketplace may, it is
true, become more fiercely contested, but to the optimists EC92
"should make the European market more, rather than less, accessible
to North American companies."[13]

The practical impact of the process formally begun when the Single
European Act came into force in 1987 will probably fall between those
two analytical poles. Many of the measures contained in Lord Cockfield's White Paper on "Completing the Internal Market" have the
potential to cut both ways, depending to a considerable extent on the
political will, objectives, and prejudices that attend their implementation. And while the optimistic perspective accepts at face value the
undeniable *economic* incentives for regional market integration and the
benefits of continued international liberalization of trade, the pessi-
mistic viewpoint reminds us of the need to take into account competing or contradictory *political* objectives and interests.

Given the fundamental importance of political will in shaping
the impact of EC92 on transatlantic trade relations, the long-standing

u.s.-European dispute in the Uruguay Round of GATT negotiations over agricultural subsidies may be taken as symbolic of North American concerns over other EC initiatives.[14] The lingering uncertainty about whether the EC and the United States have actually resolved that dispute has led some to proclaim that "the Europeans are moving too far toward a stronger regionalism that will be reflected in more protectionist trade policies."[15] Confounding the protectionism of the Common Agricultural Policy with the market-integrating EC92 program may be fallacious, since the former is "an economic mess born of the days when special interest groups ran the EC," while the EC92 can be construed as an attempt to minimize the influence of narrow-interest producer groups and enhance both competition and competitiveness.[16] Nonetheless, the longevity of the agricultural policy dispute and the inability or unwillingness of some European governments to challenge the power of those special interest groups clearly indicate that political concerns can seriously impede or distort market-liberalization plans based on even the best economic reasoning.

Our discussion of these trade-related issues could be criticized for caricaturing opposing points of view on EC92's potential impact on transatlantic economic relations. We have deliberately simplified the case, however, for our main intention in examining the likely effectiveness of supply-side reforms was to highlight the crucial part played by political will. But does the will exist to create a more open, integrated European market for defence equipment?

THE EMERGING EUROPEAN DEFENCE EQUIPMENT MARKET

The restructuring of European defence industries began some time before the dramatic transformation of East-West security relations, largely as an industry-driven process responding to pressures specific to the defence market itself.[17] As Latham and Slack have noted, "while a comprehensive understanding of the phenomenon of European defence industrial integration necessarily requires an analysis of state programmes and policies, it must begin with an exploration of the commercial logic informing the restructuring process."[18]

There is, however, some danger in assuming, as these two analysts do, that "in many ways state initiatives are of only secondary importance."[19] The leitmotif developed in the present study is that transatlantic defence economic relationships, by their very nature, are primarily and unambiguously *political* before they are either economic, industrial, or corporate.[20] Thus the comments on the implications of a European defence equipment market (EDEM) found in the *Canadian*

Defence Industry Guide have a poignant tone: "While European governments now appear willing to open their respective defence markets in
order to promote the integration of the European defence industrial
base, the degree to which they are willing to see this liberalization
benefit non-European firms is still uncertain."[21]

The fact is that since at least the sixteenth century, national governments in Europe have frequently faced the autarky/efficiency dilemma,
responding differently at different times. Their choices have been
affected by the demands of domestic economic interest groups, including defence manufacturers in particular; but they have also been
influenced by national differences in economic ideology, such as views
on the appropriate role and extent of government intervention. In the
context of the transatlantic relationship, their choices have also been
strongly influenced by national perspectives on the importance of
maintaining or developing national (or European) capabilities vis-à-vis
those of the United States. In recent years, this topic has been the
focus of much debate within the Independent European Program
Group or IEPG (now absorbed within the Western European Union
and renamed Western European Armaments Group, or WEAG).[22]

Established in 1976, partly in response to the Culver-Nunn amendment (passed by the U.S. Congress the preceding year) and partly as
a result of discussions conducted by the Eurogroup of NATO at The
Hague in November 1975, the IEPG was intended to provide a Euro-
pean-oriented forum for coordinating armaments production and
defence industrial base cooperation. For its first several years, the IEPG
remained of only marginal importance in setting European objectives.
In 1984, however, under its Dutch chairman, Jan van Houwelingen,
and with the support of U.K. Defence Secretary Michael Heseltine, the
IEPG registered a major advance by requesting a new study into measures aimed at improving the competitiveness of European defence
equipment manufacturers. The study team's two-volume report,
Towards a Stronger Europe – better known as the Vredeling Report, after
the team's chairman, former Dutch Defence Minister Henk Vredeling
– was presented to the IEPG in 1987.[23] Within a year, an "Action Plan
on a Stepwise Development of a European Armaments Market" would
be formally approved by the 13 national defence ministers at an IEPG
ministerial meeting in Luxembourg.

The long-term objectives of the action plan were the opening-up of
national defence markets in order to increase competition and efficiency, a reduction in defence equipment costs, and the promotion of
technology transfer within Europe (including support for new
research and development). To accomplish these aims, the plan set
out broad sets of policy proposals in five areas – cross-border compe-

tition, *juste retour*, technology transfer, research and technology, and the developing defence industrial nations. Within eighteen months after the release of the report, an IEPG secretariat had been established on a permanent basis in Lisbon, and defence ministers had committed themselves and their ministries to publishing defence contract information bulletins so as to enhance the transparency of procurement competitions and highlight new opportunities on a Europe-wide basis. In addition, it was agreed to form the joint research and technology project known as the European Cooperative Long-term Initiative in Defence (EUCLID).

The Vredeling Report identified "boundary conditions" that it believed would limit or hamper the creation of the new European defence market. These included policies aimed at preserving domestic employment, continued development of national industrial bases and technological capabilities, declining budgets, adequate protection for technology transfers, and the need to consider the special requirements of the developing defence industrial nations. The path to success, the report suggested, would be the continuing commitment of national governments to the IEPG's goals. It was here, "where the rubber meets the road" and rhetoric required real action, that the internal political differences over national priorities became the clearest.[24]

It is all but certain that such political differences will continue to place limitations on any industry-driven liberalizing and cooperative trends, whether at the European or the transatlantic level. The "Coherent Policy Document" tabled at an IEPG meeting in Copenhagen on 16 November 1990 is an example of this. The Copenhagen communiqué and the "Policy Document on the European Defence Equipment Market" that accompanied it together set out the basic principles of an open EDEM, which are similar to those highlighted in the action plan.[25] The Policy Document also offered guidelines on the new "contracts bulletins" and supported the British-sponsored notion of designating administrative "focal points" by which companies in other European countries could contact national procurement bureaucracies directly. Important issues, however, remained unresolved; for example, despite strong German advocacy, IEPG ministers rejected a proposal that would have forced governments to make a legally binding commitment to pursue open bidding, deciding instead to rely upon political commitment. This left room for widely differing interpretations of "openness" under pressure from domestic economic interest groups; it also left to members the tasks of monitoring adherence and utilizing dispute-settlement procedures, which are still under negotiation. One foreign observer in London noted that the "dissemination of contract information is very uneven between the members and amounts to little more than the mailing of upcoming contract listings."[26]

The clearest expression of the limitations on a truly open EDEM imposed by divergent national political interests can be found in the recognition of the requirements for *juste retour* and special provisions for the developing defence industrial countries:

Each IEPG nation participating in defence research, development or procurement activities within the European context will expect an equitable return, or *juste retour*, in relation to its contribution. This concept of *juste retour* will operate for a transitional period recognizing the need for safeguarding vital national interests in the context of the development of the open market.[27]

Governments' endorsement of this concept, it should be noted, comes despite the complaint from industry executives that it "enshrines an anti-economic principle" in a policy otherwise purported to be based on observance of market forces, and that it will therefore "severely limit the effectiveness of a common European defence equipment market."[28] As if to confirm the validity of this complaint, the Policy Document states that "it is intended that the operation of the open defence equipment market within the IEPG should offer appropriate technological and economic benefits to the [developing defence industrial] nations," without apparent concern for the obvious contradiction contained in that phrase.[29]

Not only has the behaviour of the IEPG in the European market betrayed inconsistencies stemming from members' broader political and economic differences, but the IEPG project has been similarly ambiguous with respect to transatlantic defence economic relations. On the subject of European versus transatlantic cooperation (which it presented as alternatives, not as complementary policy choices), the Vredeling Report questioned "whether the loss of a European autonomy in selected areas by such transatlantic cooperation can be balanced, in the longer term, against the immediate market advantages and the gain of some technology."[30] The more recent Policy Document stresses the non-protectionist nature of its proposals and states that suppliers from non-IEPG countries would be "generally free to compete in the open EDEM." The wording of the communiqué, however, is rather different, for it suggests that the "markets of the individual IEPG nations will generally be open to suppliers from non-IEPG countries, *consistent with their national policies and on the basis of reciprocity.*"[31]

The differences in wording and possible inferences between the Policy Document and the communiqué reflect, once again, the internal division within the IEPG between "Europeanist" and "Atlanticist" perspectives. British defence officials in London and Brussels strongly dispute the contention that the IEPG proposals could serve to lay the groundwork for European restrictions on North American imports, just as they strongly endorse the potential benefits of IEPG initiatives for transatlantic cooperation and open trade. In contrast, an official of the French defence ministry's directorate of international relations warned at the time of the communiqué's release that "if U.S. protectionism were to become systematic, we could close access [to Europe], and there would be retaliatory measures."[32] While this may be dismissed merely as verbal posturing and certainly does not accurately reflect the substance of the IEPG documents, it does demonstrate the diversity of opinions that exists within that informal institution and that may be one of the leading causes of the IEPG's current malaise. Thus it appears to us that there is very little likelihood of any real progress taking place under the agency's auspices towards the mooted transatlantic "two-way street" in defence equipment.[33]

Does this mean that IEPG initiatives are without lasting substance? Not exactly, for an examination of IEPG proposals does offer excellent insight into how and why national political interests and objectives in Europe can serve to circumscribe and direct the workings of the so-called "market logic." Divergent political demands place such obvious limitations on the development of a truly open and competitive European defence equipment market that even the Atlanticist stance of some IEPG members contains enough qualifications to make agreements at the cooperative end of the spectrum improbable, if not impossible.

That is not to say that *no* fundamental problems can be addressed within the European defence market or that the future of transatlantic defence economic relations will inevitably be marked by rising protectionism. Within Europe, a few concrete though limited steps have resulted from IEPG initiatives on the improvement of cross-border competition and the advance dissemination of new contract information; and EUCLID has spawned a number of potentially valuable research projects despite its relatively modest budget.[34] While no effective proposals have been advanced to improve transatlantic ties, IEPG members have generally remained cautious about making statements that could reinforce preexisting fears of European market closure within the U.S. Congress. By emphasizing the ambivalence and ambiguity of existing initiatives, we wish merely to counterbalance the public rhetoric of the IEPG, not to raise alarmist fears about an impending trade war.

The material considered to this point leads us to the tentative conclusion that intra-European defence industrial base relations will be characterized, for much of the next decade, by what we have termed competitive interdependence. At the transatlantic level, even though the protectionist worst-case is unlikely to materialize, the relationship between the United States and its European allies will become more problematic than it has been, containing elements of both competitive interdependence and potentially divisive competition, the latter perhaps as much through complacency as through deliberate intent. As an institutional feature of the emerging European security "architecture," the WEAG (as the IEPG is now known) is unlikely to have much influence, either in improving or worsening transatlantic relations. Far more relevant will be the preferences and interests of national governments. It is only within the realm of intra-European defence industrial and defence trade policies that institutional leadership may have a greater impact. This will be especially so in the case of the European Community.[35]

THE EUROPEAN COMMUNITY AND DEFENCE TRADE

The question of EC involvement in defence industrial base (DIB) and defence trade issues and policies may be divided into two parts: 1) the formal or legal jurisdiction of the EC in matters of defence policy in general and DIB policy in particular; and 2) whatever the legal precedent, the impact of EC market integration measures on the defence sector. Regardless of which of these two aspects is being examined, it is apparent that developments in the EC can have a major bearing on the supply-side dynamics of the transatlantic defence economic relationship.

That the EC (the Commission, the Council, or even the Parliament) has a role to play in the political and economic dimensions of security policy has been accepted for some time.[36] The EC, it should be recalled, had a hand in the coordination and implementation of economic sanctions against Iraq after the invasion of Kuwait; in its July 1990 London Declaration, NATO welcomed the "move within the European Community towards political union, including the development of a European identity in the domain of security," which it added "will also contribute to Atlantic solidarity."[37] Beyond this, however, greater controversy has surrounded the efforts of the Commission and some EC member states to add to these elements a common European defence policy.[38] Disagreements have even taken place

among the proponents of EC competency in defence policy, over
whether the new responsibilities "should essentially rest with the intergovernmental structure of the Council or the supranational concept
of the Commission."[39]

Aside from these disagreements, there has been an obvious Euro-
cleavage, with Britain and France leading two groups of EC states, the
first pursuing Atlanticism, the second Europeanism. In addition to
establishing ambitious goals and timetables in the areas of economic
and monetary union and in social policy, the Maastricht Treaty has
given both camps an opportunity to proclaim that their goals and
preferences were successfully obtained.[40] Whatever the accuracy of
these claims, the terms of the treaty did not create any special new
anxieties in the United States, largely because the outcome had to
some extent been decided earlier during intense pre-summit negotiations (notably between the French and U.S. governments) that had
satisfactorily addressed the major concerns of the latter regarding the
continued primary role of NATO in any defence matters affecting its
members.[41]

While the issue of the EC's competence in what may be called the
high politics of European defence policy was for a time resolved,
greater uncertainty remained as to Brussels' formal jurisdiction over
defence economic matters. Here the debate revolved around legal interpretations of parts of two salient documents – paragraph 1(b) of
article 223 of the Treaty of Rome (the founding agreement of the
EC), and article 30(6)(b) of the Single European Act, which marked
the beginning of the EC92 program.[42] As Rupp has observed, "in the
past, in the absence of a truly common, or single European market,
nations used article 223 as an instrument to protect their national
defence industrial interest by focusing narrowly on the first part of
para 1(b) and by ignoring the second part."[43] What this means, as
Latham and Slack note, is that although article 223 allows states to
protect their defence industries from the EC's trade and regulatory
measures, it does not formally require them to do so.[44] Furthermore,
article 30(6)(b) of the Single European Act stipulates that the signatories "are determined to maintain the technological and industrial
conditions necessary for their security" and that "they shall work to
that end both at the national level and, where appropriate, within the
framework of the competent institutions and bodies." Although their
claim is strongly resisted by those who support the IEPG and the WEU
as the most appropriate forums, a number of Commission staff members, as well as other observers, have argued that the EC's involvement
in a variety of advanced-technology R&D projects renders it just such
a "competent institution."[45]

Despite the suggestion made by the Commission in late 1990 that article 223 be abolished completely and despite its dwindling confidence in the IEPG's ability to foster successfully an open and competitive defence equipment market, the EC has not launched a frontal assault in an attempt to gather under its mantle competence over all European defence industrial base activities.[46] According to one report based on statements by senior British and French officials, "a practical agreement" was reached between the IEPG and the EC whereby "the IEPG will keep the EC 'informed' of its activities, if the EC will refrain from asserting jurisdiction over defence procurement."[47] In fact, like the IEPG and its successor the WEAG, the EC too must attempt to reconcile frequently divergent national interests and preferences: at the Maastricht summit, the various heads of state again rejected the attempt by Commission President Jacques Delors to abolish article 223. Opposition by the industrial ministers of Germany, Britain, and the Netherlands similarly stopped a French initiative to extend further an EC industrial aid package to assist in the restructuring and conversion of European defence industries facing significant difficulties as a result of declining defence budgets.[48]

As the travails of Maastricht's supporters indicate, political differences among EC members continue to hinder the organization's assumption of greater responsibility over DIB and defence trade issues; nevertheless, it appears likely that, even if the Maastricht agreement should fail to achieve its full economic promise, the integrated commercial market envisioned by the Single European Act will cause the EC's *indirect* influence to spread. If so, then Rainer Rupp is surely correct when he foresees that "at a time when dual use goods make up a large and increasing share of defence industrial supplies to the military sector, civilian EC directives will become applicable for these goods once the conditions of the Single Market have been established."[49] Interestingly, EC competition policy should make it more difficult for governments to subsidize companies whose dual-use products or technologies are also sold in the civilian market. Similarly, EC merger and antimonopoly regulations will likely give the Commission greater oversight authority in a market undergoing extensive corporate restructuring.[50]

Other avenues of possible indirect expansion by the EC into DIB and trade affairs include: recent intergovernmental agreements to liberalize such previously exempt areas of public procurement as energy, water, transport, and telecommunications; research projects in the areas of information technology, advanced communications, and industrial technologies – all part of the "framework program" for basic research; the separate EUREKA research effort focusing on applications in the fields of aerospace, communications, and most prominently, supercomputers; and, at perhaps a more mundane but nevertheless potentially important level, the harmonization of technical standards to Community-wide accepted norms.[51]

What does increasing EC involvement in European defence industrial base and trade affairs mean for transatlantic defence economic relations? Here it is probably safest to conclude (as have others) that in view of the myriad uncertainties surrounding the process of European market restructuring, no one can really say with any authority what the future will bring. Much will doubtless depend on "the modalities of change" – that is, on the particular mix of policies pursued by governments as well as on the nature of corporate activity. Intergovernmental relationships will obviously condition and possibly even determine how the EC and WEAG interpret and seek to implement policies on such issues as reciprocity, technical standards, import and export controls, and procurement. All of these, in turn, will have a bearing on the tenor of transatlantic defence economic relations.[52]

Thus it follows that if recent experience is a valid guide, there are reasonable grounds to suggest that the EC's greater involvement in such matters will create strains on both sides of the Atlantic. The attempt by the Commission to establish a new common customs tariff on European imports of defence equipment, for example, eventually faded in the face of strong opposition from Washington and Ottawa, as well as from a few European governments. In some form, however, this issue will reemerge, since this is an area of reform *required* under the Single European Act.[53] What is less certain is the degree of divisiveness that will result from these strains and disagreements.

DEFENCE ECONOMIC POLICY IN THE UNITED STATES

The debate within the U.S. government over America's own defence industrial base and defence trade policies and preferences is the final critical component of the transatlantic defence economic relationship. Despite the existence of a bounty of protectionist measures currently before the U.S. Congress and despite the recognition in some circles that massive government support for military R&D can and does constitute a *de facto* industrial policy, the Executive branch has until very recently resisted calls for more protectionist and interventionist policies. With neither Congress nor industry united in their views, the Reagan and Bush administrations were generally able to maintain their aversion to measures that smacked of an "industrial policy" or to the microeconomic interventionism advocated by a vocal school of "strategic trade" theorists.[54] Instead, the Republican White House "embraced the globalization trend rather than attempting to resist it."[55]

It is apparent, however, that even before the victory of the Democratic Party and the election of Bill Clinton as president, the Republican position was encountering growing pressure to support American industry and to promote the country's trade interests in international markets more vigorously. Even optimistic analysts tended to assume that major shifts in policy might occur should economic security issues take precedence over those of national defence, and it could not be gainsaid that by the early 1990s many Americans viewed economic competitiveness as a national security problem. Accompanying this was a second recognition – namely, that the country's manufacturing base needed shoring up. In the defence sector especially, reduced and declining budgets were resulting in massive industry layoffs, with further job losses predicted into the late 1990s. That this pressure was mounting at a time when the U.S. economy also faced severe adjustment requirements resulting from a long period of structural change, only compounded the magnitude of the problem. Whatever the outcome of the presidential election, members of Congress were likely to face growing pressures to take measures to stimulate industrial growth, even though the microeconomic policies at their disposal could only have limited long-term positive effects without sound macroeconomic management.[56]

The difficulties facing U.S. defence companies and the restructuring of the domestic defence industry will be reviewed in greater detail in the next chapter. It is nonetheless important to note here that the vulnerability of several leading U.S. defence contractors to losses in the very limited number of major new weapons platform competitions has become a matter of deep concern in Congress – a concern that has been exacerbated by the seeming indifference of the Bush administration to this issue. Proposals by Representative Mary Rose Oakar to enforce tougher "buy American" restrictions or by Senator Alan Dixon to impose new offset reporting requirements were passed in the House and Senate, respectively, during the debates on reauthorization of the Defense Production Act in 1990, but they were then put on hold as attention focused on the Persian Gulf crisis.[57] Had the proposals been submitted to the White House, they would have faced certain presidential veto. The act requires renewal every five years, however, and it will come up again in the mid-1990s, at a time when the defence industry will have struggled through a period of downsizing predicted to be worse than any in the postwar era, including that in the immediate post-Vietnam era. One thing seems certain: Congressional champions of defence industry protection may go – as have

Oakar and Dixon, neither of whom now sits in Congress – but new ones will also come. Less clear, though, is the impact of the Clinton administration's declared preference for "conversion" on the future prospects of America's defence companies.[58]

The growing emphasis on the economic dimension of security is stimulating new questions in Washington, not only about domestic defence industrial base policy but also about defence trade policy. In a period marked by such broader problems as the declining international economic competitiveness of the United States, analysts in the Congressional Office of Technology Assessment observed that the "reasons the United States collaborated with its allies in defense technology are not as valid as they once were, and U.S. policies on armaments cooperation, broadly conceived, must be reconsidered."[59] Aside from the U.S.-European relationship, this assessment is obviously relevant in the context of American relations with Japan – even more so, perhaps, than in the transatlantic case.

In a widely cited *New York Times* opinion poll conducted in mid-1990, it was reported that Americans believed that Japan's economic power was a greater threat to their security than the military strength of the Soviet Union, by a margin of 58 to 26 percent.[60] The controversy surrounding the Japanese decision in the mid-1980s to opt for a domestically sourced replacement for the F-1 fighter – which grew ever more when the United States and Japan signed a bilateral Memorandum of Understanding on the joint development of the FSX aircraft – clearly illustrated American sensitivities to what was seen as an attempt by Japan to create new domestic aerospace capabilities that could, and would in time, compete with American industry.[61]

As this example shows, a recasting of the foreign policy agenda is in progress in both countries. This is confirmed by several other disputes in which national economic interests either took precedence over, or at least severely constrained, the goal of maintaining good bilateral relations.[62] To argue, as does Friedberg, that the FSX controversy had only a limited bearing on American defence economic policies "aside from its impact on U.S.-Japan relations" and that "the movement towards military co-development was therefore permitted to go forward," seems to us to miss the point.[63] That argument underestimates both the lasting impact of American "technonationalist" criticisms of the Memorandum of Understanding – which, Friedberg maintains, unwisely placed Defense Department interests over the economic objectives of the Commerce Department – and, from a different perspective, the "bitter lesson" apparently learned by Japanese policymakers, which has strengthened the appeal of nationalistic sentiments in Japan.[64] To cite once again the Office of Technology

Assessment report, "it is probable that the FSX controversy will be revisited the next time a major codevelopment program is proposed with an ally."[65]

The U.S.-European relationship is not likely to be marked by any similar controversy over a major new weapons platform, mainly because there have been no cooperative research and development projects across the Atlantic, at least between the United States and the leading Western European states.[66] (The failed effort by Senator Sam Nunn to foster such codevelopment projects will be discussed later on.) The growing significance of the economic dimension of security in the United States has nonetheless been made plain in a number of cases. After the EC in 1988 announced its plans to apply the common customs tariff to such imports of dual-use equipment as computer chips and radar systems, Secretary of Defense Frank Carlucci warned of a possible critical reevaluation by Washington of existing bilateral memoranda of understanding regulating defence procurement and trade with eleven Western European countries. These memoranda, which were used by the Executive branch to waive "buy American" and other Congressional legislation, thus gave Carlucci the ability indirectly to threaten the EC with the imposition of damaging countervailing duties on European defence products.[67]

The dispute over the customs tariff remains unresolved, and that issue has been put aside by the EC – at least for now. Its real significance, however, may reside less in its immediate impact – though it appeared to confirm American critics' fears of a new European protectionism emerging under the EC92 banner – than in its longer-term repercussions. Senator Joseph Biden observed at the time that while crises were not unexpected in the workings of the Alliance, "this is a real watershed where U.S.-EC trade intersects NATO."[68] Linkages between EC acceptance of U.S. demands in the Uruguay Round of GATT negotiations, especially over the matter of agricultural subsidies, and U.S. policies towards NATO were later made not only by Republican members of Congress, but also by Bush administration officials, including Secretary of State James Baker and Vice President Dan Quayle, much to the discomfiture of NATO and Western European officials.[69]

Events during the second half of the 1980s also offer insights into the tenuous nature of American political support for international cooperation. Consider the fate of international joint development projects initially established with funds specially earmarked under the so-called Nunn Amendment. The Nunn-Roth-Warner Amendment to the FY1986 Defense Authorization Act directed Congressional funds to support American participation in cooperative R&D projects with the European members of NATO, in response to complaints by the Europeans that Washington was not willing to collaborate in the "upstream" (development) phase of the weapons procurement process. The rapid growth of several high-profile Nunn Amendment projects even led some observers to predict "the beginnings of an Alliance defence industrial base."[70]

By the end of the 1980s, however, the majority of these international projects had abruptly collapsed. Many of them were beset by attempts to reconcile too many participants' operational requirements within one design, with large cost increases as a result. The projects' collapse also revealed something else – namely, that the armed services and the Congress had little enthusiasm for multinational endeavours in the face of declining u.s. defence budgets and popular demands for a "peace dividend" resulting from the end of the Cold War.[71] At the same time, many in Congress did not want to be seen by their electorate to be "exporting" American jobs or otherwise assisting in the development of new foreign competitors. The failure of Senate Armed Services Committee chairman Sam Nunn to preserve the Congressional coalition in support of such international cooperative programs has also had an impact on Europeans, who now view with suspicion a Congress deemed unwilling to participate in other international defence economic agreements.

PROTECTIONISM OR
PRAGMATISM? ALLIANCE
DEFENCE ECONOMIC
RELATIONS IN THE 1990S

Examples taken from the relatively narrow domains of American DIB and defence trade policies are clearly insufficient to provide conclusive support for either side of the academic debate over the impact of changes in domestic structural arrangements – in particular, the increasingly active role of Congress – on American foreign economic policymaking.[72] Neither the demise of the Nunn Amendment projects nor the growing emphasis on the *economic* (especially domestic) dimension of defence industrial relations has resulted in the enactment of new protectionist legislation by Congress, despite the pressures exerted by some groups. The Bush administration managed continually to resist the temptation of interventionist microeconomic policies and was criticized for its apparent tacit acceptance of the probability, or even the unavoidable necessity, of a process of industrial Darwinism among the ranks of America's defence contractors.[73]

Nevertheless, it is evident that even before the November 1992 election, there had been a reevaluation of priorities by both the administration and Congressional supporters of nonintervention and international cooperation, as each side grew more sensitive to the domestic and international economic dimensions of America's security relations. In his recent analysis of the strength and consistency of relative gains-seeking behaviour in u.s. dealings with Japan over issues of trade and technology transfer (including the fsx fighter aircraft), Michael Mastanduno rightly notes that the change in each country's relative economic fortunes over the past several years "has helped to produce a serious challenge, within government and the private sector, to the ideological consensus in favor of free trade that has guided u.s. policy throughout the postwar era."[74]

As this ideological consensus has come under mounting pressure, u.s. international economic policies (including those in the defence area) have been characterized not so much by increasing isolationism or protectionism as by a growing pragmatism, a "new internationalism" that may no longer be as willing to put American national economic interests second in order to maintain good alliance relations.[75] This trend towards a more pragmatic approach is consistent with our earlier observation that policy outcomes in the future will likely fall somewhere between competitive interdependence and divisive competition. What better way of illustrating this than to refer to the debates and disagreements that have accompanied the defence trade initiative currently being undertaken at nato headquarters in Brussels – arguably the only cooperative, "free trade" proposal remaining on the transatlantic bargaining table?

Even before the u.s. ambassador to nato, William H. Taft iv, suggested, on 15 March 1990, the establishment of an international board to monitor defence trade in a manner similar to the gatt's regulation of civilian trade, a number of attempts had been made to foster greater transatlantic cooperation in defence procurement, trade, r&d, and industrial base policies.[76] The Military Production and Supply Board, established in 1949 by the North Atlantic Council, sought "to promote coordinated production, standardization and technical research in the field of armaments," with the Defence Research Directors (later the Armaments Committee) being added in an effort to improve upstream r&d cooperation.[77] The nato Basic Military Requirement procedure – a precursor to the caps – was also initiated during this period; and in 1966 the Conference of National Armaments Directors (cnad) replaced the Armaments Committee with a mandate similar to that of the supply board and the committee.

Those earlier attempts met with limited success, since there did not exist the common political will to place Alliance needs over those of individual countries' armed services and defence industries. By 1990, more than one NATO official shared the opinion of a Canadian observer that differing national interests were proving to be divisive and that the "close relationship between NATO's security policy [political] and defence production policy [industrial] was suffering. There was even a struggle to retain a NATO emphasis, as opposed to separate North American and European perspectives."[78] It was perhaps in recognition of this trend – and of the purported military and economic benefits that could be obtained from rationalization – that a scaled-down version of Ambassador Taft's proposal was established under the CNAD, in the shape of an informal study group on NATO defence trade.[79]

Among the five major areas of the study group's mandate, the primary focus has been on attempts to develop a better statistical data base on defence trade and to draft a code of conduct.[80] The former initiative is clearly an integral element in determining the size of the transatlantic armaments trade and the degree to which national markets are accessible, but the collection of the necessary statistics has proven to be very difficult; indeed, it soon reaches a point where the effort required to amass information simply becomes cost-ineffective.[81] The disclosure of export sales information for defence goods tends to be a politically sensitive issue, especially for countries with close government/industry ties, such as France. At the same time, early opposition from several larger defence industrial states ensured that third-country sales – that is, sales to non-NATO partners – would be excluded from the terms of the investigation.[82]

The objective of the proposed code of conduct – to "reduce identifiable barriers to intra-Alliance trade, be they legal, legislative, political, cultural, procedural, or attitudinal" – reflects the variety of such barriers on both sides of the Atlantic. It also acknowledges implicitly the objections of the U.S. government to what it regards as biased analyses of the relative degrees of "openness" of various national procurement competitions and defence markets.[83]

A marked divergence in viewpoints emerged in the early stages of the initiative over the priority to be given to the goal of opening defence markets on an Alliance-wide basis, versus that of first addressing the task of European market restructuring. A French-led coalition of states maintained that unless an integrated European defence market was established first, opening transatlantic defence trade would offer U.S. firms an unfair advantage over European firms, given the vast differences in market sizes and scale economies. Supporting this position were developing defence industrial nations such as Greece, and smaller defence industrial countries such as Spain and Belgium. In their view, NATO "should not be involved in setting rules, even voluntary ones, for cooperation in development projects and trade in developing technologies."[84] France expressed its preference for trans-atlantic relations to be maintained through existing bilateral memo-randa of understanding, with the Western European Union being vested with responsibility for advancing intra-European defence trade. Had France participated in the initial stages of the CNAD study group's discussions, according to one French official, the initiative would have taken a dramatically different form.[85]

A second substantial divergence in preferences centred on the prod-ucts that should be included in the purview of the proposed code of conduct. Again, a French-led grouping insisted that the code should cover only the supply of "off-the-shelf" equipment and maintenance – a view perhaps akin to the notion of a "three-tiered" armaments market (although curiously reversed in its logic).[86] Against this approach was an American-led group stressing that since most national defence ministries prefer to purchase equipment designed specifically to meet their operational requirements, such a limitation would render the code useless.[87] A NATO discussion paper prepared in December 1991 remained inconclusive on the subject, stating that the member states would seek to apply the principles of open market operations at or above an as-yet undetermined level of cost.[88]

Related to the issue of scope and coverage was the demand by several European countries that *juste retour* provisions be accepted and included in the code. This requirement, however, was criticized by Washington as "yet another form of offset compensation for imports of defence equipment," inhibiting the open trade and rationalized production that were the intent of the Taft initiative and, for that matter, of the IEPG's original mandate.[89] Defending their support of *juste retour*, Belgian officials pointed out the importance of considering not only the needs of the developing defence industrial nations but also of the smaller defence industrial countries, for whom open com-petition as described in the code of conduct could only have limited appeal: "Until now, as historically all large and medium size countries tended traditionally to be protectionist, offset has been so far the only existing method for small countries to oblige larger countries to involve their industries on the subcontracting level." The smaller countries, according to this perspective, needed some guarantee that they would receive a share of subcontracting work, perhaps through the inclusion of specialized (i.e., "niche market") industries in new programs "from the R&D phase as subcontractors, even when it is not

clear whether these countries intend to acquire the equipment."[90]
Again, such a position is an interesting inversion of other arguments
for a three-tiered defence market, based on "managed" free trade,
competing consortia, and collaboration at increasing levels of value
and complexity. In either case, the Bush administration remained
opposed to such differentiation, since it implied too much government intervention in the market.[91]

The last major obstacle confronting supporters of the CNAD study
group and the code of conduct was the lack of credibility of the U.S.
position at NATO in the eyes of Europeans who had already witnessed
American withdrawal from the collaborative international projects
envisioned under the Nunn Amendment. With varying degrees of
scepticism, European delegations at NATO doubted that the idea of a
defence trade agreement would be acceptable to Congress. They also
insisted that Congressional approval would be an essential prerequisite
before they could ever agree to open European markets to North
American industries. The vagaries of Congress, to say nothing of the
unpredictability attached to the awkward appropriations process by
which the U.S. Department of Defense's budget is determined, have
reinforced the long-held preference of European governments for
avoiding transatlantic collaboration wherever possible, chiefly because
of U.S. restrictions on technology transfer and third-country sales.[92]
To assuage such European concerns, U.S. representatives at NATO have
suggested a number of measures that could usefully be taken to
improve European access to the U.S. market (in some cases, even
without direct reference to Congress); European officials have argued,
however – at times disingenuously – that the White House would
ultimately back away from the initiative it had originally proposed.[93]

CONCLUSION

The concerns expressed by the representatives of the various member-
states during the discussion of the defence trade study and the proposed code of conduct highlight yet again the intensely political
nature of the Alliance defence market. The initial suggestion of a
"defence GATT" was quickly replaced by more modest objectives.
Progress towards even those objectives, however, repeatedly faced
what, in another context, Thomas Callaghan has referred to as "first-
order attitudinal and structural obstacles" and "second-order attitudinal problems."[94] Callaghan's own preferred solution to the problem
of a fragmented Alliance defence industrial base – the signing of a
"two-pillar treaty" – presupposes that North American and European
governments have the political will to accept such a formal arrange-

ment.[95] As the defence trade study illustrates, however, formal recognition and commitment remain a long way off. Certainly, Europeans feel this willingness to be nonexistent in Congress; at the same time, our earlier discussion of IEPG and EC activities suggests that the preferences of European governments in this regard are also weak, and even at times contradictory.

The halting progress of the defence trade initiative through the Conference of National Armaments Directors and the numerous disagreements between the major players are evidence that NATO member governments may ultimately be unable to craft even a "second-best solution" to the problem of ensuring national security in an era marked by declining threats and budgets in the context of an increasingly competitive global economy.[96] While not a high-profile project, the code of conduct would signal the Allies' ability to address post-Cold War problems of cooperation in defence matters that their civilian counterparts had not totally accomplished in the Uruguay round of the GATT. If NATO collaboration cannot achieve at least this level of success, however, then the balance between competitive interdependence and divisive competition will have swung towards the latter, to the undeniable detriment of Alliance defence economic relations.[97]

CHAPTER THREE

Corporate Strategies and Responses in a Changing International Defence Market

Our analysis of the Western Allies' policies and initiatives directed at both the demand and the supply sides of their defence economic relations leads naturally to a consideration of changes and trends within the defence market itself. What are the immediate responses and medium- to long-term strategies of companies involved in defence-related business? To what extent can corporate leadership resolve the dilemmas with which national governments and intergovernmental organizations have been grappling? Can the private sector – either within Europe (for example, through the IEPG's efforts) or on a transatlantic basis, achieve some rational response to the challenge posed by the current climate of defence industrial Darwinism and, in doing so, optimize the Allies' individual and collective need to procure the best possible military hardware in the most cost-effective manner? Can it do so without jeopardizing the survivability of the defence industrial base of those states that choose to preserve some comparative advantage in the production of defence goods?

In attempting to answer these questions, it is important to have a clear view of the size and nature of the NATO defence market and of some unusual aspects of this market, including the dynamics of intra-NATO defence trade. Among market-related issues that are specific to the defence sector are those contained within the rubric "structural disarmament." Our examination of this and some other peculiarities of the defence market is followed by a review of the strategies guiding European and North American defence industries as they seek to maintain or improve their economic viability and profitability in a rapidly changing environment. We conclude by revisiting the question that informs this chapter: can industry provide the impetus to effect greater transatlantic defence economic cooperation?

NATO DEFENCE TRADE:
SIZE OF THE MARKET,
SCOPE OF THE PROBLEM

The most immediate problem one encounters in trying to attach a monetary value to the NATO defence market is the dearth of accurate defence-trade statistics.[1] Not only are governments loath to make public the information they do possess on their defence exports, which can in many cases be politically sensitive, but contractors are not always obliged to provide such details even to their own governments and certainly not to make such data available for use by potential competitors. Moreover, methodological and technical differences often make comparisons of such data as may exist difficult. With these caveats in mind, NATO has relied on figures gathered by the U.S. Arms Control and Disarmament Agency in its reports on defence trade. These figures are also used here.

Over the five-year period from 1984 to 1988, total defence trade within NATO amounted to $21.7 billion, or $4.34 billion a year on average (see Appendix Table A.1 for national figures).[2] During this same period, total annual defence spending in Europe and in the United States is estimated to have reached $150 billion and $290 billion, respectively, of which some $30 billion and $75 billion, respectively, were directed to the annual procurement of defence equipment.[3] In each case, the majority of procurement contracts were made with domestic suppliers.

The significance of defence-related sales by individual industry sectors (aerospace, electronics, shipbuilding, land systems, etc.) and by specific companies is discussed below. In a broader macroeconomic context, the impact of defence trade is relatively small, as a share of both imports and exports of NATO members (see Table A.2). When considered in terms of high-technology trade, however, defence looms larger, whether as part of the imports of developing defence industrial countries or of the exports of larger countries.[4] For the latter, with the exception of Germany, sizable defence export surpluses can have an important offsetting effect when set against deficits in other areas of high-technology trade (see Table A.3).

This last point reaffirms the fundamental characteristic of the defence market – namely, that its logic is primarily political rather than either economic or even military. As one NATO study reminds us, "procurement decisions are most often based on national priorities, backed or influenced by a wide constituency of interests, aimed, besides satisfying varied military requirements, at bolstering national economies through the maintenance or creation of employment, strong capital investment, gains for balances of payments, and the protection of national technological and industrial bases."[5] As a result of this dominance of national political priorities over economic efficiency and military requirement, it is difficult to talk of a defence trade market in the same breath as other commercial sectors, since in practice, as one Canadian official puts it, "there is really no NATO defence market, no European defence market, and no North American defence market."[6]

Similarly, if the common definition of trade is adopted – that is, the production of commodities in respect of which a state has a comparative advantage and the exchange of those commodities with other states for goods it cannot produce competitively – it can be said that there is very little defence trade in NATO. In fact, the term transatlantic military trade is misleading, since so little of it, in the words of that same Canadian official, "involves the buying or selling of complete systems or even subsystems. Most of it involves various forms of barter: licensed production, co-production, offsets, etc., whereby the 'seller' compensates the 'buyer' for his purchase, in whole or in part."[7] Not surprisingly, with most if not all governments preferring to sell and not buy, naked or disguised barter plays a major role in intra-Alliance defence trade.

In the Alice-in-Wonderland environment of transatlantic defence economics, terms such as "market" and "trade" take on meanings that diverge from their more commonplace, civilian ones – often to the chagrin of analysts and corporate planners alike. There are, however, some additional trends within this so-called market that are to a large extent technological rather than political in inspiration; indeed, because these trends may directly clash with political realities, defence industries may find themselves uncomfortably sandwiched between conflicting imperatives. One such trend – a very important one – is structural disarmament.

STRUCTURAL DISARMAMENT, DUAL-USE TECHNOLOGY, AND THE NATO DEFENCE MARKET

The decline in various countries' procurement budgets following the end of the Cold War and the collapse of the Soviet Union has exacerbated the problems that already plagued the Alliance defence market, buffeted by divergent political forces and defined by its fragmentary structure. Some observers argue that the phenomenon of structural disarmament dates back to the dawn of the Industrial

Age; if so, it can be said that its importance has grown with the technological revolution that has occurred since the end of the Second World War – in particular since the late 1950s.

As described by Thomas Callaghan, Jr., who originated the phrase, structural disarmament occurs when the market represented by a nation's defence budget plus exports (the "structure") is too small to bring armament development and production costs down "to a level either politically acceptable for governments or, equally, affordable to industry."[8] The most celebrated explication of this trend comes from Norman R. Augustine, chairman and chief executive officer of Martin Marietta Corporation in the United States, who observed in 1980 that the unit cost of much high-technology equipment seemed to be increasing by a factor of four every decade (by a factor of two in the case of ships and tanks). Other analysts have estimated that unit costs of major platforms (especially aircraft) have increased by as much as 8 to 10 percent annually above inflation, mainly as the result of the rising fixed costs of research and development and of new production technology. The problem, as Augustine pointed out, was that "other relevant parameters, e.g., the defense budget" either did not grow at an equal rate or have actually declined.[9]

Hypothetically – in Augustine's perhaps not entirely facetious example – the result of constantly rising unit costs, measured against defence procurement budgets that increase more modestly or even decline, could be that by the year 2054 (based on 1980 budget projections) the entire u.s. defence budget would allow the purchase of just *one* tactical fighter aircraft. For other NATO countries, however, the impact of such trends ceased to be a laughing matter long ago. Indeed, following the cancellation of the Avro Arrow program and the signing of the bilateral Defence Production and Defence Development Sharing Arrangements with the United States in the late 1950s and early 1960s, Canada became the first of the larger defence industrial countries of the postwar era to succumb to Augustine's Law, effectively abandoning domestic development of all major weapons systems or platforms with the exception of ships.[10]

With costs rising rapidly and defence budgets peaking and then declining, not only have fewer platforms been purchased with each new generation fielded, but the number of new program starts has also fallen and the time periods between new contract competitions have lengthened.[11] As a result, even successful contractors face constantly diminishing production runs, with economies of scale becoming more difficult to achieve, including in the United States. Losing competitors face the possibility of being driven out of the market for new defence systems altogether, since they may not be able to maintain existing production lines and retain essential R&D or skilled personnel until their next successful bid. Such are the implications of structural disarmament.

A related trend, of more recent origin, is the growing importance being accorded the dual-use technologies. How might this affect defence manufacturers and their market? While defence budgets face a severe squeeze, civilian high-technology markets have expanded and are likely to continue to do so, notwithstanding the recent recession. The result, to some observers, is that compared with the situation in the late 1980s (see Table A.3), "defence's share of high-technology markets will have fallen to around one-half its present level by the end of the century" despite the potential boost to sales provided by the demonstration of the value of much advanced-technology weaponry during the Gulf War.[12]

Increasingly, the vaunted spin-offs from defence R&D to the civilian sector are being replaced by a spin-off in the opposite direction, with commercially developed products or technologies becoming ubiquitous in defence applications; composite materials, microelectronics, semiconductors, and new production techniques using advanced robotics are a few well-known examples. Partly as a result of this trend, defence departments and manufacturers alike are under growing pressure to adopt commercial specifications and standards where feasible – an option that has the added attraction of reducing some costs.

The emphasis on advanced-technology weaponry and the growth of dual-use technologies will likely have important consequences for the composition and nature of the defence industrial base. William Walker explains that these trends "imply a still more decisive shift towards an electronics-based industry, particularly at the systems level: the displacement of industrial resources from hardware to software, and from technology systems that are lumpy and loosely connected, to those that are more diffuse but strongly interconnected through modern communications techniques."[13] The "Japan model" of defence industrialization, as we have labelled it elsewhere, could therefore become more prominent over the next ten to twenty years – a possibility foreshadowed in the increasing dependence of U.S. defence industries and the Department of Defense on imports of Japanese materials or components.[14]

The policy issue of foreign dependence in "critical" defence technologies or products, which achieved some notoriety in the United States during and after the Gulf War, is a central element in the concerns of governments over maintaining independent national DIBs and technological capabilities.[15] This issue was alluded to in our discussion of the political nature of the defence market; here, we simply note some other possible implications – in particular, the obsolescence of ministerial regulations that still strictly enforce the separation of companies' defence- and civilian-related R&D and production facilities, and even their personnel! This latter question, brought up periodically by American industry executives as they seek to adapt to their new business environment, leads us more directly into an examination of corporate responses to the trends noted above, both in Europe and the United States.

CORPORATE STRATEGIES IN THE EVOLVING DEFENCE MARKET: THE WESTERN EUROPEAN RECORD

It is a truism that privately owned defence corporations must ultimately be able to show a profit from their business in order to continue in that business. In the defence industry, however, success on the bottom line has become more difficult to attain for several reasons. In particular, fragmented markets and rising costs already make the achievement of the minimum efficient scale of production beyond reach in national European markets, and problematical even in the United States.[16]

Table 3.1 compares the number of prime contractors producing major platforms and weapon systems in the United States and Europe, and gives their average annual output. These figures show, for example, that in the mid-1980s there were eight European prime contractors in the aerospace sector, each producing an average of only 37.5 aircraft a year compared with six "primes" in the United States, each with average annual production levels of 100 aircraft.[17]

Manufacturers in Europe's larger defence industrial countries (Britain and France, in particular) have traditionally pursued export sales as a crucial method of increasing unit production and hence improving efficiency and reducing unit costs. These markets, however, became smaller and more competitive as market saturation manifested itself in the late 1980s and as new national defence industries began to offer their products.[18] Between 1984 and 1989, French exports of defence equipment reportedly fell from approximately FF62 billion to FF20 billion. Aircraft manufacturers such as Avions Marcel Dassault were unable to reach the levels of export orders that would have forestalled the need for basic corporate restructuring.[19] (Even with their longer production runs, many American defence companies too have been obliged to undertake significant restructuring projects that resulted in large-scale layoffs.)

Table 3.1
Average Annual Volume of Defence Equipment Sold Per Firm, United States and
Europe, mid-1980s[1]

	Aircraft		Tanks		Ships		SAMs[2]		ATGMs[3]	
United States	100	(6)	300	(2)	1.2	(10)	2,500	(4)	5,000	(5)
Europe	37.5	(8)	100	(5)	0.6	(23)	1,000	(7)	4,000	(5)
U.S.:Europe	2.7:1		3:1		2:1		2.5:1		1.25:1	

Source: Steinberg, *Transformation of the European Defense Industry,* p. 13.
1 The number of firms is shown in parentheses.
2 Surface-to-air missiles.
3 Anti-tank guided missiles.

These restructuring activities in the larger European defence industrial countries (Britain, France, Germany, and Italy) may be divided
into two distinct but complementary approaches – the consolidation
of domestic manufacturers to produce "national champions" within
each country, and the development of transnational linkages.

The process of domestic rationalization began as early as the 1950s,
mainly through the use of mergers and acquisitions (m&a), and by
the mid-1980s was well advanced in the United Kingdom, France, and
Germany; in Italy, much of the domestic DIB was by then controlled
by a pair of state-owned holding companies. This movement has
continued since then; indeed, it has accelerated under the pressures
of declining post-Cold War defence budgets. In the United Kingdom,
for example, GEC and Siemens of Germany joined in a takeover of
Plessey in 1989 to form British Aerospace, the third-largest defence
electronics company in the world after Hughes Aircraft of the United
States and Thomson-CSF of France.[20] The purchase of Ferranti
Defence Systems by GEC, after Ferranti's ECR 90 radar system had been
selected for the European Fighter Aircraft program, "strengthen[ed]
their portion of avionics and allow[ed] immense scope for rationalization of the industry."[21] Since then, GEC has acquired Ferranti's
guided missile division and has announced an interest in seeking to
purchase the missile-manufacturing subsidiary of British Aerospace,
British Aerospace Dynamics.[22]

The pursuit of "critical mass" in the face of more difficult market
prospects also lay behind the merger, in France, of Aérospatiale's
holdings in Crouzet, SFENA, and Électronique Aérospatiale with the
General Avionics Branch of Thomson-CSF to form Sextant Avioniques
SA, the largest avionics company in Europe and one of the largest in
the world. Similarly in Germany, the amalgamation of Daimler-Benz's

subsidiaries – Messerschmidt-Boelhow-Blohm, Dornier, AEG, and Motoren und Turbinen Union (MTU) – into a new conglomerate, Deutsche Aerospace (DASA), brought together approximately 70 percent of the German industry to create the world's fifth-largest aerospace company. The Messerschmidt group had previously merged with VFW-Fokker and also owned a controlling stake in the armoured vehicle manufacturer Krauss Maffei.[23] Finally, in Italy the state-owned Istituto per la Ricostruzione Industriale (IRI) holding group, which includes among its members Aeritalia, Agusta, and Selenia, was reorganized into two separate groups – Finmeccanica for defence and STET for telecommunications – in order to further rationalize that country's defence industry.[24]

The creation of "national champion" firms such as British Aerospace, DASA, or Sextant Avioniques has led to a reduction in the number of companies competing within individual national markets. It has not, however, successfully addressed the fundamental problem of the fragmented European defence market; nor has it been able to ameliorate the overcapacity that still plagues the industry. The figures in Table 3.1 offer a clear example of the problem created by the presence of too many firms competing for too few new orders; simply put, the production capacity of the European defence industry is as much as 300 percent above what is required to meet existing government defence requirements.[25] A recent study by the Stockholm International Peace Research Institute (SIPRI) suggests that between 185,000 and 350,000 jobs could still be lost in Europe's defence industries by 1995, with employment levels falling from some 1.5 million in 1985 to 815,000 in 1995.[26]

The SIPRI analysis argues that "the triple challenge of speedy technological advance, economic integration of civilian industries, and deep cuts in arms spending demands solutions within a larger framework than is available at the national level."[27] European industries have in fact, as indicated above, already attempted to work on a broader basis, seeking to form new transnational linkages. In doing so, they have adopted three main strategies: horizontal integration, sectoral consolidation, and complementary groupings.[28] Formal mergers and acquisitions have been largely intranational, although there have also been, to a lesser extent, some transatlantic (U.S.-U.K.) initiatives. More common have been equity exchanges and "economic interest groups" (EIGs), both means of establishing corporate ties with more security and predictability than are provided by ad hoc collaboration on individual programs. Measures such as these limit the potential risks of legal entanglements associated with formal mergers and acquisitions of companies regarded as national political or security assets.[29]

By the early 1990s, three "transnational clusters" (or axes) appeared to be developing within the European defence industry as a result of these corporate initiatives. The first linked British Aerospace with Thomson-CSF in the area of missiles and avionics, although this cooperation looked more promising at the outset than it has turned out to be. The second is the Franco-German pairing of Aérospatiale and Deutsche Aerospace, who have made rather more substantive progress through the creation of Eurocopter, today the second-largest helicopter manufacturer after Sikorksy of the United States. The third cluster, involving GEC of the United Kingdom, Siemens of Germany, and France's Matra, focuses on defence electronics and space technology.[30]

Together, these three dominant clusters comprise most of Europe's leading aerospace and defence electronics companies. Along with the principal engine manufacturers – Rolls-Royce of the United Kingdom, SNECMA and Turbomeca of France, and MTU of Germany (itself part-owned by DASA) – they make up the first tier of the European DIB. Below this level is a second tier, of diminishing size, composed of independent companies such as Westland, Thorn-EMI, and Racal of Britain; France's Dassault Aviation and Dassault Électronique, and GIAT; Germany's Krupp-Mak, Krauss-Maffei, and Rheinmetall; Italy's two public holding companies, EFIM and IRI/Finmeccanica; and the Spanish state-owned aeronautics company CASA.

Both national consolidation and transnational linkages have proven to be useful strategies in the face of rising costs and declining demand, but given the continuation of excess capacity, politically drawn boundaries of the past can and do continue to cause difficulties. In some cases, even simple national consolidation may clash directly with domestic political priorities, thus hobbling the attainment of the necessary conditions for a more open, integrated European defence market. The prospect of the decay or outright loss of a country's capacity in a particular sector, should its sole "national champion" fail to obtain a share of a major new contract in its area (possibly the only such contract likely to materialize for a decade), will very probably prove unacceptable to the governments of the larger European countries. Under these circumstances, they are unlikely to accept cross-border liberalization of defence trade unless it comes with an adequate protective layer of compensating mechanisms. "National champion" firms have similarly problematical implications for the attainment of such goals as reducing R&D and procurement costs, and improving the efficiency and competitiveness of defence industries.[31]

One might be tempted to assume that the development of transnational clusters is evidence that a more open and integrated European defence market is emerging as a result of corporate activities and initiatives. Closer examination of a number of structural trends shows, however, that this "evidence" is weak at best.[32] First, although there still exist opportunities for further domestic consolidation, the pace is slowing. At the same time, the outlook for transnational mergers and acquisitions remains dim. Why should this be so? In the main, because transnational consolidation flies in the face of governments' tendency to seek to protect critical sectors of their DIB capabilities, even at the cost of having to accept considerable inefficiency. Italy and Spain have been singled out in this regard because of their insistence on rationalizing their state-owned holding companies instead of encouraging transnational consolidation.

Because of their awareness of the various legal and other obstacles placed by governments in the path of formal m&a activities, corporations have leaned towards less formal but nevertheless extensive strategic alliances (the above-mentioned EIGs). Economic interest groups undoubtedly foster improved corporate information exchanges and business relationships, although some analysts question the impact that this may have ultimately on control and accountability.[33] At the same time, the extent to which EIGs will improve the competitiveness of European industries remains uncertain, and some observers continue to express doubts about the "viability of strategic alliances in the absence of concrete collaborative programs."[34]

Finally, it cannot be assumed that EIGs will proliferate or even that existing ones will survive in the market of the 1990s. Successful ventures such as the Deutsche Aerospace-Aérospatiale Eurocopter must be set against the decision made by British Aerospace and Thomson not to proceed any further with Eurodynamics, despite its having won approval from both London and Paris. James Steinberg deems it "perhaps noteworthy that the Eurodynamics negotiations broke down at the same time Thomson-CSF received a large order from Saudi Arabia for the Crotale air defense system (a program that would have fallen within Eurodynamics.)"[35] This suggests that the companies involved may have found Eurodynamics' complementary grouping approach incapable of generating sufficient cost savings. (Eurocopter by contrast was a horizontal grouping.) It may also be that Thomson determined that its newly improved export prospects should be kept within the company. This case serves as a reminder that defence contractors remain economic competitors even though market constraints may occasionally prompt them to become collaborators of convenience.

CORPORATE RESTRUCTURING
ACTIVITIES IN THE UNITED
STATES

Attempts to adjust to changing market realities are also evident in the
U.S. defence industry. At first glance, the size of their market for
defence equipment and the profits being reported by many major
defence contractors in the United States appear to belie the idea that
the American defence industry is entering into a turbulent period. In
his testimony before the House Armed Services Research, Development, and Procurement Subcommittee on 28 April 1992, Deputy
Secretary of Defense Donald Atwood pointed out that U.S. defence
procurement spending in FY1993 would surpass $50 billion, with an
additional $40 billion for R&D.[36] Meanwhile, corporations such as
General Dynamics, Grumman, Lockheed, Northrop, and Thiokol
experienced large increases in their net earnings for the first quarter
of 1992 – as high as 44 and 40 percent, respectively, for General
Dynamics and Grumman.[37] U.S. defence companies continued to
dominate the international defence market, with sixteen of the top
twenty-five firms (based on 1990 defence revenues; see Table A.4),
and four of the first five, being American. The negative impact of
structural disarmament, already strongly felt in Europe and in Canada,
seems to have been kept more or less at bay in the United States until
now.

Appearances, however, can be just as deceiving in defence industrial
circles as elsewhere. The reality is that deep cuts have taken place over
the past seven years in American defence spending, and more are in
the offing. In the aerospace sector, for example – an area hard-hit by
the contraction of defence budgets during the past decade – Department of Defense (DoD) expenditures on aerospace products plum-
meted from $44.4 billion (in current dollars) in 1987 to $28.8 billion
in 1994. When inflation is factored in, the decrease in procurement
approximates 50 percent over the period.[38]

The aerospace sector is not alone. Significant problems are facing
the overall U.S. defence industry at each level (or "tier") of contractors. Between FY1986 and FY1993, the country's defence spending
diminished by some 30 percent, and it is expected to shrink by a
further 12 percent from the 1986 total by FY1997 – a total decline of
42 percent over the decade. The procurement budget, still apparently
impressive at $54 billion for FY1993, is less than half of the 1986
amount of $120 billion. Should the Clinton administration be as
determined as its predecessor to maintain stable funding levels for
research, development, testing, and evaluation, this would likely trans-

late into even deeper cuts in procurement spending, which can be expected to trend downward along with force levels.[39]

The apparent paradox of high or even record profits being reported during a period of declining defence spending and uncertain business prospects is seen by industry financial analysts as an instance of the "supernova phenomenon" – hardly an auspicious metaphor, given that stars reach their brightest level just prior to their implosion. The image of the supernova nonetheless offers a parallel worth meditating, for the final production phase of a defence contract, during which companies recoup their investments, is always the most profitable under DoD contracting terms. It is also the moment when companies begin to lay off employees if there are no new orders, contributing to the illusion – for that is what it is – of robustness. Ironically, as one analyst explains, "companies are able to cut their costs and book higher profits on a more mature program base only because new business is drying up."[40] With fewer or no new orders and with shrinking backlogs, the coming years are seen by many industry analysts to be a period when "supernova" becomes the dominant metaphor for the industry.

Structural disarmament may only recently have begun to be viewed with real anxiety by observers in the United States. This does not mean, however, that all was well in the defence industrial base before its onset; there have been expressions of concern for some years about an impending structural crisis in this sector, albeit for other reasons. In his 1992 analysis of the implications for the defence production base of DoD's new Five-Year Defense Plan through to 1997, then-House Armed Services Committee chairman Les Aspin argued that "if we follow the Department's plan, by the end of the [Plan] we will be out of business entirely in several defense industries, and imminently out of business in several others. And in those remaining sectors, a significant contraction of funding levels and programs occurs."[41] Aspin's worries are illustrated clearly in Table 3.2, which depicts the decline in the number of different system types (though not in the numbers of units) to be produced during and after the current Defense Plan. The hardest-hit sectors obviously will be heavy armoured vehicles (including guns and cannons) and shipbuilding; in the latter case, the five existing yards building Navy vessels may be reduced to as few as two, while tank production capabilities could be lost entirely.

Whatever the national security utility of Defense's new policy on reconstitution and its new acquisition strategy, the American defence industry obviously faces a significant period of restructuring and overall reduction.[42] Already burdened by high debt loads and poor bond

Table 3.2
Number of Program Types in Production, United States, 1992 and 1997

Sector	1992	1997	Post-FYDP[1]
Airframes	25	16	6
Guns/cannons	5	2	0
Hulls	9	2	1
Heavy vehicles	0	0	0
Strategic missiles	7	5	2
Tactical missiles	20	13	8

Source: Aspin, "Tomorrow's Defense From Today's Industrial Base," 3.
1 FYDP = Five-Year Defense Plan.

ratings – and hence by rising costs of borrowing capital – prime contractors have pursued cost-cutting reorganization strategies that have reduced their total workforce from 4.2 million employees in 1988 to 3.8 million in 1990, with 800,000 additional jobs expected to be lost by 1995.[43] To some extent, these cuts are simply beyond the industry's control: when McDonnell Douglas lost the A-12 contract, it had to lay off some 6,000 workers; should the F-15 aircraft production facilities be closed, a further 7,000 jobs may be lost.[44]

Faced with such uncertain prospects, the major U.S. defence contractors have responded in a variety of manners, including downsizing or consolidation in "core" defence businesses, the purchasing of contracts through mergers and acquisitions – which frequently implies divestiture of defence businesses by other companies – and diversification either within the defence sector or into new civilian markets, often through dual-use technologies. Strategic alliances within specific sectors also have begun to be explored.

An important factor affecting the companies' range of strategic choice tends to be the role played by defence contracts in their total revenues (figures for 1990 are provided in Table A.4). Several prime contractors are more than 85 percent defence-dependent – in particular, Loral (100 percent), Northrop, Martin Marietta, General Dynamics, and Alliant Techsystems. While these companies have sought to diversify into closely related non-defence markets – often in such areas of government procurement as air-traffic control and information systems – downsizing and concentration on core defence activities or future technologies appear to be a common theme of their adaptation effort.[45]

For McDonnell Douglas and Raytheon, both with defence business accounting for approximately half of their total revenues, the identi-

fication of critical "core competencies" that must be maintained within
the corporate structure is a primary response to the declining defence
market.[46] Like most of the defence industries in the United States,
these companies view diversification or the politically appealing notion
of conversion as realistic alternatives to only a very limited extent.
Neither approach is sufficient to compensate for the loss of manufacturing as defence business continues to decline. And while conversion
may be a popular electoral phrase at the moment, historically it has
proven to be an extremely difficult path to follow for defence contractors, especially those involved in platform production rather than in
the provision of electronic kit. Accordingly, downsizing, diversification
within defence, or concentration on core activities and the "pulling
in-house" of previously subcontracted business have been the principal
responses of the large u.s. defence contractors to the tightening
domestic defence market.[47]

In addition to these internal corporate responses, companies that
intend to remain active in the u.s. defence market have sought to
acquire divisions being sold by other contractors that are divesting
themselves of peripheral businesses or leaving the defence market
altogether. More recently, strategic alliances within sectors have also
begun to appear. In one example of the latter development, Alliant
Techsystems, itself formed by Honeywell's spin-off of its Defense and
Marine Systems division in September 1990, has acquired Olin Corporation's Ordnance Division and Physics International in return for
the transferral of 22 percent of its common stock to Olin. The deal
will make Alliant the sole supplier of 120–mm tank ammunition to
the u.s. government, eliminating competition in that area, and at the
same time reduce Olin's dependence on defence contracts.[48] Similarly,
Hughes Aircraft's bid to acquire General Dynamics' Air-Defense Systems Division would make the former one of the largest tactical
missiles manufacturers in the United States while reducing overcapacity in that sector through the consolidation process that might be
assumed to follow a successful completion of the transaction.[49] Finally,
following their 1986 joint venture to seek u.s. Army contracts for the
next-generation armoured vehicles to be built around a common
chassis, fmc's Defense Systems Group is believed to be currently
pursuing a permanent alliance with General Dynamics' Systems Division, since "with the downsizing of the military, there probably will
not be enough business for two [independent] companies."[50]

Clearly, the larger u.s. defence contractors are responding to their
new business environment in various ways that will see a restructuring
of the domestic defence industry. Despite the Bush administration's

avowed intention to "let the market decide" and despite the view of
some industry executives that the best position for the government to
take is to "get out of the way," it is rather less clear how far these
corporations will be able to proceed without meeting political intervention either from the Clinton administration or, more probably –
and probably more immediately – from Congress.

One issue that will bring almost automatic Congressional involvement in monitoring defence contractors' activities is the fate of the
subcontractors and small businesses that make up the lower tiers of
the defence industrial base. In discussing their intentions to develop
in-house capabilities for work that was previously subcontracted in
order to maintain their own employment levels, executives of some
larger contractors readily acknowledge that the most worrisome issue
is not their own prospects but those of the subcontractor base. These
smaller companies are often heavily or entirely defence-dependent
and frequently rely on contracts from a single prime contractor. In
addition, they tend to be marginal organizations with very limited
backlogs of work and little financial capacity to weather a prolonged
downturn in business. At times, they are mainly commercial suppliers
of dual-use technologies. Despite their size, these smaller defence
suppliers are often critical, "because they develop much of the innovative and leading-edge technologies needed for next generation
weapons systems."[51] Thus a 1990 report from the Office of Technology
Assessment argued plainly that Congress would be obliged in the early
part of the decade "to choose between managing the down-sizing of
the defense industrial sector or letting it be dismantled piecemeal" by
corporations pursuing the bottom line.[52]

The strength of political support for existing legislation such as
Small Business Set-Asides indicates where the preference of Congress
would lie under these circumstances: after Congress received from the
Pentagon a report analyzing the condition and future of the u.s.
defence industry in early November 1991, its response was that "allowing the defense industrial base to shrink by free market forces is not
what we would call a strategy."[53] Both Congressional and industry
officials are now calling for the creation of a national strategy to
support the DIB rather than allow a process of industrial Darwinism
to determine which contractors will survive. No solutions have yet
emerged from the industrial-base debates, but the proposals recently
presented by the House Armed Services Committee chairman in
response to the Pentagon's new acquisition strategy and to the notion
of reconstitution, suggest that Congress intends to play an active (even
a proactive) role in helping to shape the defence industrial base in
the remainder of this decade.[54]

CONCLUSION

In seeking to determine whether and to what extent the activities of defence industries could replace government initiatives in support of a more open Alliance defence market, we have examined corporate restructuring strategies within both the European and u.s. defence markets. This analysis has revealed a central theme – namely, that both are political markets to a significant degree, driven by a logic that does not necessarily match that of industry and that tends to set strong limits or "boundary conditions" on the ability of market imperatives to determine the structure of the market and of defence trade relationships within it. Does this focus on the two geographically separate markets skirt the possibility that a wider transatlantic defence market may be emerging? Is our emphasis on the distinctiveness of the Alliance's defence markets misleading?

We think not. To begin with, it is apparent that industry-initiated m&a activities of a transatlantic nature have been very limited, in either direction: not only is the Atlantic not a two-way street, it hardly rates as even a one-way path. Between 1986 and 1988, of a total of 42 acquisitions made by American companies, 37 were in the domestic market, three in the United Kingdom, and one in France (the other was in Canada). American companies have shown very little interest in pursuing formal transatlantic industrial linkages, which is especially surprising given the advent of EC92 and the commonplace business reasoning that "being there" is a critical element in successful market penetration. British companies were, it is true, more active, making 20 acquisitions in the United States, along with 24 in the United Kingdom and one each in Canada, the Netherlands, and Germany. The other leading European defence industrial country, France, saw its companies make only five acquisitions, four in the United States and one at home. Thus, of 90 acquisitions accomplished by companies of these three NATO members, 62 were made within their own markets and 28 on a transatlantic axis, with only four of the latter involving acquisitions of European businesses by u.s. companies.⁵⁵ If governments hope to hand over the initiative to industry in establishing patterns of transatlantic cooperation, the record of formal mergers and acquisitions offers little concrete demonstration of such an inclination or capability, with the single exception of u.k. manufacturers.

Moreover, as our review of European corporate activities indicated, there are evident factors limiting the extent to which industrial restructuring strategies in EC countries can proceed before they run up against national political interests and "boundary conditions." Much the same is true of the appreciation by European governments of the merits of transatlantic defence trade and defence economic relations. While the Bush administration was ostensibly committed to the notion that industry and the market must decide the future of the defence industrial base and defence trade, with government merely playing a "permissive" rather than a leadership role, this position had less appeal in the eyes of Congress. The perspective of many in that latter body may be glimpsed in the following passage from the previously cited Office of Technology Assessment report:

The dilemma for policy makers is that the interests of the u.s. defense companies may not coincide with the future national interests of the United States ... international collaboration can increase u.s. dependence on potentially unreliable foreign sources to unacceptable levels, erode the middle tiers of the u.s. defense industrial base, take business away from u.s. companies and jobs from u.s. workers, and transfer valuable technology to competitors that may later be used to penetrate civilian markets in the United States. Perhaps most important, industry-to-industry collaboration reduces government control over the distribution of advanced defense technology.[56]

The controversy over the u.s.-Japan FSX program, though perhaps an extreme example given the otherwise volatile nature of that bilateral relationship, may be a harbinger of future such disputes if the concerns expressed in the report eventually become policy initiatives.

Our examination of the progress and prospects for corporate-led defence market restructuring convinces us of the wisdom of Callaghan's observation, cited at the end of chapter 2, that substantive transatlantic defence economic cooperation required political leadership and sustained political will. Since the collapse of the government-negotiated Nunn Amendment projects, several government officials in the United States and Europe (most notably in Britain) have expressed the wish that defence companies be allowed to lead the way in seeking out and establishing future collaborative ventures on an efficient and profitable basis. In practice, however, although companies may have greater leeway, their activities remain subject to numerous political limitations. The nature of the defence market is such that the establishment of more open trade and improved defence economic relations depends finally on the actions of governments that are the "only buyers in the arms market in the Alliance, who control export sales and who are in most nations the only ones able to finance the development of products."[57]

PART TWO

The Domestic Context

CHAPTER FOUR

The Defence Industrial Base: Domestic Policy Context and Industry Review

Directly or indirectly, changes in the international economic and security environment, governmental policy initiatives related to defence economic relations, and corporate responses to both of the above have a powerful and unavoidable impact on the export-oriented Canadian defence industry. But government policies pertaining to that industry are no less affected by external variables. Over the past four years since the outbreak of the Persian Gulf crisis and the rapid conclusion of the war that followed, the impact of these factors has been highlighted by a series of parliamentary debates over Canadian export policy regarding defence products, following the approval of General Motors' sale to Saudi Arabia of 1,117 light armoured vehicles (LAVs) produced in London, Ontario. More recently, a proposed sale of frigates by Saint John Shipbuilding to Saudi Arabia has whetted parliamentary concern over sales of weapons platforms to non-Allied recipients, especially those situated in troubled regions such as the Middle East.[1]

Whatever other issues it raised, the fact that the proposed LAV sale led to hearings on the criminal code and on the Export and Import Permit Act suggests another policy context that may set "boundary conditions" for the Canadian defence industry – namely, the political and economic realities of the domestic defence market. To be sure, the export policy review has not exactly dominated public discussion in Canada, not even among those few people who take a serious interest in procurement issues. Two other matters – the dispute over the perceived favouritism shown to Quebec by former Defence Minister Marcel Masse in the awarding of several major new defence contracts and the controversy surrounding the support given by his successor Kim Campbell to a prior decision to purchase fifty EH-101 helicopters (at a total program cost of more than $5 billion) – have received far more publicity.[2] Whatever the merit of the criticisms levelled at the two ministers, the fact that attacks such as these are made so regularly clearly indicates that one must not lose sight of the domestic context when examining the recent politics of Canadian defence acquisition.[3]

Accordingly, this chapter begins with a review of the domestic policy environment within which the Canadian defence industry has evolved. We also explore the salient contours of the contemporary policy context, paying special attention to the roles and interests of the major actors, including those in key federal government departments. We then summarize the dominant characteristics of the Canadian defence industrial base before concluding the chapter with a brief analysis of the sectoral structure and composition of the industry.

THE DOMESTIC POLICY ENVIRONMENT: HISTORICAL BACKGROUND

The history of the Canadian defence industrial base (DIB) since World War II has been characterized by two main trends. The first is closer cooperation with, and integration into, the U.S. defence industry and market; the second is the shift away from the domestic production of major platforms towards a concentration on subsystems and components.[4]

The origins of the first trend can be traced back to the Ogdensburg Declaration, signed on 18 August 1940, in which Prime Minister Mackenzie King and President Franklin Roosevelt agreed to coordinate defence production, and from which would emerge the Permanent Joint Board on Defence. This declaration was significant for two reasons: for Canada, it was a recognition that this country was part of North America, with vital interests linked to continental defence and cooperation with Washington; for the United States, it marked an awareness of Canada's importance as an element in continental military and industrial preparedness.[5]

King and Roosevelt met again on 20 April 1941, eight months after their Ogdensburg encounter, at the president's private residence in New York's Hudson River Valley. The result of this second meeting – the Hyde Park Declaration – signalled their intention to "develop a coordinated program of requirements, production, and procurement."[6] This second statement of purpose was a major step on the road to a North American defence market and fostered the expectation that the border between the two countries would, in effect, be eliminated almost completely with respect to all defence-related concerns, whether purely military or defence economic. Defence production from that time would increasingly be contemplated in continental rather than national terms, though it has to be said that this perspective has been more evident in Canada than in the United States.[7]

Since the early 1940s, some fifty bilateral defence production agreements have been signed by Ottawa and Washington, conforming to the spirit of the Ogdensburg and Hyde Park Declarations. In particular, an exchange of notes on 26 October 1950 reaffirmed the principle of joint defence production and resource sharing set out in the latter declaration, through the issuance of a new Statement of Principles of Economic Cooperation, which was subsequently incorporated into the U.S. armed-services procurement regulations. Bilateral defence economic transactions increased rapidly during the 1950s as a result of the outbreak of the Korean War and of subsequent mobilization efforts, with U.S. military procurement from Canada reaching $300 million in FY 1952. Canadian purchases from the United States between April 1951 and December 1952 totalled approximately $850 million.[8] Once the Korean conflict ended, however, these levels fell rapidly and both governments tended to favour their domestic industries in a shrinking market. However, to the amount of defence equipment being traded should be added the sums transferred under the U.S. Defense Production Act, both to obtain "strategic minerals" for the National Defense Stockpile and to expand Canadian productive capacity in some of these minerals (especially nickel).[9]

The 1950s also witnessed the rapid expansion of the Canadian defence industry under the leadership of C.D. Howe's new Department of Defence Production, established in 1951. By 1957, for example, the industry was producing a variety of piston and jet engines (including, among the latter, the Orenda and Iroquois); it had also developed a strong electronics sector and was selling small numbers of aircraft to the United States and shipping much larger numbers to the European allies.[10] This swelling in Canadian defence production capabilities was taking place even though, once the post-Korean War demobilization began, neither Ottawa nor Washington was particularly anxious to expand continental defence economic cooperation; indeed, it could be argued that the stagnation in bilateral procurement was the cause of this outward thrust.

By 1958, however, the Canadian defence industry was facing a crisis and Canada became the first NATO member to experience structural disarmament, although no one identified the problem in those words at the time. Despite undeniable technical successes and achievements, Canada's defence industry suffered the effects of the collision between the spiralling costs of advanced-technology weapons platforms and a limited domestic market. The crisis hit home with the cancellation of the CF-105 Avro Arrow aircraft; in abandoning that program, Canada was effectively also abandoning future domestic development prospects for entire major weapons systems. In this new context, Ottawa and Washington agreed in 1959 to the Defence Production Sharing Program (also known as "Arrangement," thus its acronym, DPSA), the essence of which, from the Canadian perspective, was the "removal of obstacles that prevented Canadian firms from bidding for U.S. defence contracts on an equal basis with their U.S. competitors, and the consolidation of these gains by embodying them not only in U.S. procurement regulations, but in the behaviour of procurement agencies and of U.S. and Canadian firms."[11]

When the DPSA was reviewed four years later, a new provision was added to the original objectives, stating that, henceforth, each side should seek to maintain "a rough long-term balance in reciprocal defence procurement at increasing levels." (During the late 1980s, this goal was to come under critical reexamination in the face of persistently large American surpluses – an issue to which we shall return in chapter 5.)[12] Also in 1963, both sides signed a memorandum of understanding regarding cooperative R&D projects, especially with respect to joint funding and permission for Canadian firms to bid on American defence R&D contracts funded solely by the U.S. government. The resulting Defence Development Sharing Arrangement (DDSA) was intended to complement the DPSA by helping Canadian industry to take part in the early stages of new systems development aimed at meeting future Pentagon requirements.[13]

As a result of the Arrow decision and the subsequent signing of the DPSA and DDSA, the defence industry in Canada "increasingly evolved into a subsystem/component supplier to both the DoD and American prime contractors. Other export opportunities for specialized Canadian products evolved in large part from this relationship with the United States."[14] Whatever arguments might be made about the sovereignty implications of this dependence on access to the U.S. defence market – or, for that matter, on whether there existed any realistic alternative to dependence if maintaining defence industrial capabilities was deemed to be necessary – the new relationship clearly did make the domestic industry vulnerable to shifts in the trade and economic policy climate of the United States. And as neither set of sharing arrangements held treaty status, they were and remain open to alterations, restrictions, or simple evasions on the part both of Congress and of successive administrations – a flaw that was exposed about a decade after they had been signed.

As part of a comprehensive review of the United States' international economic relationships, Treasury and Commerce Department officials sought in 1971 to eliminate a number of bilateral Canada-U.S. trade irritants. Among those irritants, they cited a Canadian surplus in defence trade (largely a result of Department of Defense procurements during the Vietnam War), as well as the 10-percent preference given by Ottawa to Canadian companies seeking the award of new domestic defence contracts. Although the trade talks were broken off in 1972, the intrusion of the Treasury and Commerce Departments into the domain of bilateral defence economic relations, and the linkage of such issues to broader U.S. economic policy concerns, marked a significant departure from American practice of the previous few years. With the U.S. Department of Defense no longer the sole manager on its side of the relationship, the sharing program became more "vulnerable to modification, or even termination, through bargaining trade-offs for what Canada perceived to be highly questionable criteria."[15]

It is perhaps difficult to justify the accusation implied in the term "highly questionable criteria," given Ottawa's own constant focus upon the economic aspects of the DPSA and DDSA (particularly the former), but in retrospect this episode can nonetheless be seen as a harbinger of the change in the nature of the bilateral defence economic relationship that occurred by the late 1980s and early 1990s. The defence trade balance during the past decade has shifted heavily in favour of U.S. industry; even so, the general economic malaise in the United States during the past few years has fostered a sense that the country's trading partners are "taking advantage" of it, and this has led to renewed pressures – from the Congress rather than the administration, this time – being directed at the defence-sharing arrangements. Concomitant with this rise in resentment in the United States has been a call by the Canadian defence industry for the bilateral defence trade relationship to be placed on the same treaty basis as trade in the non-military sector. This shows clearly that defence company representatives recognize the critical importance of access to the U.S. defence market and are keenly aware of their present vulnerability to political interventions by Congress in response to pressure from domestic interest groups in the United States.[16]

While the Canadian industry's sense of vulnerability was triggered by the Nixon administration's interventions in the early 1970s, the defence policy review initiated at about the same time by the government of Prime Minister Pierre Elliott Trudeau promised to have a more severe and immediate impact on the structure and composition of the domestic defence industry. The details of the defence policy review need not occupy us here; suffice it to note that for Canadian defence producers, the failure to carry through on procurement plans mooted by the Pearson government, coupled with a virtual moratorium on new procurement projects, was to result in "a major erosion of Canada's military capabilities and ... a concomitant erosion of Canada's defence industrial base."[17]

Until the Defence Structure Review was initiated in December 1974, the domestic aerospace and defence industry relied on such civilian and export sales as it could find to maintain at least some of its rapidly deteriorating capabilities.[18] The second phase of the review, which was completed in November 1975, established a revised funding formula for the Department of National Defence (DND) whereby the budget would be indexed to inflation and capital equipment procurement funds would increase by an additional 12 percent a year until such time as they accounted for 20 percent of total defence spending.

The funding increases resulting from the review proved invaluable for the rebuilding or expansion of what had since 1959 become the major elements of the Canadian defence manufacturing base – aircraft components, defence electronics (especially systems integration), ships, small arms, and light armoured and other vehicles. Of course, those increases in funding were from a base that had been lowered substantially as a result of earlier spending reductions imposed by the first of Trudeau's defence reviews in the late 1960s. Reports published at the close of the Trudeau era suggested that the government had only approved slightly more than half of the procurement funding estimated to be required to cover the necessary replacement of obsolete equipment until the end of the century.[19]

The period from the late 1960s to mid-1970s was further noteworthy because two "givens," or parameters, of future procurement policy became established: tight budget constraints accompanied by vacillating government direction; and the requirement that offset provisions be attached to all major equipment purchases from foreign sources (including the United States). The deferment, scaling-back, or outright cancellation of projects previously proposed under Prime Minister Lester Pearson, the period of spending freeze, and then the reversal of policy in the Defence Structure Review resulted in a pattern in Canadian defence procurement decisions that came to resemble nothing so much as, in the words of one commentator, "ad hoc obsolescence management."[20] It was this unpredictable, short-term, and fundamentally reactive procurement environment that the 1987 Defence White Paper, *Challenge and Commitment*, was supposed to correct, with its emphasis on long-term planning, greater and more dependable funding for "essential" procurement projects, and better industrial-preparedness planning.

The 1987 White Paper, or more precisely its subsequent gutting in the April 1989 budget, merely continued (albeit in dramatic form) the trend established in the early 1970s.[21] The familiar cycle of procurement proposals, policy reversals, and new proposals at further-reduced levels was on display again in the span of only a few months between late 1991 and early 1992, beginning with the unveiling of what was supposed to have been the country's "new" defence policy in September 1991. This new policy lasted until February 1992, when as part of its budgetary revisions the government announced an additional force structure reduction of 1,000 troops and the reversal of its decision to retain a stationed task force of 1,100 troops in Europe after 1995. In a similar display of pinchbeck consistency, Defence Minister Marcel Masse announced on 7 April 1992 a $1.8 billion procurement plan for 100 new helicopters and 229 light armoured vehicles, to be acquired respectively from Bell Helicopter Textron (Mirabel, Quebec) and GM Diesel Division (London, Ontario); but he also cancelled the planned procurement of a $2.8 billion batch of multirole combat vehicles, which had been announced the previous September.[22]

The vacillation and unpredictability of the Mulroney government in the matter of defence policy, and the undeniable influence that broader financial or other economic policy considerations had on defence policy, were not a departure from the trend established during the late 1960s but rather its most recent iteration.[23] Whatever the validity of the criticisms directed at former Defence Minister Masse (principally that he unduly "favoured" Quebec firms), the debates over the Bell Helicopter Textron contract also highlight the second given of the defence procurement policy process in Canada – namely, the requirement for various forms of offsets and "regional industrial benefits."

The effective abandonment in 1959 of domestic production of major non-naval weapons systems or platforms to meet the needs of the Canadian Forces, which implied that a proportionate amount of DND procurement dollars would be spent with foreign suppliers, "provided the catalyst for a 'new' comprehensive defence-purchasing strategy."[24] Beginning with the competition to provide the new long-range patrol aircraft and later with the new fighter aircraft program, the "issue of industrial benefits to Canada from weapons procurements emerged, and was to remain, as a primary political and economic consideration in defence decision-making."[25]

The use of offsets or industrial-benefits provisions was viewed as a valuable means of maintaining some domestic defence industrial capabilities and reducing the potential political fallout resulting from the expenditure of large sums of DND money outside Canada. As two students of the issue have put it, offsets and industrial benefits were attractive in that they enabled the "central purchasing agency to place major contracts with offshore suppliers and simultaneously guarantee substantial orders for domestic firms."[26] Beginning in 1986, there was a shift in emphasis away from quantitative measures of benefits and offsets towards such qualitative and long-term gains as the inflow of technological knowledge. Such gains were considered to be much more valuable than the earlier "build-to-print orientation of recent military procurement," which had been criticized in the 1983 Report of the Advisory Committee on Aerospace Development as precluding "any real state-of-the-art improvement in Canadian engineering or design."[27]

The implementation of the industrial-benefits policy in the 1970s served to reinforce the preexisting trend towards integration of Canadian defence companies into the U.S. defence market as specialized subcontractors. Because of the need to fulfil the new offset requirements, U.S. prime contractors intensified their relationships with Canadian suppliers and in some cases established subsidiaries in Canada. These two trends – integration and specialization – were strengthened with the creation in 1987 of the North American Defence Industrial Base Organization (NADIBO), although under the current rapidly changing environment that organization has become comatose, at least temporarily.[28]

By the early 1990s, these facets of the Canadian defence industry were combining with two dominant characteristics of the domestic policy environment pertaining to defence procurement issues – uncertainty resulting from budgetary constraints and from the lack of long-term leadership and direction on the part of the government; and the use of procurement budgets, such as they are, in the pursuit of domestic economic and political policy objectives – in a manner reminiscent of the concerns raised in the early 1970s about access to the U.S. market. A defence industry heavily dependent upon, and integrated into, the North American defence market today faces U.S. industries that are increasingly bent upon maintaining their own production capabilities and employment levels. The use of industrial-benefit requirements, especially by Canada but also by some other NATO allies, is being criticized in the United States as a pernicious form of "double-dipping," and Congress has been pressing for the review of existing bilateral defence industrial and trade memoranda of understanding, purportedly to take U.S. economic interests more fully into account. At the same time, the Canadian defence industry must seek to plan as best it can in the face of myriad uncertainties over the future of DND procurement budgets and of government policy turnabouts and pressures for further defence budget reductions to generate a "peace dividend" from the ending of the Cold War. The domestic policy context becomes more important, yet also more difficult to fathom.

THE CONTEMPORARY DOMESTIC CONTEXT

In a 1988 article written for the defence journal *Forum*, W.L. Claggett, sales manager of Defence Product Sales at General Motors of Canada's Diesel Division, discussed the "government–industry duet" that characterized the normal operating environment for defence industries based in Canada. Claggett identified some fifteen offices in five government departments and agencies with which his division was in routine contact in its pursuit of defence contracts at home and abroad.[29] A major concern raised in the article, and expressed at numerous defence industry conferences, was that "it is often difficult to determine who is supposed to occupy the leadership role," especially on the issue of international defence sales.[30]

In truth, "duet" is a misleading term, because it understates the chaos that reigns in the defence-industrial concert hall in Canada. To begin with, in discussions of the domestic policy context and the policy-making process pertaining to the defence industrial base, many analyses tend to leave out perhaps the most important bureaucratic actor, since it is one without a direct and immediate presence. We refer to the Department of Finance, which plays a powerful role in establishing the conditions within which the other, more directly involved, departments must operate. As two DND officials have noted, "the government has set the broader fiscal context for defence policy – and, indeed all government operations – through its commitment to reduce Canada's accumulated national debt ... This fiscal context has specific implications for the Department of National Defence [since] the defence budget is seen as a discretionary item."[31]

In the 1989 federal budget, planned defence expenditures were to be reduced by $2.74 billion over five years; the 1990 budget subtracted a further $658 million from future DND coffers. The defence policy announced in September 1991, as modified in the February 1992 federal budget, included additional reductions of $258 million for 1992–93 and $272 million for 1993–94, so that "in all, since 1989, [projected] defence spending has been cut by close to $6 billion."[32] The Chrétien government's first budget, unveiled in late February

1994, did something novel: it actually reduced defence spending instead of simply paring back "projected defence budgets." Although the oft-cited figure of $7 billion in defence cuts between 1994 and 1999 involved some elimination of projected increases, there was no blinking the fact this time: actual defence spending in current-year dollars would be reduced. From a figure of $11.3 billion in 1993–94, defence spending is to decline to $10.8 billion in 1994–95 and $10.5 billion in 1995–96. By the latter date, it is estimated that defence spending as a share of gross domestic product (GDP) will have shrunk to 1.5 percent.[33]

Within this general context of budgetary constraints, defence companies must still seek a livelihood; in doing so, they find themselves dealing with the multitude of departments and agencies customarily referred to in most studies of the domestic policy environment for defence industry issues. Table 4.1 summarizes the relevant federal government actors, including those specific directorates or offices within departments with particularly significant defence industry-related roles; the mandates or areas of responsibility of the departments and directorates or offices; and the main policy instruments at their disposal.[34] The table represents the wide variety of actors, mandates, and instruments with which defence industries in Canada must attempt to deal.[35] It also indicates the number of sources of assistance – in planning, marketing, and finance – to which these industries may turn. From the industry's perspective, the bureaucracy is far from being entirely constraining, not to say menacing; there is also a beneficial side of the story, as shown in Table A.5, where the notes offer insights into the potential advantages associated with multiple and overlapping bureaucratic mandates.

However beneficial some aspects of this bureaucratic web of jurisdictions may be, the competing and often contradictory demands on industry continue to draw criticism – and not only from the defence companies. One issue, in particular, can be guaranteed to raise eyebrows: the requirement for industrial and regional benefits. These are of special interest in the United States, where much scrutiny has been brought to bear on whether industrial and regional benefits requirements (IRBs) violate the spirit of the DPSA and DDSA. They have also featured largely in the domestic policy debate. IRBs have proven to be a useful policy tool with which successive governments in Canada have sought to direct defence expenditure towards the achievement of regional economic objectives.[36] Their value has inhered primarily in the fact that defence spending represents such a large proportion – more than a third – of the federal government's discretionary funds

Table 4.1
Canada's Defence Industrial Base: Major Federal Government Actors and Policy
Instruments

Department/agency and selected key directorates	*Defence industrial base-related mandates/ activities and policy instruments*
Department of National Defence – Maritime/Land/Air Doctrine and Operations – Associate Deputy Minister (Materiel) – Director General, International and Industry Programs (includes DDIR) – Chief, Research and Development	User department: – establishing current and future supply requirements – R&D and life-cycle support – international cooperative programs (IJDPS); industrial preparedness planning and analysis in DDIR – in-house R&D for Canadian Forces, using CRAD budget (Defence Industrial Research Program)
External Affairs and International Trade Canada (EAITC, now DFAIT) – International Marketing Bureau, Aerospace and Defence Program Division	Primary responsibility for defence trade activities and promoting international trade: – prepare profiles of short- and medium-term export market opportunities for key sectors (defence and civilian aerospace and marine products – provide potential foreign customers with information on Canadian industrial capabilities; and assist Canadian companies' export efforts – increase access to U.S. RDP defence and commercial markets via DDSA and DPSA; and manage RDP defence arrangements with European nations, including Task Force on Europe 1992 recommendations – enhance/maintain Defence Program Strategy of "Going Global" – export controls and permit programs
Supply and Services Canada/Canadian Commercial Corporation (SSC/CCC, now DGS/CCC)	SSC/DGS is the department responsible for handling all DND contracts in Canada; CCC facilitates foreign (especially U.S.) purchases of military items on a government-to-government basis. – collect information on defence procurement and DIB capabilities (e.g., Defence Industrial Base Review 1987, Federal Procurement Database) – Canadian Content Policy; Open Bidding Policy; and Procurement Review Board (non-defence items)

Table 4.1
(cont'd)

Department/agency and selected key directorates	Defence industrial base-related mandates/ activities and policy instruments
Industry, Science and Technology Canada (ISTC, now IC and SC)	Mandated to plan and implement industrial support programs in Canada relating to regional industrial development, trade and commerce, including defence industries. – Defence Industry Productivity Program (DIPP): oversight of DIPP funds – Program for Export Market Development (PEMD) coordination – Industrial and Regional Benefits Policy as part of Canadian Annual Procurement Strategy (CAPS) – preparation of industry profiles and statistical analyses; and emergency planning coordination
Export Development Corporation (EDC)	Government financing, guarantees and insurance for international sales – restricted to Canadian content only of defence products

Source: Compiled from Claggett, "Government-industry duet"; Canadian Defence Industry Guide, 1992; Chief, Research and Development, the Defence Industrial Research Program, Department of National Defence; Your Way to the Government Market: Access to the Federal Procurement Database; Sandor, "Notes for a Speech"; and R. Thomas, "Canadian Annual Procurement Strategy."

and that, unlike other forms of discretionary expenditure, it is bound by neither legal agreement nor statutory obligation.[37] Equally significant, GATT restrictions and Canada-U.S. Free Trade Agreement conditions that limit the discriminatory use of procurement so as to favour domestic industry do not apply to matters related to national security and defence expenditure.[38] Despite these advantages, both the use of defence spending to pursue non-defence objectives and the more particular impact of IRB requirements on the Canadian defence industrial base have come under critical scrutiny at home for several reasons.

First, although the IRB policy established in 1986 by Industry, Science and Technology Canada (ISTC, now Industry Canada and Science Canada) considers the foremost priorities in procurement to be operational requirements, competition, and accessibility, followed by lesser objectives such as industrial and regional development, IRBs can nonetheless determine who will win and who will lose the competition for contracts. As one analyst has summed it up so well, "a satisfactory IRB proposal cannot make an otherwise unsatisfactory bid acceptable.

The converse, however, is also true. An otherwise satisfactory bid can lose because of an unsatisfactory IRB proposal."[39] Mindful of this, companies bidding for defence contracts have had to juggle the competing demands of the user department (DND) and the department judging the IRB proposals (ISTC/IC), with the former insisting on efficiency in resource allocation (that is, on achieving the lowest cost of producing a given level of defence capability) and the latter emphasizing regional equity.[40]

A second criticism of the IRB process has been that by frequently involving the establishment of new production facilities in Canada, it has served to stimulate overcapacity, thereby exacerbating the defence industry's dependence on exports. Companies involved in high-technology production, it has been remarked, "require very rich diets," and it is far from certain that they can find sufficient new work once their original contracts have been completed.[41] While the industrial benefits policy of the past twenty years has served to facilitate the establishment in Canada of some companies and production capabilities not hitherto present, the focus on investment in new companies becomes counterproductive for the economic health of the industry when it creates excess capacity. By dint of increasing overcapacity, this policy may weaken or undermine established companies' prospects. Accordingly, officials at ISTC, as well as industry representatives, have been suggesting that the IRB requirements associated with future defence contracts should place greater emphasis on supporting *existing* production facilities in Canada, not on creating new competitors.[42]

That it confronts defence contractors with confusing departmental overlapping and creates excess capacity have not been the only charges levelled against IRB policy; according to industry executives testifying before the Senate Special Committee on National Defence in 1984, the policy in force at that time provided merely "low tech scraps of weapons systems developed abroad in return for the political illusion of jobs" and was clearly intended chiefly to make defence budgets more palatable to cabinet and to public opinion.[43] The use of defence spending to achieve economic policy goals has itself been criticized because "other public expenditures may be just as effective, if not more so, in influencing regional patterns of employment and incomes," despite the ostensible advantages of defence expenditures alluded to earlier.[44]

The IRB policy revisions announced by the federal government in May 1986 were intended to allay those criticisms. The new policy concentrated on such qualitative benefits as technology transfer and R&D to be performed in Canada; investment and product development; and licensing agreements. The aim was "to create long-term, sustainable economic activity in Canada that results in goods and services which are internationally competitive."[45] In addition, in order to streamline the process and reduce the administrative load on smaller Canadian companies, ISTC indicated that in the future it would not seek IRBs on contracts valued at less than $100 million; instead, IRB requirements would be applied only to major crown projects.[46]

The procurement of the Martin Marietta-Oerlikon Buhrle air defence/anti-tank system (ADATS) to meet Canadian Forces requirements for a low-level air defence capability, because of the industrial benefits arrangements associated with the project, has been touted as an example of how the new IRB policy should work. The Oerlikon contract involved "certain world product mandates with export possibilities, technology transfer and investment in the defence industrial base, combined with a regional development programme which satisfies DND's needs."[47] Since 1986, when the choice of the new system was made – or, more to the point, since 1989 when the above comments were written – the changing international security environment and the decision to withdraw all Canadian troops from Europe and close the two Canadian Forces bases in Germany have left the question of export potential in serious doubt while effectively eliminating the original DND rationale for the entire project. In fairness, this may be less an observation on the logic of either the IRB requirements or the procurement selection process than on how quickly the external security context has been transformed and how ad hoc defence policymaking by the federal government can sometimes contradict its own recent and costly procurement choices.

Nevertheless, the low-level air defence project did not address the concern expressed about creating new companies or projects in Canada that would depend on exports to survive. In the end, this may prove to have been a major flaw, given changing market conditions, though it was initially considered an excellent opportunity.[48] The Oerlikon contract did offer work for a number of existing high-technology industries in Canada, including Litton Systems Canada, CAE Electronics, Devtek Corporation, Dowty Canada, Lavalin Incorporated, and Spar Aerospace. However, if the long-term value of the project to these companies depends on success in obtaining extensive export sales, as seems to be the case, then the final judgment on the procurement program is likely to be less positive than the one made in 1989.

Aside from this particular controversial example, a number of possible changes in the management of industrial policies – not just those pertaining to the defence sector but others of a more general nature regarding all government procurement – suggest that the difficulties created by the complex departmental web of regulations and responsibilities have been recognized and that complaints from industry groups such as the Forum for Industrial Participation (formerly the Canadian Industrial Benefits Association) have been heard in relevant government offices. Formal evaluation of the long-term economic benefits – industrial and regional – actually attained from the new IRB policy has not yet been undertaken, partly because of the short lapse of time since the new policy's inception. Nevertheless, a review of that policy has been set into motion to identify means of improving its implementation. Moreover, the Canadian content policy announced by Supply and Services Canada (currently Public Works and Government Services Canada), effective from 1 April 1992, was intended to simplify all government procurement procedures by replacing with a single set of guidelines the eleven policies previously existing affecting "Canadian content."[49]

Although still in their early stages, it is apparent that neither the IRB review nor the new Canadian content policy has resolved the problem of competing government objectives and mandates – a problem cited both by industry groups and by federally appointed study teams such as the Defence Industrial Preparedness Task Force.[50] However, the measures adopted should at least reduce the burden of paperwork and additional time facing companies seeking to fulfil IRB demands or to determine whether their products meet Canadian-content levels. At the same time, there is concern that the revised federal regulations on content policy might expose Canadian manufacturers to competition from international companies, some of which receive considerable support from national governments. Be that as it may, it seems safe to predict that, insofar as the domestic policy context is concerned, current priorities will remain largely unchanged, with defence trade and procurement continuing to play second fiddle to domestic political and economic realities.

CANADA'S DEFENCE INDUSTRIAL BASE: A SECTORAL ANALYSIS

Despite some rather exaggerated claims and occasional trivializations to the contrary, the first and most general remark to make regarding defence production in Canada is that there does not now exist, and has never existed, a "military-industrial complex" comparable to what is found in the United States, the larger European countries, or for that matter, even in neutral Sweden.[51] Any claims that Canada has a military lobby of some 500,000 to three million members with the military, economic, political, and bureaucratic clout to distort the country's defence policy would seem to be betrayed by the relatively quick and comprehensive demise of the 1987 White Paper, as well as by subsequent (and repeated) program deferments and cancellations, the frequent zigzags in government procurement plans, and the demonstrated power of other departments (such as Finance and ISTC/IC) to press their competing claims on limited public funds.[52] The complicated reality of the domestic policy context is far removed from caricatured versions of a military-industrial complex, even though defence lobby groups certainly do exist (as they do for any other industry), and even though former high-ranking military officers are found in the executive ranks of the corporate sector, where their understanding of DND requirements and knowledge of remaining personnel can offer some advantages to their new employers.

The second point worthy of note, partly derivative of the first, is that the macroeconomic impact of Canadian defence industries is limited, whether measured as a percentage of gross national product, of trade, or of the total domestic workforce.[53] Admittedly, within particular industry sectors and geographic regions, its importance can be much greater, a point we highlight below.

Third, and again at this very general level, the defence industry is incapable of fulfilling the equipment needs of the Canadian Forces, even after (or despite) the reductions and revisions announced in September 1991, February 1992, and February 1994. Indeed, it has been neither structured nor tasked to fulfil those needs since the late 1950s.

One particular characteristic of the Canadian defence industrial base is that it is composed primarily of small and medium-size enterprises, with sales of under $100 million per year. Foreign ownership of defence industries is also comparatively high – at more than 60 percent – in relation to the situation in other countries, and it is especially prevalent among the largest firms. This reflects, for the most part, the decision in the late 1950s to abandon domestic development of major systems, but it also is a consequence, as we have argued, of subsequent IRB policies requiring foreign companies competing for DND contracts to establish production facilities in this country. Finally, the Canadian defence industry is characterized by an extremely heavy dependence on exports in order to remain economically viable, with the largest percentage being sent to the United States.

Within the defence industry, the major areas of strength are in aerospace, electronics, and communications, where there exists some capability for total systems-design integration. This capability, however, requires considerable technical and financial support, and this can be obtained or developed most easily by the subsidiaries of larger foreign companies, such as Paramax Electronics (prior to the EH-101 cancellation) and Oerlikon Aerospace.[54] Significantly, although there has been growth in western Canada and although the shipbuilding industry in the Atlantic provinces is almost entirely defence-dependent, defence production has been geographically concentrated in Ontario and Quebec, particularly in the "golden triangle" of Toronto-Ottawa-Montreal.[55]

A number of other basic strengths and weaknesses of the Canadian defence industrial base – opposite sides of the same coin, to a large extent – are commonly cited. Take the case of the integration of Canadian and American defence production via DPSA and DDSA and, at an administrative planning level, via NADIBO; this can and does offer Canadian companies favoured access to elements of the much larger U.S. market. Geographic proximity can itself be an advantage, in part as the Pentagon seeks to maintain a reliable variety of "planned producers" of essential defence-related goods. But integration also causes a number of immediate and potential difficulties, not the least of which is the uncertain status of the bilateral defence economic sharing regime. As we indicated earlier, without formal treaty status for the sharing arrangements, the access of Canadian-based industries to the American market will remain subject to gradual erosion through the application of nontariff and other barriers. It will also be hostage to any rise of protectionist sentiment in Congress, either as a result of rapidly declining domestic U.S. defence budgets or because of perceptions of protectionist policies or intentions elsewhere (EC92 and the IEPG's initiatives, for example).

Additionally, the reinvigoration of defence industry capabilities in Canada in the latter part of the 1970s, and the use of industrial benefits requirements to expand these capabilities, have resulted in a defence industry with internationally recognized expertise in a variety of fields including flight simulators, gas turbines, major aircraft components, inertial navigation systems, microwave land systems, and other technologies geared towards specialized needs in aerospace and naval subsystems or components.[56] These specialized capabilities have in turn given Canadian companies competitive advantages in individual niche markets and facilitated their export-sales orientation. However, this comes with a price tag – one that becomes less affordable during periods of lean international markets. As long as these technological skills have remained predominantly Canadian, the niche markets have been reasonably secure. Increasingly, however, as foreign companies or governments respond to a much reduced market and to the growing

Table 4.2
Defence Industry Sector Profiles, 1988–90[1]

Sector	Number of establish- ments	Employ- ment	Total sales	Exports	Exports/ total sales	Defence- dependent	Exports to United States
			($ millions)	($ millions)	(%)	(%)	(%)
Aerospace	200	63,650	5,990.0	4,175	70	30	70
Defence electronics[2]	150	26,330	1,723.0	1,381	80	100	80
Shipbuilding & ship repair	47	12,250	1,568.4	36.4	2.3	90	11
Instrumen- tation	475	25,871	1,952.0	791	40.5	n.a.	69

Source: Industry, Science and Technology Canada, Industry Profile series (Ottawa, 1990–91).
1 Figures refer to ISTC 1990–91 sector profiles reporting results for 1988 (aerospace), 1989 (defence electronics, shipbuilding) and 1990 (instrumentation).
2 Trade and employment statistics for the defence electronics sector are also included within the totals for the aerospace sector.

high-technology composition of defence products, competition in these niches can be expected to become much fiercer. As well, governments may be more inclined to favour domestic producers.

Dependence on niche markets, whether in the United States or overseas, also requires that Canadian industries retain a skilled workforce, capable of adapting quickly to changing industrial processes and techniques. The recent recession may mask, but it does not eliminate, the chronic structural reality of the Canadian defence industry in this instance: the industry has traditionally faced shortages, or at least uncertain availability, of skilled production workers, experienced technologists, and engineers. In addition, the adoption by defence companies – especially second- and third-tier firms – of computer-aided design and manufacturing capabilities, total-quality-management techniques, just-in-time inventory controls, and concurrent engineering has been lagging and may result in their being increasingly vulnerable to competition from such new suppliers as South Korea, Taiwan, and Indonesia.[57]

The core of the domestic defence manufacturing base remains the aerospace and defence electronics sectors, which in many cases are closely integrated: the aerospace industry statistics for trade and employment presented in Table 4.2, for example, include those for defence electronics and space technology companies. The table illustrates the basic composition of the defence industry, based on the most recent estimates available at the time from ISTC; lacking from the sectors listed is that of land systems, for which ISTC (or its successor, Industry Canada) as yet does not produce a sector profile.

Obviously, care must be taken lest one read too much into these summary statistics. As mentioned above, the trade and employment figures for the defence electronics industry cannot be added to those for aerospace, shipbuilding, and instrumentation, since they are included as well within the aerospace statistics (as the avionics subsector). This caveat aside, one interesting finding, confirmed by discussions with officials of what was then ISTC, is that of the total sales for the Canadian aerospace industry in 1988 (almost $6 billion), only 30 percent were obtained from defence contracts. Among this latter set, 70 percent of sales dollars were derived from exports and 30 percent from domestic Canadian defence procurement. As a rough rule-of-thumb, therefore, the aerospace industry in Canada looked to domestic defence contracts in 1988 for $539.1 million, or 9 percent, of total sales – a share that had remained unchanged since at least 1985.

Although as a proportion of defence sales the domestic market is still significant (at roughly 30 percent), the aerospace industry as a whole is certainly cushioned from the immediate impact of declining domestic defence spending. This does not, however, take into account the importance of domestic sales either to individual manufacturers or as a demonstration of a product's acceptance by DND; that latter point could, in turn, become a significant factor for other potential buyers.

The preponderance of foreign ownership is evident in both the aerospace and defence electronics sectors, especially among the larger firms. Despite the purchase of de Havilland (previously owned by Boeing Aircraft Canada, a subsidiary of the U.S. defence contractor) by Bombardier – a move with undoubtedly major implications for the domestic aerospace industry since it established a single, integrated manufacturer (a "national champion" perhaps?) – six of the top ten aerospace firms in Canada are foreign-owned. Among the ranks of the ten leading defence electronics companies, seven are subsidiaries of foreign parents. In both cases, the majority of foreign owners are located in the United States.[58]

The shipbuilding and ship repair industry, relatively small in comparison with the aerospace sector, is largely Canadian-owned and almost entirely dependent on domestic government contracts. The two largest shipyards in eastern Canada – MIL in Quebec and Saint

John Shipbuilding in New Brunswick – possess approximately half the industry's capacity. It is worth noting that the two major naval programs – the Canadian patrol frigate and the Tribal-class update and modernization program – have both involved foreign subsidiaries (Paramax Electronics, owned by Unisys Corporation; and Litton Systems Canada) as suppliers of naval subsystems and for systems integration.[59]

The last sector that we wish to highlight briefly here is one not included in Table 4.2 – land systems. The pivotal companies in this precinct of the industry are Bombardier, General Motors' Diesel Division, and UTDC, although Oerlikon Aerospace and the Western Star Truck Company have gained some public prominence of late as a result of the criticisms directed at the low-level air defence procurement and the award of the light support vehicle wheeled (LSVW) truck contract, respectively. The GM plant, a subsidiary of General Motors of the United States, has also come under intense scrutiny, given that its sale of LAVs to Saudi Arabia was the occasion for parliamentary hearings on Canadian exports of defence-related products.

Our sectoral review here has necessarily been abbreviated, intended merely to set the stage for our next chapter, in which we focus on the economic viability of the Canadian defence industry in the light of current market conditions in Canada and the United States, as well as overseas. Those conditions, a product of both governmental and private-sector decisions, increasingly take on a Darwinian aspect, and the remaining chapters are devoted to an assessment of the ability of the Canadian defence industry to engage in this struggle of the fittest.

CHAPTER FIVE

Defence Production: Changing Markets and Economic Viability

If it is deemed advisable that a technologically advanced defence production capability be retained in Canada, beyond the confines of some form of limited, state-owned arsenal, then it follows that the defence industry must also be commercially viable. For this, three essential conditions must be met. First, Canadian-based manufacturers must maintain, and perhaps even expand, their access to the larger u.s. defence market. Second, in order to cushion their business against fluctuations or adverse trends in that market, other international purchasers must be cultivated. Finally, to provide business incentives within the domestic defence industrial base and increase imports from the United States – with a view to stimulating further export flows southward under the "rough balance" provision of the DPSA – the Canadian government must increase its own defence capital expenditures.[1]

In this and the following chapters, we set out to meld our earlier discussions of demand- and supply-side factors into an assessment of the marketing environment within which the Canadian defence industry must operate. Taking the question of the continuing viability of this country's defence industrial base as our framework for analysis, we will examine the recent evolution of the domestic defence industry, focusing, *inter alia*, on corporate and governmental initiatives and policies. Our inquiry will begin by considering the third of the market conditions introduced above – namely, domestic Canadian defence expenditures and changes in DND equipment requirements. Budgetary analysis will serve as our jumping-off point at this stage, for as one defence analyst has correctly observed, "much of what passes for defence policy formulation in Canada these days revolves around questions of the budget; how much the Forces have to spend, and, more importantly, what they intend to spend it on."[2] This budgetary perspective will provide a handy means of determining both the priority given by the federal cabinet to national defence relative to other federal government programs, and within DND itself, to different branches of the armed services. This perspective will also provide insights into Ottawa's decisions about force posture – and about associated equipment requirements – by highlighting changes in the allocation of funds between personnel, operations, and maintenance, on the one hand, and capital, on the other.

CANADA'S DEFENCE BUDGET

The two major issues of interest in the context of the defence budget are the trends in the relative priority given to defence and the impact on equipment procurement of the funds specifically appropriated for the *capital* component of expenditures. We are hardly the first writers to draw attention to this dual aspect of DND's contemporary funding "crisis."[3]

It could be argued that talk of a crisis in defence funding is misplaced, perhaps even alarmist. After all, the absolute level of defence expenditures, whether measured in budget-year or constant-dollar terms, has risen steadily since the early to mid-1970s, following the Defence Structure Review. Between 1980 and 1990, for example, the defence budget grew from roughly $5 billion to slightly over $11 billion; it reached nearly $12 billion in FY1992–93 before declining to $11.3 billion in FY1993–94.[4] However, it would be erroneous to infer from these figures that DND has been able systematically to advance its departmental interests at the expense of competing departments or that defence budgets have grown at a "disproportionately" high rate in Canada.[5]

Relative to both gross domestic product and total federal outlays, post-1945 defence spending in Canada peaked during the Korean War, reaching nearly 7.5 percent of GDP in 1952. In subsequent years, it actually fell sharply until the 1970s, recording a low of 1.6 percent in 1979, when it began to stabilize. By 1990, despite the apparent commitment of the Conservative government towards defence, the defence/GDP ratio was only slightly higher than its postwar low, at not quite 1.8 percent. Thus, over the past two decades, defence spending has remained below 2 percent of GDP, and the 1979 mark is likely to be eclipsed by the end of this decade, when that figure may decline to 1.5 percent as a result of GDP growth and further defence cuts.[6] As a share of total federal government expenditures, defence spending declined from a peak of 43.4 percent in 1952 to a low of 7.8 percent in 1982, rising to 8.1 percent in FY1991–92. As with the GDP measure, this latter indicator suggests that a steady state has been reached (at around 8 percent of federal outlays) since 1975; however, that proportion is expected to slide to 7 percent during the remainder of the 1990s.[7]

The downward relative trend of defence expenditures over the past twenty years reflects both Ottawa's greater emphasis on social programs, which rose from 26.5 to 36.1 percent of federal spending between FY 1989–90 and FY1991–92, and the large debt charges arising from these and other programs (including defence). Public debt servicing accounted for 25 percent of total federal government spending in FY1993–94 – more than three times the amount expended on national defence.[8] Defence will no doubt have to absorb its share of budget cuts in response to the government's ongoing fiscal difficulties (as well as to a changing and, at least temporarily, less menacing strategic environment), but it would be idle to believe that further defence budget reductions can do much to solve the deficit problem in the absence of more radical macroeconomic policy measures.

If the critics of defence spending in Canada tend to overstate their case, might not the same argument be made respecting those who see not too much but too little public spending on defence? At the aggregate level, recent figures do not suggest an imminent crisis. As Dan Middlemiss notes, although defence does consume a much smaller share of GDP than it did in the 1950s, as well as a reduced share of total federal outlays, "this is now a smaller percentage of a greatly expanded economy," and the general levels appear to have been quite stable. A more significant indicator, however, both for DND's operational capabilities and for the prospects of its suppliers of defence-related products, is the ratio of the budget allocated to personnel, operations, and maintenance as opposed to capital expenditures – that is, expenditures on major equipment, buildings and facilities, and research and development.

While there is no *a priori* "correct" ratio, DND statements and defence analysts have customarily claimed that in order to maintain a capable and modern fighting force, regularly supplied with updated equipment, the department must allocate between 25 and 35 percent of its budget to capital programs. The 25–percent figure was initially accepted in the 1964 Defence White Paper; in the statement of Canadian defence policy made in April 1992, Defence Minister Marcel Masse noted that his department would seek to raise the capital share from just below 22 percent to 26 percent over the next five years, "while a target figure of 30 percent will be maintained."[9] The 1992 defence policy statement added that in order to achieve this higher relative level of capital spending, the share allocated to personnel must be reduced, with R&D expenditures remaining at their previous level of 5 percent.

If past experience is any guide, there is not much likelihood that these targets will be attained. Indeed, one might be excused for viewing Masse's April 1992 statement as yet another incarnation of "*déjà vu* all over again" (in Yogi Berra's famous words). Since 1959, the 25–percent goal has been met in only one five-year period, 1984–88; since then, the proportion of capital spending has actually fallen, to nearly 21 percent in 1991–92. The "target figure of 30 percent" may make for good reading, but it has so far proven to be a will-o'-the-wisp, not once having been reached since the 1950s. Nor is the February 1994 budget, with its frontal assault on DND infrastructure costs, likely to contribute significantly to the attainment of that target; at best, a capital share of between 23 and 25 percent of defence spending can be anticipated.[10]

This failure to match rhetorical commitment with actual outlays is hardly unique to this country, and thus the shortfall in capital budgets does not amount to a crisis when Canada is compared with the rest of NATO. But in light of the long-term impact of the 1972 allocations to capital of only 7.8 percent, that failure has nonetheless created a serious cumulative shortfall in expenditures on equipment that, when measured in terms of the nominal target of 30 percent, amounts to some $19 billion since 1965. It is in this sense that one can claim that DND today faces an urgent need to replace obsolete or obsolescent equipment and that its operations have been impaired by a "chronic funding problem of crisis proportions."[11]

THE "CRISIS" AND THE DEFENCE INDUSTRY

Although equipment obsolescence may seriously undermine DND's ability to fulfil even its normal post-Cold War operational tasks – to say nothing of the equipment needs associated with the expanded commitment to peacekeeping and "peacemaking" mooted by the Liberal government – it would be reckless to think that this will generate substantial new domestic contract opportunities for Canadian defence companies. The April 1992 policy statement, for example, while arguing that the military must have "the tools to do the job," also recognized that higher priority needed to be accorded to other national economic and social policy objectives. Accordingly, the statement enjoined DND to "search rigorously for the minimum necessary in each category of expenditure"; the limited resources available for the capital budget under these circumstances "will be used frugally on the highest priority items." This might be taken to imply that equipment that has become entirely obsolete and genuinely unsafe will be replaced, even though the example of the "low level air defence" (LLAD) contract suggests the opposite.[12]

The "new" policy of DND for capital acquisitions during the second half of the 1990s, as set out in the Conservative government's defence policy statement, emphasized multi-purpose roles for the Canadian Forces. This implies a constriction of the range of equipment types and also suggests that procurement of systems whose performance has already been demonstrated in the field may be desirable. That, in turn, would probably translate into fewer new contracts – though some individual contracts might be somewhat larger – and into an even greater emphasis on off-the-shelf procurement. The policy statement also indicated that equipment upgrades would be evaluated critically against their cost and that "unique Canadian solutions that require expensive and risky research, development or modification of existing equipment" would be avoided. In summary, "shortening the procurement cycle" would appear to be the continuing approach of the Liberal government.[13]

It is difficult to determine exactly how all this will affect those Canadian companies which specialize in unique technologies for DND requirements, but in general terms it seems likely that the policy will reduce their incentive to engage in new R&D activities. The interviews that we conducted suggest that there will be greater emphasis, by both companies and federal government departments, on further developing existing products rather than creating new ones.[14]

Although DND's professed intention to seek to allocate a larger proportion of the Defence Services Program (DSP) to capital expenditures may make excellent sense from a military-operational point of view, there are good reasons to expect that economic and political factors will impede the department's ability to do so, all the while continuing to erode the purchasing power of existing capital funds. Such macroeconomic variables as fluctuations in the exchange rate and the rate of inflation can reduce the real value of the defence procurement budget. Inflation is a significant concern, as the Treasury Board no longer compensates DND for its full impact; the shift from the DND Economic Model to the GDP deflator in economic analysis means, in the words of one observer, that the "*real* [i.e., adjusted for true defence-related inflation] growth in defence spending has been overstated by about 1.7 percent annually," on average, since FY 1985–86.[15] Variations in the exchange rate are also significant, since DND procures much of its equipment from outside Canada because of the specialized nature of the domestic defence industrial base.

Such fluctuations affect the capital portion of the defence budget more than any other element, for two main reasons. First, most of DND's acquisitions of major new equipment (except ships) since 1959 have been from the United States, but the Canadian dollar has almost always traded below par with the U.S. dollar during this period – by more than 20 percent in recent years. Second, the long-standing tendency for the costs of advanced-technology defence products to increase at a rate surpassing that of "normal" inflation – that is, the trend towards structural disarmament, to which we referred in chapter 3 – did not simply end when the Cold War did. Whether or not DND succeeds in meeting its stipulated goal of spending 26 percent of the DSP on capital by 1995–96 – and we think it will not – these pressures will continue to erode the purchasing power of the defence procurement dollar.

Apart from these more or less purely economic factors, domestic political and policy issues have intruded in such a way as to constrain DND's freedom to decide the fate of its own budget. In order to reduce spending on other portions of the DSP, the department been trying to reduce the excessive domestic infrastructure it had retained from a time when the Canadian Forces were much larger. Eliminating redundant or underutilized facilities – which means, essentially, the closure of a large number of bases across Canada – would in turn allow DND to reduce the relatively large number of civilians in its employ who perform support and administrative functions for this oversized infrastructure.[16]

Despite occasional reports to the contrary, both DND and the community of defence analysts in Canada recognize that as many as half of the twenty-eight bases operating in early 1994 are redundant. The appointment by Marcel Masse, in mid-1992, of an advisory group to analyze the issue of base closures amounted, in effect, to little more than a means of laying the groundwork for yet another debate on the subject and, more to the point, shelving the politically contentious matter until the 1993 federal election had taken place.[17]

One should not single out the governments of Brian Mulroney or Kim Campbell for criticism, however. Previous governments and political parties were equally adept at skirting the issue of infrastructure rationalization as the armed forces were being steadily downsized. In that respect, the federal budget unveiled on 22 February 1994 really did constitute something new – and not entirely unwelcome to the Canadian Forces' military leadership. What Finance Minister Paul Martin announced that day was nothing less than an attack on DND "overhead," ordering that twenty-one departmental facilities (including four bases) be closed and that an additional seven facilities be reduced. These measures, coupled with further reductions and restructuring at National Defence Headquarters, will pare some 16,500 positions – slightly more than half of them civilian – from DND rosters by 1998.[18]

But even if the issue of pork-barrel politics, as represented by excess infrastructure, is now resolved – and we are not convinced that it is – DND's capital expenditures will continue to be affected by political considerations, and in particular by the expectation that all major crown projects (and, indirectly, smaller contracts as well) should provide industrial and regional benefits (IRBS). To our knowledge, no systematic analysis has been done of the financial premiums paid by DND in order to meet the new IRB objectives; but as one observer puts it, "this requirement still adds costs, complications and delays to DND's equipment procurement programmes," and it is often the cause of acrimonious debates and intensive lobbying by political and business interests alike, as well as jockeying between federal departments "who seek to exploit it as an economic policy instrument."[19]

What does all this mean with respect to the capital spending targets announced in the April 1992 defence policy statement? The "bad news" for the Canadian defence industrial base is that the 26-percent target is unlikely to be attained, while the 30-percent level is clearly a fanciful figure, unrelated to the real world. However, the "good news" is that the attack on overhead makes it unlikely that there will be a repeat of the nightmare of the early 1970s, when capital acquisition nearly disappeared as a legitimate defence budgetary aspiration. But even if the government remains firm in its determination to weather the resistance mounted by a variety of groups affected by the February 1994 defence cuts, the actual purchasing power of capital appropriations will continue to be eroded by factors largely beyond DND's control. And the government's fiscal restraint policy will continue to force the department to squeeze its capital expenditures – in absolute if not in relative terms – in order to meet the demands, realistic or not, for further reductions in the defence budget.

THE POLITICS OF CONTRACTING

While the effectiveness of DND's efforts to bolster the capital portion of the DSP remains the key to the long-term prospects of the domestic defence market, this topic receives relatively limited public consideration. Far more attention, by comparison, is lavished on individual contract competitions and awards, not least because of the political controversies that major contracts regularly stir up between winners and losers, and between supporters and critics. By way of illustration, we consider a small sample of these contracts, including both ongoing and proposed future projects.

When Defence Minister Masse announced on 7 April 1992 that General Motors' Diesel Division had been awarded a contract for 229 light-armoured vehicles (LAVs) to replace DND's 25-year-old Lynx vehicles, senior department staff and other defence analysts applauded the decision. They saw it as an earnest of Ottawa's commitment to reequip its military with modern systems – in this instance, systems that had been combat-proven by U.S. forces in the Persian Gulf War.[20] At the same time, they were aware that the $800 million LAV contract award followed the cancellation of existing plans for a much larger, $2.8-billion program for new multi-role combat vehicles. To be sure, the LAV contract provided General Motors with valuable additional work to supplement its Saudi Arabian order (and a possible Australian one) for the same vehicle, but the government's decision to abandon the earlier acquisition program illustrated the unpredictability and vulnerability of capital procurement plans to other policy considerations.

The decision to withdraw all Canadian Forces personnel from Europe, announced in February 1992, effectively negated any possibility that the obsolescent Leopard C1 main battle tank would be replaced. While a domestic tank production capability would not have been considered in any event, the substantially scaled-down LAV contract and the $200-million "light support vehicle wheeled" (LSVW) contract (awarded to the Western Star Truck Company of Kelowna, British Columbia) constituted the only two major domestic manufacturing projects to be undertaken for the land systems sector of the defence industry.[21]

In the aerospace sector, DND's capital-equipment acquisitions plans during the first half of the 1990s initially revolved around two key projects, with a very distant third possibility. The two contracts (one still under way and the other cancelled by the new Liberal government) were both within the rotary-wing subsector – the "utility tactical transport helicopter" (or UTTH), and the controversial and short-lived "new shipborne aircraft" (NSA). At the same time that the LAV award was being announced, Defence Minister Masse also gave notice of a contract for 100 new Model 412 helicopters from Quebec-based Bell Helicopter Textron Canada, worth approximately $1 billion. The primarily commercial design of the Bell helicopter could be modified for military purposes, and the aircraft was intended to replace Canada's aging fleet of 116 CH-136 Kiowas, CH-135 Twin Hueys, and CH-118

Iroquois in a variety of roles, including troop and supplies transport, inland search and rescue, and emergency medical evacuation.[22]

For this Canadian subsidiary of a large American manufacturer, the UTTH contract involved the creation of some fifty to 100 additional jobs, depending on the required rate of production after the start of delivery in 1994 and on the company's ability to remain an active participant in the Canadian helicopter market. The vast majority of Bell Helicopter's sales are made abroad, with 260 Model 412s already in service in the United States, Japan, Germany, Norway, and Egypt.[23] The announcement of the contract, however, was immediately greeted with a number of widely reported accusations that Masse had deliberately directed the work to the Mirabel-based firm without adequate opportunity for competitive tendering from a rival manufacturer, Eurocopters Ltd. of Fort Erie, Ontario (previously MBB Helicopter Canada).

The criticism of some of Masse's public statements, especially those regarding the disparity between Quebec's share of the defence procurement pie and its percentage of the national population (with the former being smaller), may well have been justified. But even if it was not, there arose a perception within federal departments that the minister was determined to make Quebec "Canada's arsenal," and this, it has been argued, did considerable damage to government officials' morale.[24] Criticism of the contract procedure itself, or of the choice of the Model 412, appears by contrast to be neither accurate nor reasonable. One industry publication, *The Wednesday Report*, noted that the selection criteria were known well in advance, that Eurocopter personnel were less critical of the final decision than media and political or other commentators, and that the selection process compared very favourably, in cost terms, with "the unending cost of the NSA acquisition process."[25]

The decision to increase the number of helicopters in the UTTH contract from the original figure of forty to 100 raised further speculation, especially given Masse's remarks on increasing Quebec's share of defence expenditures. Again, however, this choice was consistent with DND's policy of rationalizing its equipment inventory as it modernizes its forces: as indicated earlier, the greater number of Model 412s will be used to replace at least three types of helicopters now in service. This, it is argued, will enable DND to make long-term savings in operating and maintenance costs, as well as simplifying future training requirements.

The logic of force modernization and rationalization may also be glimpsed in the case of the NSA program through which older Sea

King and Boeing-Vertol Labrador helicopters were to be replaced by the EH-101, tendered by E.H. Industries (EHI) of Montreal. In this ill-fated and highly controversial instance, most of the public debates in Ottawa focused not so much on the particular choice of helicopter or the geographic location of the manufacturer of the aircraft as on the financial and political affordability of the project in the context of the post-Cold War era and the continuing domestic fiscal constraint. Although EHI's original $5-billion proposal (for fifty-seven units) was reduced to fifty helicopters at a total acquisition cost of $4 billion, and subsequently to forty-three helicopters, the entire project came under considerable criticism and was eventually cancelled. Even those who supported the need for a new helicopter to replace aging Sea Kings and Labradors suggested various alternatives, such as the purchasing of fewer EH-101s with more limited advanced-technology features or consideration of alternative products such as the Sikorsky Seahawk, a Eurocopter model, or a new Sea King.[26] We shall return, in the next chapter, to a discussion of the debate that surrounded the EH-101 program prior to its cancellation and of the impact of that decision.

Apart from these high-profile and generally well-known capital acquisition plans, the April 1992 defence policy document contained a small shopping list of potential new major equipment programs for both the aerospace and shipbuilding industries. The study of a fixed-wing aircraft, presumably intended to replace the CF-18, suggested in the policy review, has led to little or no debate. This may be linked to its relatively distant time horizon, beyond the current fifteen-year planning cycle.[27] Somewhat more immediately relevant are two proposed naval programs – one for six new conventional submarines, and a second for a fleet of six corvettes – which are beginning to attract greater attention from critics and advocates alike.

With its two principal navy contracts – the much troubled Canadian patrol frigate (CPF) and the Tribal-class "update and modernization project" (TRUMP) – theoretically scheduled for completion by 1996, the domestic shipbuilding and ship repair industry, more than any other subsector of the defence industry, faces an uncertain future. As indicated earlier, this industry remains especially dependent for new business on domestic government contracts, and in particular on those from DND. The proposed new programs, as they are currently defined, call for six new submarines to replace the older Oberon-class vessels, along with the corvettes; however, no firm timetable has been suggested for the latter program, although DND did initially state that the submarine project would not begin until 1994. The start date, of course, presupposed that the conventional submarine proposal will not meet the same fate as that of its nuclear-powered predecessor, announced in the 1987 Defence White Paper.[28]

Without work on these new major naval programs being undertaken prior to the completion of the CPF and TRUMP contracts, the Canadian Maritime Industries Association has warned that Canada stands to lose a large portion of its existing shipbuilding and ship repair industry. The association has proposed that the submarine and corvette programs be started soon and that the procurement methodology be changed so as to replace the boom-and-bust pattern of intermittent large contracts by a more constant production of warships at a lesser rate.[29] Some critics of the proposed new programs, who suggest instead the procurement of additional frigates to take advantage of the current CPF production, thereby improving scale economies as well as support costs, might accept this latter suggestion of carefully regulated production rates to maintain industry workloads. Others, however, have expressed the view that domestic shipbuilding should be phased out *entirely* and replaced by off-the-shelf procurement of naval vessels from abroad (most likely from the United States), which they argue would be more cost-effective. These analysts suggest that Canadian-based companies could then focus on such tasks as installing new systems into the vessels to meet Canadian naval requirements. In this way, they argue, an industry that perhaps remains artificially supported by government contracts could take a route similar to that already travelled by the more internationally competitive aerospace industry, abandoning platform development and production in favour of concentration on specialized, high-technology markets.[30]

THE CANADIAN PROCUREMENT HORIZON DARKENS

If, as suggested by P.H. Wall, one of the chief conditions for maintaining the economic viability of Canadian defence production is an expansion of government procurement, then the business prospects for the domestic defence industrial base generally are shrinking along with the real purchasing power of the capital portion of DND's budget. Given the forty-year record of failure of capital budgets to approach stated government spending targets – and even without taking into account the preferences and objectives of the current government – there is little reason for DND or the defence industry to expect capital spending to meet the 1992 target figures. Rather, the speed with which the EH-101 contract was cancelled suggests that market conditions for

Canadian defence contractors will only continue to become more difficult in the future. It will become increasingly difficult to support individual major crown projects, however necessary they may be in order to counter the "rust-out" and obsolescence of current equipment, in the face of fiscal constraint, emphasis on deficit reduction and other social programs, and a popular press much enamoured of the phrase "peace dividend."

As explained above, the capital portion of the Canadian defence budget is especially vulnerable to the erosion of its purchasing power for macroeconomic and technological reasons (exchange rates and "defence inflation") largely beyond the control of DND, as well as to the more obvious domestic political pressures linked to non-defence industrial and regional economic benefits requirements. Whatever their domestic political value, even in justifying defence programs, these requirements result in a premium being paid by DND on many of its most important equipment procurement contracts, thus further eroding already scarce capital funds.

To all of these pressures, DND has responded in two main ways that may directly affect the domestic defence market. First, it has sought to improve the capital portion of the DSP. Second, it has begun to rationalize its equipment inventory as it replaces older equipment. If successful, this policy should allow for greater economies in operating, maintenance and training costs, as well as in unit prices (assuming, in the latter case, that production is not stretched out over inordinately longer periods of time). In addition, off-the-shelf procurement of proven platforms has become even more widespread.

The impact both of these pressures affecting the DND capital budget and of the department's new procurement approach on defence manufacturers' business plans and strategies will be assessed in the next chapter. Here, a few broader points about the evolving nature of the Canadian defence market are in order. First, although their export orientation helps to cushion, to some extent, the aerospace and avionics sector, as well as the defence electronics industry, the "constant inconstancy" that characterizes government defence procurement seriously undermines the ability and willingness of industry to make the essential long-range plans or to risk the investment commitments that would maintain its international competitiveness. Second, because the shipbuilding and ship repair industry is almost entirely dependent on domestic demand, uncertainty over future government procurement plans portends a monumental structural crisis during the next half-dozen years that can only further complicate the industry's search for business strategies other than those dictated by short-term survival needs. Finally, it is worth noting that, to the extent that DND is able to reduce regular force levels to less than 67,000 in order to pursue its spending targets for capital, an ironic longer-term result will be that less equipment of many types will be required for the lower troop levels.[31]

Apart from this uncertain and shifting domestic political context, the recent examples cited above – the light armoured vehicle and the Bell Model 412 and EH-101 helicopters – suggest a trend towards fewer new contract opportunities and fewer units being ordered in these contracts. The LAV order was scaled down considerably from earlier DND proposals, and the contract for 100 new Bell 412s, though larger than the first estimate of some forty or fifty, nonetheless is intended to replace 116 existing machines. The long, drawn-out debate and review of options for the EH-101 program also suggests another result of financial constraints and alternate government political priorities – that industry can no longer assume that major procurement contracts, even when they are signed, will not in the future be cancelled as either governments or priorities change. At one time, defence critics would argue, perhaps justifiably, that, once begun, programs took on a life of their own and could not be cancelled. That is no longer the case: for industry executives, especially, long-range uncertainty is the only constant in the Canadian defence market.

Two purposes are said to be served by strong or improved domestic demand for defence – the provision of business incentives to domestic producers; and the increase in Canada-U.S. defence trade, since higher levels of imports of American platforms or major systems are presumed to be compensated for by more exports to the United States under the "rough balance" provision of the production-sharing arrangements. While we have dealt with the former issue, the latter appears to us a dubious contention, not simply because of the long-term imbalance in bilateral defence trade in favour of the United States or of the pressures on new capital procurement programs in Canada, but also, and perhaps mainly, because of changes in the crucial U.S. defence market.

U.S. DEFENCE PROCUREMENT
AND MARKET ACCESS IN THE
1990S: THE BUDGETARY
PERSPECTIVE

When considering the North American bilateral defence-trade relationship in the light of those numerous changing market conditions outlined in earlier chapters, it is useful to take two different, though related, approaches to the question of the likely prospects for Canadian companies seeking to win contracts from the U.S. Department of Defense (DoD). The first is budgetary; under this rubric, we seek to ascertain trends in U.S. defence spending, especially for procurement, and to ask how these might affect industry subsectors as well as types of procurement programs. The second approach is politico-economic; here, we speculate on the manner in which the pressures of defence austerity might influence the views of both the administration and Congress on matters of defence industrial base and defence trade, most particularly in the bilateral context. Will the access of Canadian companies to the vital U.S. defence market be altered? If so, what will be the consequences?

In chapter 1, we made passing reference to the Pentagon's Six-Year Defense Plan for 1992–97 in the context of our selective review of some countries' post-Cold War defence budgets. In chapter 3, we set out in greater detail the moderately critical response to DoD budget plans and the new procurement strategy that was issued by Wisconsin Representative Les Aspin, the influential chairman of the House Armed Services Committee who later became Secretary of Defense, and we highlighted Aspin's own suggested alternative procurement strategy, intended to mitigate the adverse effects of budget cutting on the U.S. defence industry. We now revisit the budgetary element more thoroughly before moving on to discuss the political repercussions of defence austerity. Needless to say, some of these repercussions have already begun to be felt in the Canada-U.S. defence trade relationship.

Table 5.1 sets out U.S. defence budgets since 1985 in terms of both actual outlays and procurement budget functions, and it compares the totals in both current dollars and constant 1991 dollars. The proposed spending figures from FY1992 onward, it should be noted, were calculated prior to the election of the Democratic administration. The new president's spending plan, however, included relatively limited cuts beyond those already planned by the Bush administration, totalling US$60 billion over five years; thus, the overall trends are broadly similar.

The figures reveal that defence spending peaked under the Reagan administration and has been declining since the end of the 1980s, especially when measured in constant dollars. They provide a graphic illustration of the declining purchasing power of defence dollars: the FY1991 outlay in current dollars, for example, was over $40 billion higher than in FY1985, but in constant dollars the 1985 total represented an additional $12 billion in purchasing power. Between FY1986 and FY1991, virtually identical outlay totals in current dollars hid a

Table 5.1
U.S. National Defence Expenditures, by Outlay and Procurement Year, 1985–95

	Outlay		Procurement	
	Current $	1991 $	Current $	1991 $
	(Billions)	(Billions)	(Billions)	(Billions)
1985	252.7	310.8	70.4	86.6
1986	295.2	354.5	74.3	89.2
1987	282.0	329.2	80.7	94.2
1988	290.4	328.3	77.2	87.3
1989	303.6	329.5	81.6	88.6
1990	299.3	314.9	81.0	85.2
1991	298.9	298.9	79.1	79.1
1992	295.2	–	74.3	–
1993	292.0	–	68.8	–
1994	286.7	–	67.2	–
1995	288.6	–	68.6	–

Source: U.S. Government, *Budget, FY 1992*, 30–6, 38–44.

1 When the table was prepared, the 1992 figures had been enacted, while the 1993–95 figures had been proposed.

constant-dollar decline of over $55 billion. Likewise, while the current-dollar procurement budget rose from $70.4 billion in FY1985 to $79.1 billion in 1991, this nonetheless represented a decline in constant dollars (and purchasing power) of almost $7 billion. Not taken into account by these figures is the additional impact of "defence inflation," which results from the constant pressure for technological improvements in equipment performance – another way of expressing the trend towards structural disarmament.

Other measures of this declining priority for defence in Washington's budget process can be cited. One is the shrinking share of defence spending in relation both to other federal government expenditures and to GNP. From 1983 to 1989, defence accounted for more than 26 percent of total federal outlays, peaking at about 28 percent in FY1986 and FY1987. By 1992, however, that share had sunk to just above 20 percent. As a percentage of GNP, national defence spending from FY1983 to FY1988 was constantly above 6 percent, peaking at 6.5 percent in FY1986; by early 1992, that share had dropped below 5 percent; today, it is closer to 4.5 percent. Government forecasts, based on trends prior to the change in administrations at the White House, anticipated that defence would account for 19 percent of all federal outlays and 3.8 percent of GNP by FY1996.[32] These forecasts, however, are likely to err on the *high* side, given the domestic priorities of the Clinton administration, even though the president has signalled that he intends to insure that the United States will remain committed to developing high-technology weaponry.[33]

Declining DoD procurement budgets have already begun to affect market opportunities for individual Canadian companies, some of which participated in a number of those multinational programs initially funded under the Nunn Amendment. Two of those programs – the "autonomous precision-guided munition" project and the NATO frigate replacement project – were cancelled following withdrawal or uncertain financial support by the United States. The decision by the U.S. Navy to cut its purchases of sonobuoys from 425,000 a year to 100,000, so as to reduce spending on this equipment from $190 to $60 million a year, was expected to prove detrimental to the export sales of Hermes Electronics of Dartmouth, Nova Scotia, which supplies the Navy with the SSQ-53D sonobuoy. The decision will also likely force two large American manufacturers, Magnavox Electronic Systems and Sparton, to pursue new orders outside their traditional domestic market, perhaps including the relatively small but stable Canadian one.[34]

The cancellation or collapse of new international joint development projects, the reduction of existing procurement programs and export opportunities, and potential competition from U.S. suppliers in the Canadian market and abroad are the most problematical and direct consequences of cuts in Washington's defence budget, at least from the perspective of Canadian defence manufacturers. On a more positive note, tighter R&D budgets in the United States may encourage American companies and DoD officers to seek greater cooperation with their Canadian counterparts in order to make use of Ottawa's financial support, however modest in comparative terms, of industry through the Defence Industry Productivity Program (DIPP). This outcome remains largely speculative, however, as it depends on maintaining DIPP funding levels in the face of domestic financial constraints and some public criticism, to say nothing of the (remote) possibility that the DIPP might become an issue in GATT discussions on subsidies.

It is the longer-term political consequences of declining defence budgets that will prove of greatest importance in determining the conditions of market access for Canadian companies pursuing exports to the United States. In particular, as budget cuts and program cancellations cause large-scale layoffs in the American defence industry, Congress has come under increasing pressure to control the downsizing of the industry and to assist those local economies and individual companies most severely affected by the process.[35] This intervention has usually taken two forms – financial and other types of support for domestic industry and workers; and a critical review of the terms of current defence economic arrangements with the United States' military allies and trading partners.

Pressure has mounted for Congress to "do something" to cushion the full force of post-Cold War defence budget reductions on industry and related workers, as well as on DoD personnel; the Bush administration's avowed *laissez-faire* stance towards issues of economic adjustment and industrial policy only exacerbated these pressures. A 1992 report by the Office of Technology Assessment (OTA), a Congressional advisory and analysis group, estimated that defence spending would decline from $287.5 billion to $235.7 billion between 1991 and 1995, while defence industry employment would fall from 2,900,000 to about 2,300,000 and some 500,000 DoD military and civilian jobs would be pared. Should budget cuts be deeper than DoD was estimating, total defence-related employment would, according to the OTA, fall from 5,990,000 in 1991 to some 4,600,000 by 1995 and approximately 3,600,000 by the end of the century – an overall loss of nearly 2,400,000 defence jobs in a single decade.[36] In one U.S. defence sector alone, aerospace, nearly a third of all jobs were lost between 1990 and 1994.[37]

Bearing in mind the interests of their constituencies, the Democratic members of both the House of Representatives and the Senate introduced adjustment assistance packages. The House proposals, passed on 4 June 1992 as part of the $270-billion defence authorization bill for 1993, specified $1 billion as the first installment of a multi-year aid program, with measures to provide new job training, assistance to state and local governments for the creation of alternative job opportunities, and early retirement benefits for laid-off workers. Industry could receive up to $150 million to fund consortia for the development of dual-use technologies, with a further $50 million for direct DoD investment in firms that could or would not otherwise invest in "critical technologies." Finally, as a demonstration of its special interest in small business, Congress directed that an additional $125 million – still part of the $1-billion total package – be made available to these companies through the provision of information services and advice on defence technologies.[38]

The House package was considerably larger than the Bush administration's proposed measures, even if slightly smaller than the Senate package announced on 21 May 1992. Support for both was strong in the previous Congress, particularly with reference to the administration's proposals, which were regarded as inadequate for those "unprecedented times." With the Democrats having lost control of the Congress, however, it would be surprising if new Congressional initiatives were to bear greater fruit in coming years, unless defence spending increases.[39]

THE POLITICAL ENVIRONMENT

The budgetary perspective is a valuable approach for identifying relevant trends in U.S. defence expenditures, as well as some of the more direct implications for individual procurement programs or market sectors in which Canadian companies have a stake. In order to grasp the full meaning of the contemporary challenge to the bilateral defence-trade relationship, we must turn to an analysis of the political and economic consequences of the downsizing of the American defence industry during the late 1980s and early 1990s. Above all, a clear understanding of Congressional involvement in American defence economic relations is critical. How might the changing attitudes in Washington affect the relatively successful Canada-U.S. defence trade agreements? And how will they affect Canadian access to the lucrative U.S. defence market?

Criticisms of the bilateral defence-trade agreement or of the balance of defence trade have recurred throughout the thirty-five-year history of the DDSA/DPSA.[40] Each country has at times had reasons for desiring revisions to the terms of the production-sharing arrangements, in particular. And both countries have faced domestic demands for change, although until recently most of the criticism directed against the sharing arrangements tended to come from Canadian groups irritated by the continuing imbalance in defence trade in favour of the United States.[41] Despite this, both types of arrangements continued to operate comparatively successfully, probably in large part because they were pursued at a non-political, bureaucratic level. The NADIBO, established in 1987, added another layer to the bilateral cooperation on DIB-related matters and, at the same time, sought to promote greater awareness in both countries – but especially on the part of DoD procurement officers and politicians – of the national security benefits of including Canadian companies as "domestic" American suppliers.[42]

Despite these achievements, however, the unprecedented adjustment problems faced by the defence industry and the entire economy in the United States have placed the bilateral relationship in a crucial transition period. In response largely to Congressional directives that it take domestic economic interests more fully into account in the future, the Pentagon initiated a reevaluation of existing bilateral memoranda of understanding pertaining to defence research, development, and production (RDP).[43] While the contents of the reevaluations remained confidential at the time of writing, their tone, intent, and broad parameters can be established with a reasonable degree of confidence from comments made by government officials on either side of the border during our research.

Given the greater emphasis on domestic economic benefits or implications that marks the RDP review process, the central U.S. concern about defence trade with Canada is the latter's inevitable demand for extensive offset provisions associated with any major procurement contracts. This is viewed by critics in the United States as a form of "double-dipping" in a supposedly security-oriented arrangement that already provides Canadian companies with favoured access to the American defence market. In response to this point and to other questions regarding the appropriate role of the Canadian Commercial Corporation in aiding these companies' sales drives, officials in Ottawa have long pointed to a variety of protectionist legislation and practices that inhibit or restrict access to DoD contract competitions.[44]

The initial American report on the bilateral development and production-sharing arrangements that circulated between government departments in Washington and Ottawa and generated part of the current pressure on the relationship, has been described by Canadian officials as a mediocre study that never grasped the realities of Canada-U.S. defence trade. At best, the Gibson Report was seen as an early data-gathering exercise to be used as a starting point for fuller debate and negotiation. Opinion on the significance of the RDP review process itself was and remains mixed, with some Canadian officials suggesting that it was simply part of internal Pentagon and Washington politics and would fade away without any major impact.[45]

At least one observer has noted, however, that the present circumstance may be different. A DND internal discussion paper of 1991 recommended the negotiation of a new defence economic arrangement: "Based on years of successful cooperation, [this] should be negotiated in the near future, and in fact will be, whether we want to or not. Based on early indications from the U.S. side, it will be a challenge for Canada to maintain even an equivalent of the status quo."[46] The broad-ranging Defence Economic Review and the conditions of confidentiality under which it took place – quite unlike those normally attending such policy discussions – are indications of the seriousness with which the possibility of a long-term negative impact was viewed. Contributing to the reluctance of Canadian government officials to disclose the substance of their review process in any detail, of course, may be the fact that any policy recommendations would likely entail changes in IRB requirements, in the terms of the DPSA, or in other measures affecting industry and local economies – all subjects with highly sensitive political implications.

Canadian industry executives often insist that it is not potential future protectionism that concerns them so much as the existing array of restrictive legislative measures and informal practices surrounding the U.S. defence market. Small Business Set-Aside legislation, "black" (i.e., classified) programs, and the "no foreign" designation – which can hinder the participation of Canadian companies even though Canada was considered as part of the American DIB in proposed amendments to the Defense Production Act – are the obstacles most frequently cited in this regard.

Notwithstanding these apprehensions, one must bear in mind that even with all of the above restrictions attending the U.S. procurement process, Canadian suppliers do have access to a market of roughly US$20 billion. At the same time, however, Canadian government officials in Ottawa and Washington repeatedly argue that of this market, Canadian industries obtain, on average, much less than 5 percent, either through DoD direct acquisition or through subcontracts made with American prime contractors.[47]

In the opinion of these Canadian officials, one of the chief obstacles to increased defence sales by Canadian companies to the United States – which currently stand at 9 percent of all foreign contracting in that market, in absolute terms roughly equivalent to the share of defence contracts awarded to the state of Nebraska – is their inability to operate well in the highly political American defence procurement marketplace. This is partly a function of the relatively small scale of most Canadian firms, which even in less uncertain economic times leaves little financial leeway for employing sales representatives and market analysts on a permanent basis in Washington. However, it also results from an unwillingness to take certain risks, especially those necessary to obtain essential marketing expertise. As valuable as it may be, the aid provided by government agencies such as the Canadian Commercial Corporation and by trade commissioners cannot substitute for more aggressive marketing by the manufacturers themselves.[48]

It should be clear that there is no single factor determining the overall success, or lack thereof, of Canadian defence industries in the American market. Budget cuts may have a direct or indirect impact, either by constricting DoD's demand for specific products or by heightening Congressional anxieties about the vitality and viability of the American defence industry. On the other hand, many of the programs now facing cancellation, reduction, or deferment in the United States do not involve Canadian firms since they primarily concern major platforms – with one notable exception, heavy armour.[49] Congressional protectionism, though lamented by Canadian industry executives, is not the entire story, and Canadian officials are correct in noting that those still-considerable u.s. defence market opportunities are inadequately pursued by the majority of Canadian manufacturers.

As long as the review of defence economic agreements continues in both countries, concrete details on existing bilateral defence trade arrangements will be difficult to obtain. One can, nevertheless, speculate. It is our hunch that a consequence of the review process could well be cooperative pacts that are more specific regarding *what* is to be purchased, and *how* it is to be "traded."[50] We shall return to this hunch in the next chapter.

THE OVERSEAS MARKET AND CANADIAN DEFENCE PRODUCTION

The u.s. defence market will undoubtedly remain the most attractive target for Canadian defence exporters. Still, the overseas defence market is a third critical element affecting the future economic viability of the Canadian defence industrial base. In order to continue to operate at anything like its current level, the Canadian defence industry will, at times, require marginal revenues through sales outside North America. This essentially means Europe, though there are some notable, and often well-publicized, exceptions.[51] The DPSA and DDSA are not Canada's only bilateral defence-production compacts; since the early 1960s Ottawa has entered into bilateral RDP agreements with nine European countries (Belgium, Denmark, France, Germany, Italy, the Netherlands, Norway, Sweden, and the United Kingdom). Agreements with Spain, Australia, and possibly also South Korea, may be added to these existing RDPs in the future.

The original aim of the RDP agreements was to identify "*defence projects* of sufficient bilateral interest to warrant the contribution of funds by both nations to *develop and produce products* to meet the requirements of each or both armed forces and agreed third markets."[52] Differences of opinion exist as to the success of the RDP agreements for Canada, and industry has often been critical of their orientation. The RDP "success story" most commonly cited is that of the CL-289, an unmanned reconnaissance drone jointly developed by Canada, Germany, and France, which shared equally in its $2-billion development costs.[53] The RDP agreements and process did indeed contribute to this program, but as one observer has noted, "in all likelihood, it would have occurred in the absence of RDPs with Germany and France." Other than the CL-289, very few joint projects have been attributed directly to the RDP agreements.[54]

Mixed opinions similarly exist regarding the utility or appropriateness of Foreign Affairs' continuing mandate over the RDP process, with critics arguing that "the original objectives have been eroded and have evolved into mainly commercial and trade related objectives." A more positive assessment, by contrast, is that "the evolution of all RDPs towards more commercial and trade related objectives reflects changes in the defence industry and the need for increased government support to achieve sales."[55] Notwithstanding its lacklustre record, the existence of the RDP program could, in theory, offer industry opportunities for meeting the future defence requirements of various European governments.[56]

That, at least, is the theory. Experience suggests, however, that access to European defence procurement contracts for Canadian industry hardly depends upon the existence of the RDP agreements. Their importance in this regard is marginal at best. The mere existence of specific bilateral accords means very little in comparison to the broader transatlantic defence economic and defence trade dynamics that are developing as the United States and Europe adjust to their new international and internal political-security and economic environments.

Thus it must be acknowledged that the prospects for greater defence economic cooperation and increasing defence trade seem very limited, in the transatlantic dimension especially. Declining defence budgets, fewer procurement dollars, industry restructuring, and large layoffs continue to make the major NATO states very reluctant to spend any significant portion of their defence revenues outside their domestic markets. The NATO defence trade initiative, discussed in chapter 2, made only very slow progress in the face of this reluctance, despite the otherwise clear logic favouring increased cooperation to achieve the purported economic and military benefits of equipment standardization.[57]

Potential markets outside either the United States or Canada's NATO or RDP partners, however valuable, are controlled and restricted by export regulations; the debates associated with the General Motors sale of the LAV to Saùdi Arabia, whatever their final implications for Canadian export legislation, will make both industry and government even more hesitant to try to find new markets in the Middle East and elsewhere in the Third World. The indirect export of Canadian defence products as components of U.S. equipment sold in those markets may also be affected as American firms seek to maintain their own workloads.[58]

Since 1985, the external environment – conditioned by political, security, and economic considerations – of Canada's defence industry has undergone a period of rapid and, at times, bewildering change. The demand for defence, and hence for defence production, has declined in its chief export markets. The defence industry is globalizing and becoming more fiercely competitive, while its political salience has become more acute as the domestic economic costs of post-Cold War industrial restructuring trigger electoral alarm bells in a number of countries. In this environment, how might Canadian manufacturers and government officials respond? That is the question we attempt to answer in chapters 6 and 7.

CHAPTER SIX

Defence Industrial Darwinism? Industry and the Dynamics of Adjustment

The period from the late 1980s to the mid-1990s will prove to be a decisive one for the economic viability of Canadian defence production. Momentous changes in the international security structure have had significant consequences for the demand for defence, lessening the public's willingness to pay for investments in national security, at least of the traditional military variety. At the same time, juxtaposed with trends in the international economy, changes in supply-side factors in the international defence market have transformed defence economic policy and industrial base issues into politically contentious subjects both between and within the member states of the North Atlantic Treaty Organization. The Alliance's defence trade initiatives have repeatedly come to an impasse as a result of politically inspired obstacles, with the resolution of one difficulty merely leading to the emergence of another.

The pressure to preserve an industrial capacity deemed to be critical for national security is especially strong in the United States, where it is estimated that the Department of Defense's supplier base shrank from some 120,000 companies in 1982 to 40,000 by 1987, and to many fewer today. In Canada too this Darwinian trend has been evident: at the end of the 1980s, the number of Canadian companies supplying goods and services to the Department of National Defence dropped by between 25 and 35 percent as enterprises either went bankrupt or chose to move out of the defence business.[1] Mergers, takeovers, and acquisitions have also played a part in changing the makeup of the domestic defence industry.[2]

This chapter focuses on these and other changes that have occurred in the Canadian supply side in response to both demand- and supply-side pressures originating in the United States and overseas.[3] After examining the adjustment efforts undertaken by a number of companies in the aerospace and electronics sectors, held jointly to be the pillar of whatever Canadian defence industrial base emerges from the current shakedown, we evaluate how Ottawa has managed defence-related issues and policies, including IRBs, DIPP grants, and other subsidies in support of defence exports. We highlight those structural changes which are developing in the defence industry in response to two sets of variables – corporate reorganization strategies and government policy initiatives – so as to project where the "government/industry duet" is likely to take Canadian defence industries during the coming years of Darwinian struggle.

CORPORATE RESTRUCTURING
ON THE LEADING EDGE:
THE CASE OF THE AEROSPACE
SECTOR

As the preceding chapters have suggested, the evolution of the defence industry in Canada has by no means reached a terminal point; if anything, the pace of change can be expected to accelerate. Perhaps as a result of this, the collecting of reliable data on corporate adjustment strategies in the post-Cold War defence market can be a daunting task. Manufacturers naturally are reluctant to divulge too many financial, technical, or other details, while even government departments charged with oversight of industry or trade matters cannot always obtain suitable data from all segments of the defence industry.[4]

In the case of the aerospace and electronics sectors, however, the relatively modest size of the industry and the predominance of a few major firms tend to counterbalance such drawbacks. In the aerospace industry, the ten leading firms account for approximately half of the total annual industry output, and the top twenty firms for more than 80 percent. The defence electronics industry is marked by an even greater degree of concentration, with the ten leaders in 1989 producing some 75 percent of that sector's nearly $2.4-billion revenue. Accordingly, our analysis here will focus on these groups of manufacturers, all of which are included under the general rubric of aerospace, although we will also have a word or two to say about companies in the shipbuilding and ship repair, land systems, and instrumentation sectors.

By restricting the scope of our industry study, we hope to identify major trends and developments within each sector primarily by highlighting the actions or preferences (or both) of a few principal corporations. Such an approach can only provide general insights into current restructuring strategies; obviously, each company will have a specific mix of product lines and other characteristics that will necessarily influence its behaviour. Nonetheless, we believe that the strategic choices of the leading firms often have implications for others within their sector, as well as for the lower-tier suppliers with whom they have subcontracting arrangements.

Over the past few years, defence industries in the United States and Europe have been undergoing a period of far-reaching realignment. As we argued earlier, this process predated the ending of the Cold War, at least to some extent, since it came as a result of existing defence market pressures and other political changes (especially EC92). Nevertheless, the radical transformation of the international security environment did add a much stronger impetus for defence budget cuts, in the process swelling public demands for a peace dividend.

The Canadian defence industry, including the aerospace sector, has not been immune to those pressures. The stability that marked the ranks of the leading aerospace companies in Canada throughout the 1980s gave way in the early 1990s to a restructuring drive that may have only begun to gather momentum with the sale by Boeing of Canada's de Havilland division to the Bombardier group, which already included Canadair. Table 6.1 illustrates the stability of the aerospace industry during most of the 1980s: of the twenty leading companies listed in 1989, only three were not in that group prior to 1985. Among the top six (Pratt & Whitney, Canadair-Bombardier, Boeing, Litton Systems, McDonnell Douglas, and CAE Electronics), there had been few changes in rank ordering.

The 1991 ISTC survey assessing corporate rankings did, as can be glimpsed from its forecast for 1994 company standings, anticipate greater fluidity in the aerospace sector during the early 1990s. The moderate decrease in employment levels at Pratt & Whitney Canada appears to be conforming to the expectations of ISTC analysts: the 2 April 1992 announcement of an additional 400 jobs to be cut, mainly at the firm's Longueuil (Quebec) headquarters, brought total employment at its major facilities to 7,885, down from some 8,500 in 1990–91.[5] Despite declining international export orders for Pratt & Whitney's highly successful lines of aircraft engines, this subsidiary of United Technologies in the United States will retain the second-largest engineering department among Canada's privately owned aerospace companies and will continue to dominate all other firms as the primary recipient of federal DIPP funding.[6]

A far more fundamental change in the organizational structure of the Canadian aerospace sector, however, was neither reflected nor anticipated in the ISTC report. After Boeing's initial attempt to sell its de Havilland aircraft division to the Franco-Italian consortium of

Table 6.1

Leading Aerospace and Other Defence Companies in Canada, 1989–94[1]

	Year				Country of	Location of
	1985	1988	1989	1994	ownership	major plant
Pratt & Whitney Canada Inc.	1	1	1	2	United States	Longueuil, Que.
Canadair/Bombardier Inc.	2	2	2	1	Canada	Dorval, Que.
Boeing of Canada Ltd.[2]	3	3	3	3	United States	Downsview,[2] Arnprior, Ont.; Winnipeg, Man.
Litton Systems Canada Ltd.	5	4	4	9	United States	Downsview, Ont.
McDonnell Douglas Canada Ltd.	4	5	5	4	United States	Mississauga, Ont.
CAE Electronics Ltd.	7	7	6	6	Canada	Montreal, Que.
Canadian Marconi Company	11	13	7	10	United Kingdom	Kanata & Cornwall, Ont. Montreal, Que.
Spar Aerospace Ltd.	6	6	8	7	Canada	Mississauga, Ont. & St. Anne, Que.
General Electric Canada Inc.	–	8	9	12	United States	Rexdale, Ont.
Rolls-Royce Industries Canada	9	10	10	11	United Kingdom	Montreal, Que.
Bristol Aerospace Ltd.	10	14	11	18	United Kingdom	Winnipeg, Man.
Raytheon Canada Ltd.	8	11	12	–	United States	Waterloo, Ont.
Bell Helicopter Textron Canada	–	19	13	8	United States	Mirabel, Que.
Standard Aero Ltd.	18	9	14	13	United Kingdom	Winnipeg, Man.
Computing Devices Company	13	12	15	17	United States	Nepean, Ont.
Garrett Canada[3]	12	15	16	14	United States	Rexdale, Ont.
Menasco Aerospace Ltd.[4]	16	16	17	15	United States	Oakdale, Ont.
Devtek Corporation	–	18	18	20	Canada	Kitchener & Scarborough, Ont.; Dartmouth, N.S.
Bendix Avelex Inc[3]	14	17	19	16	United States	Montreal, Que.
Walbar of Canada Inc.[4]	15	–	20	–	United States	Mississauga, Ont.

Source: Compiled from Industry, Science and Technology Canada, sector profile series, various years.

1 Ranked by sales in 1989; the ranking for 1994 is projected only.

2 Prior to the sale of the de Havilland division to Bombardier.

3 Garrett and Bendix Avelex are operating divisions of Allied-Signal Aerospace Canada, a U.S.-owned subsidiary of Allied-Signal Corp.

4 Menasco and Walbar are divisions of Coltec Industries Inc. (formally Colt Industries) of the United States.

Aérospatiale and Alenia was nullified by the European Commission, which deemed that such a sale would create a near-monopoly in the European commuter aircraft market, the company found buyers for its Downsview, Ontario subsidiary in Bombardier and the provincial government of Ontario. Having purchased de Havilland originally from the Canadian federal government in 1986 for a cash payment of $90 million, Boeing invested almost $400 million in plant and other improvements, and received from Ottawa $161 million as compensation for existing deficiencies at the Downsview facility. Despite the improvements, Boeing was unable to make de Havilland a profitable enterprise, with industry analysts citing its labour structure and high operating costs as the chief problems. Given that the American parent company was seeking to reduce its debt load as part of its own broader restructuring plans, it came as no surprise that it should divest itself of de Havilland, selling it in January 1992 for a $70-million payment accompanied by the transfer of $190 million in liabilities to the new Canadian owners.[7]

For Bombardier, already owner of Canadair of Montreal (as well as Short Brothers of Belfast, Northern Ireland), the acquisition of de Havilland offered a number of potentially valuable "considerations" in both the defence and commercial aerospace markets. In the commercial market, Canadair's Regional Jet and the de Havilland Dash-8 series aircraft were considered complementary, while the Lear jet was produced by Learjet, Bombardier's U.S. subsidiary. Therefore, even before engaging in any additional efforts to diversify its business further, the new company would be able to offer a wide range of products and could spread its management overhead costs over an expanded business base in order to make its entire aircraft group more cost-effective. Finally, cheaper procurement of parts and the ability to subcontract work out within the group were additional benefits that could serve to reduce costs and improve competitiveness.

The defence side of Bombardier's expanding aerospace activities now includes the six versions of the Dash-8 currently in service with the Canadian Forces; Canadair's prime contractorship for technical and systems engineering support on the CF-18 from its Mirabel facility; the Canadair CF-227 Sentinel and CL-289 unmanned aerial vehicles, the latter produced in conjunction with Dornier GmbH of Germany and SAT of France; and, though not military products but still something aimed at government procurement markets, the CL-215 and newer CL-215T amphibian water bombers.[8] It is worth noting that part of the financing attending the purchase of de Havilland was a $170-million federal government loan in the form of DIPP funds for restructuring, as well as the promise of assistance in seeking foreign aircraft sales by the Export Development Corporation.[9] This funding was arranged despite an earlier statement by Science Minister Bill Winegard that the federal government would *not* become financially involved with the company, following the European Community's objection to the sale attempted by Boeing with Aérospatiale and Alenia.[10]

In the event, neither the federal nor the provincial government was willing to risk the consequences of Boeing's being unable to secure a purchaser for de Havilland. The company had already announced that it would lay off 1,300 of its 3,700 employees in 1992, and its possible complete closure would have been an exceptionally damaging blow both to the local economy and to the Canadian aerospace industry. A 1990 study prepared by the Aerospace Industry Association of Canada estimated that almost half of de Havilland's Dash-8 sales were made in Canada, creating over 350 million dollars' worth of orders for its 2,000 smaller suppliers.[11] As a result of the de Havilland-Bombardier arrangement, possibly large labour force reductions were avoided (at least temporarily), although future employment levels depend upon the new management's success in obtaining greater orders for their aircraft. On a negative note, orders for the Dash-8 dwindled from 104 in 1989 to only thirty-two by 1991 because of the recession and of potential buyers' uncertainty regarding de Havilland's prospects.

Closely related to the improvement of export sales and international competitiveness, and of equal significance for Bombardier and for the Canadian aerospace industry in general, is the integrating effect of the acquisition of de Havilland on company and industry alike. As one analyst has explained,

[the] purchase gives Canada a fully integrated aircraft company for the first time, one that can compete in the global marketplace ... It means Canadian suppliers will deal with one major aircraft manufacturer, which could, over time, ease marketing and production problems emanating from juggling the demands of two separate companies.[12]

While stressing that the critical element in achieving export success is the ability to bring to the defence market the best product at the best price, Robert Brown, president of Bombardier's Canadair group, had pointed out a few months before the deal that compared with their American and European counterparts, Canadian defence producers were still too fragmented to generate the critical mass necessary to produce competitive advanced-technology systems.[13] The new company, which brings together Canada's two major airframe manufacturers along with extensive engine and avionics capabilities, may thus be

seen as a step that goes some distance towards creating in Canada a
rationalized and vertically integrated aerospace sector and a "national
champion" manufacturer in a manner clearly parallel to that in the
European defence industry, described previously.

If the conglomeration of Bombardier/Canadair/de Havilland was
seen to be a positive element in the corporate restructuring among
the leading defence and aerospace companies, it should be recalled
that there is another side to the coin. Following its divestiture of de
Havilland, Boeing Canada Technology retained two operating divisions, in Winnipeg and Arnprior. The Winnipeg facility designs, man-
ufactures, and supplies aerial and surface target systems for domestic
and export markets, while the Arnprior plant is primarily concerned
with servicing the needs of the Boeing Commercial Airplane Group,
a task that accounts for 75 percent of its total business.[14] However,
prospects for the remaining 25 percent – which is focused on the
repair, overhaul, and modification of the Canadian Forces' fleet of
Boeing helicopters – appear to be limited and to depend on decisions
yet to be made regarding a successor to the ill-fated EH-101 procurement contract.

The basis of the Arnprior division's defence business since at least
the end of the 1970s has been the modification and modernization,
and after 1986 the repair and overhaul, of the CH-113/113A Labrador
search-and-rescue helicopter and the CH-147 Chinook (now retired).
The decision to phase out both models and to replace them in the
search-and-rescue role by the EH-101 would therefore have meant the
loss of an important component of Boeing's Canadian defence market
after the sale of de Havilland, as well as the loss of the basis of the
Arnprior division's current defence business. However, the controversy
surrounding the purported need for, and cost of, the EH-101 program
raised the possibility of a reprieve, especially if the Conservatives were
to lose the 1993 federal election. Boeing's vice-president, George
Capern, proposed as one alternative that his company modernize the
Canadian Forces' thirteen existing Labrador helicopters for approximately $10 million each, as well as recall and modernize a number of
the Chinooks.[15] The July 1992 announcement by the Defence minister
that the EH-101 program would proceed as planned, however,
appeared at the time to mean an end to Boeing's involvement in the
Canadian military helicopter market. As the last Labrador was retired
and replaced by the EH-101, the Arnprior division either would have

to obtain subcontracting work on that or other programs, or else move out of the defence sector altogether.

Of course, the fate of the EH-101 acquisition program subsequently postponed this rather dismal scenario – dismal at least from the perspective of those at Boeing who sought to retain defence contract business. But eventually the obsolescent helicopter airframes will have to be replaced, and Boeing could again face a difficult future as part of Canada's defence aerospace industry; it could even become another casualty of the post-Cold War contraction.[16] This is not to suggest, of course, that such a fate would necessarily do significant harm to other parts of Boeing's aerospace activities in this country. As noted earlier, with most of the Arnprior division's business being directed towards servicing its commercial aircraft operations, trends in civil aviation will do more to affect overall employment and other corporate matters.

The fact that Boeing's parent organization chose to divest itself of the ostensibly unprofitable de Havilland facility while Bombardier decided to acquire it as part of its own restructuring plans, amply illustrates the point made by an executive of Bombardier – namely, that restructuring is a management tool that can be used not only for retrenchment but also for expansion.[17] It may be, as well, that the latitude enjoyed by suppliers in making such choices depends to a large extent on their degree of dependence upon government defence contracts. Neither Boeing nor Bombardier looks to defence for the bulk of its revenues and neither of their major aerospace subsidiaries are defence-dependent; while Canadair's level of dependence approached 100 percent in the mid-1970s, that figure had declined to only 10 percent by the early 1990s.[18]

For companies such as Bombardier, Pratt & Whitney, Boeing Arnprior, or McDonnell Douglas Canada – all of them major elements of the Canadian aerospace industry – the civilian market remains critical, though the defence sector has provided a valuable source of additional revenue historically. Among even the leading companies, however, there are others that look to the Canadian and international defence markets for a significant part of their revenues, ranging from virtually 100 percent in the case of Paramax Electronics to 60 percent for Litton Systems Canada and 40 percent for CAE Electronics. To understand more completely the range of pressures affecting Canadian defence industries, and their possible responses, therefore, one must review the types of strategies that have been adopted by these suppliers and the various problems that they currently see themselves as facing.

The EH-101 contract was to have been a critical element in sustaining the long-term economic viability of Paramax Electronics, a Montreal-based company employing approximately 1,100 people.[19] In a relationship somewhat akin to that between Boeing Canada and the de Havilland division, Paramax Electronics until late 1991 was the Canadian subsidiary of a U.S. firm, Unisys Corporation, though it operated through a lower level of the parent organization, Unisys Defense Systems.[20] Also like Boeing's de Havilland division, Paramax Electronics' parent company during 1991 pursued a restructuring strategy that involved divesting itself of its defence sector. On this occasion, however, the divestiture did not involve the sale of the Canadian company; instead, in October 1991 Unisys Corp. announced that it was creating a new, U.S.-based company, Paramax, consisting of both Unisys Defense Systems and Paramax Electronics. Thus the restructuring of the American parent corporation did not lead to any restructuring and rationalization of the Canadian defence industrial base, as occurred in the Boeing-de Havilland case.

To some extent, Paramax may be considered an atypical Canadian defence manufacturer, and hence not a representative example: it was established when its parent company was awarded the systems-integration contract for the Canadian patrol frigate (CPF), and has been a single-contract supplier since then. Obviously, it also became virtually entirely dependent on the domestic defence market for its revenues, which amounted to approximately $300 million a year.[21] For these very reasons, it can serve as an exemplar of the problems facing domestic defence industries in a changing and uncertain business environment. Finally, as one of Canada's leading software-engineering and systems-integration firms – even without the corporate backing it once enjoyed from Unisys Corp. – Paramax is a useful case study in its own right.

With work on the CPF program drawing to a close, Paramax in the early 1990s faced a growing need to win new defence contracts in order to sustain itself. Thus it strongly supported the Canadian Forces' proposed acquisition of the EH-101 helicopter as the new ship-borne and search-and-rescue aircraft, since Paramax would be E.H. Industries' prime contractor in Canada. If the selection favoured the EH-101, Paramax stood to gain something else it sought – potential new export sales through future international orders for the helicopter.[22] The announcement that cabinet had approved the procurement of the Anglo-Italian helicopter, when it finally came in late July 1992, thus provided Paramax executives with welcome news as the company's estimated $1.8-billion share of the program over the next thirteen years offered a measure of stability while the company sought to broaden its business base both within and beyond the defence sector.

Even if the EH-101 program had been continued, however, Paramax would still have been left in the precarious position of being a single-contract company in a market particularly prone, at times, to changes of direction based as much on political bargaining and electoral politics as on any military operational needs or prior strategic analysis. Recognizing this problem, a senior Paramax executive (who was also a former Canadian chief of the defence staff) noted at a small industry investment seminar held in 1990 that "there is a need to diversify, to get away from this one contract syndrome. The big question is where, and how do we do it?"[23]

THE LURE OF DIVERSIFICATION

As we saw earlier, the notion of diversification can take two basic forms – either *within* the defence sector but across a range of products and applications, or *out* of defence and into commercial markets. While Unisys Defense Systems became involved in civilian markets through such offerings as air-traffic-control, weather-radar, postal-sorting, and data-fusion systems, Paramax in Canada still had not advanced further by the early 1990s than planning a modest expansion into similar commercial areas involving the integration of large electronic systems.

Expansion by defence manufacturers into non-defence products and markets, as Paramax executives themselves were quick to point out, is difficult for a number of reasons. Primarily, success in such ventures often entails winning contracts in competition against existing and well-established, civilian-oriented companies with more experience and understanding of the methods best suited to this very different type of market, and with management and other personnel also familiar with commercial requirements. To an increasing extent, competition will also become fiercer as more defence firms in Canada, the United States, and Europe look towards commercial sales as an alternative to the dwindling defence market; defence electronics companies such as Paramax especially may experience this, as many begin to examine non-defence government procurement opportunities.

The difficulties of diversifying out of the defence sector are especially great in the case of Paramax by virtue of its heavy reliance on military contracts – a reliance that other defence industry executives interested in pursuing new commercial markets have also noted in their own cases.[24] As in the case of Boeing, predominantly commercial companies may thus be tempted simply to divest themselves, where possible, of their defence industry holdings or to spin off defence subsidiaries into independent units, as did both Unisys Corp. and Honeywell in the United States.[25] Another option, however – one actively pursued by Paramax – is to seek to broaden the range of products targeted at the defence sector both for traditional security requirements and for the new roles that have been mooted for the armed forces.

Among the traditional types of defence contracts that were being sought by Paramax executives in Canada, two longer-term prospects of varying potential were identified. The more likely, given Paramax's status in the original program, was seen to be the mid-life update and modernization of the CPF, which would take place in the next decade. Rather less certain, the possible acquisition of new, conventionally powered submarines would also create opportunities for systems integration and training contracts. However, after the public criticism of the nuclear-powered submarine program proposal in the 1987 White Paper – and with the example of the EH-101 cancellation in mind – it is difficult to imagine that any Canadian government would be prepared to contemplate pressing ahead with the conventional submarine program.

Less traditional security-related roles for which DND and the Coast Guard could be used, and which would therefore generate some specific new requirements, include drug interdiction as Canada becomes a major route for drug traffickers seeking to move their goods into the United States; the protection and monitoring of Canadian fisheries and other resources; interception of illegal immigrants off either coastline; and countering environmental threats such as major oil spills (again emphasizing coastal roles). Finally, in a mixture of traditional and newer concerns, a growing demand for humanitarian-relief or peacekeeping forces of all types, such as ground forces in the former Yugoslavia or technical experts searching for Iraqi nuclear weapons information, and perhaps for new and large-scale U.N. peacekeeping forces, could generate specialized equipment requirements.[26]

Whether more or less traditional in their nature, and whether short-, medium- or longer-term in their time horizons, there is a clear and common thread running throughout all of these possible defence market opportunities (also identified by Paramax executives, among others) – specifically, their emphasis on advanced technologies, especially the use of automatic data-processing techniques. Specialization in niche-market technologies and the absence since the late 1950s of major platform manufacturers may cushion the Canadian defence industry from the dramatic restructuring seen as necessary in the United States and already well under way in Europe, but Canadian aerospace and electronics industry executives and analysts alike recognize that a degree of restructuring and rationalization is inevitable. In this regard, "high technology and low cost are going to be the discriminators that eventually will decide which companies do well in this very demanding and very challenging environment, and which do not."[27] As well as the rationalization process under way in the aerospace sector, new industry consortia and strategic alliances, such as the two groups that competed for the Canadian Forces' supply-system upgrade contract, are thus likely to increase in frequency and may take on a more permanent though informal character, again as has occurred among European defence manufacturers.[28]

For defence-dependent aerospace firms in Canada, diversification either within or outside the defence sector has gained in importance as the demand for defence has declined internationally. One should not exaggerate the decline of the domestic defence market, which is still estimated at some $20 to $25 billion throughout the 1990s, but as we have already established, that market faces a variety of challenges ranging from macroeconomic variables to the rising cost of technology, all of which serve to strain the real purchasing power of whatever defence funding is made available.[29] Declining defence budgets in the United States and in Europe tend to make export opportunities more difficult to find and to increase competition for each contract. Support for increased Canadian defence exports is, in any case, precarious at best; certainly industry requests for non-NATO defence exports will be a highly contentious policy issue over the remainder of the decade.[30] The relocation of defence manufacturers out of Canada – whether by subsidiaries of parent U.S. and European corporations or by Canadian-owned companies moving to low-cost countries such as Mexico – is also a possibility that cannot be precluded.

The variety of characteristics among the leading aerospace and defence companies in Canada makes the drawing of generalized lessons from case studies a difficult task, and it would be unwise to press such lessons too far. At least one observation, however, can be made without attaching too many caveats: the most far-reaching changes in the structure and composition of the Canadian defence industry appear to be the result of corporate strategies pursued by those companies *least* reliant on the defence sector for their total sales. Whether through divestiture (Boeing) or through acquisition (Bombardier), such companies have the greatest margin for manœuvre, especially at a time when uncertainty surrounds major defence programs, even after the formal announcement of a contract award.[31]

By contrast, defence-dependent companies such as Paramax, Litton Systems, or Canadian Marconi must look towards diversification within defence to secure their future or else face a slow (or perhaps, at times, a faster) erosion in their business and in employment levels. At Canadian Marconi, for example, employment has fallen by 35 percent over the past two years; the EH-101 cancellation had an immediate and detrimental impact on employment levels at Paramax, but the company continues to rely heavily on the defence sector and, unlike Litton Systems Canada, on the domestic market in particular.[32]

Before we conclude this analysis of restructuring trends in the aerospace industry, it is important to note that corporate strategies have not been directed towards a broadly defined and coordinated rationalization of the DIB; the Bombardier/Canadair/de Havilland grouping may, it is true, constitute a major step towards an integrated aerospace industry, but Bombardier executives are the first to stress that their corporate emphasis has been simply on protecting cash flows.[33] Our comment is certainly not intended as a criticism of such aims; rather, it serves to make the point that there is generally little or no broader vision or goal motivating companies' behaviour. If deemed necessary, efforts to direct the restructuring of the defence industrial base in light of the changing defence market must be the responsibility of government officials charged with appropriate mandates.

The characteristics of the Canadian defence industry – specialized niche markets, advanced-technology components, and subcomponent supply – have so far cushioned it from some of the pressures that have faced or are now facing European and U.S. platform manufacturers. At the same time, the export orientation of most companies has limited the impact of declining real defence spending in Canada. Some significant industry restructuring has taken place, in response both to market forces predating the end of the Cold War and to more recent events. As the international defence market shrinks further, pressures for restructuring will grow; how these pressures are translated into reality will depend to a considerable extent upon government policy choices, most of which have begun to be debated but have not yet captured the degree of sustained and serious public attention that they both merit and require.

CHAPTER SEVEN

The Dilemmas
of Policy in the 1990s

In one of the regrettably few academic discussions of federal government policies affecting the defence and aerospace industries, Jeanne Kirk Laux argues that the government faces a dilemma or "paradox" in its attempts to design and implement policies to support a competitive domestic defence industry. Acceptance of neo-liberal ideology and the signing of trade agreements such as the GATT have devalued the traditional methods of preserving and encouraging this industry through protectionism, procurement, and public ownership. Laux suggests, however, that "permanent state interests place limits to liberalism in a competitive global economy" as "governments are finding functional equivalents for the forbidden forms of intervention."[1] In the case of the Canadian aerospace industry, these functional equivalents include promotion-oriented protectionism in the form of R&D subsidies and export financing, as well as the total exclusion of defence production and defence suppliers from the terms of the Canada-U.S. Free Trade Agreement.

That the federal government has a major role to play in determining the structure, composition, and location of the defence industry – and indeed its economic viability – has been clear since at least the late 1950s, with the negotiation of the DPSA and then the DDSA. Our analysis of these and other political-economy instruments is divided into the three geographic (or market) contexts employed throughout this book – the Canadian, North American, and overseas contexts.[2] We do, however, emphasize again the interlocking nature of these instruments; and in our discussion below we shall be mindful of how they can and do affect each other, whether in a convergent, divergent, or even outright contradictory fashion.

The meaning of terms such as "industrial strategy" and "industrial policy," as well as the politically acceptable limits of state intervention in the workings of the market, have long been the subjects of extensive debate among academics, government officials, industry representatives, and other analysts in Canada and elsewhere. One such analyst has succinctly noted that the "one generalization to be made about industrial policy is that this term means different things to different people."[3] Examples of differing interpretations abound, ranging from more philosophical inquiries into the purpose to be served by such a policy to taxonomies of the terms in common usage.[4]

SUBSIDIZING THE DEFENCE INDUSTRY IN CANADA

Rather than become embroiled in these broader issues, we will focus here on debates concerning specific policy instruments and agreements with potentially significant consequences for the Canadian defence industry. These include industrial and regional benefits programs (IRBs), the Defence Industry Productivity Program (DIPP), and other subsidies; the Defence Development and Defence Production Sharing Arrangements (DDSA/DPSA) review; the North American Free Trade Agreement (NAFTA); international joint development projects; and the Export Act review. Despite the welter of differing views on industrial policy, one thing seems apparent: just as in the international trade arena, so too in the defence sector the 1990s will be a time of transition in which adjustment to rapidly changing circumstances will be a primary public policy concern.[5] Less clear is what the long-term goal of adjustment in the domestic defence industry could or should entail.

A number of contemporary *domestic* policy initiatives and debates have potentially significant consequences for leading defence producers in Canada. Some of these we have already introduced in earlier chapters – for example, DND target percentages for capital procurement budgets, IRB requirements, and the perceived personal preferences of former Minister of Defence Marcel Masse – but we shall update and expand upon this list below. Other issues – especially the future of DIPP funding and other government subsidies, and the current popular "buzzword" of conversion – have only recently come to the fore. Our discussion of these issues will be divided along the previously employed lines demarcating the overseas international and North American contexts; this is admittedly somewhat artificial, but it does aid clarity and could suggest a potentially useful new direction for policy.

Stable and predictable budget guidelines for future capital equipment procurement and for R&D would offer both DND and defence manufacturers a valuable basis upon which to establish plans, whether for reequipment programs or for investment in plant and technology improvements. As we have seen, the target percentages announced by successive governments (including the last Conservative one) have been little more than politically expedient symbolic gestures. Thus, while budget guidelines may be predictable, they are anything but stable, and the persistent shortfall in spending on new capital equipment can be expected to continue.[6] Nevertheless, should the Chrétien government maintain its commitment to the unpopular and hard choices on the issue of base and other facility closures announced in the February 1994 budget, the *relative* capital spending targets announced in April 1991 could still be at least approximated, if only because personnel, operations, and maintenance expenditures will shrink more radically than capital outlays. This may, however, be small comfort for Canada's defence industry, which lives in the world of *absolute* expenditures.

The critical domestic policy issues (other than budgetary) that are frequently cited by defence industry and government officials as they ponder the future of Canadian defence production include the industrial and regional benefits requirements associated with major contract awards, as well as government assistance in the financing of industrial R&D or other forms of investment. Neither major policy instrument, it should be recalled, falls under the control or supervision of DND; rather, both are within the mandate of Industry Canada (a successor, since mid-1993, to Industry, Science and Technology Canada), and despite the recommendations of the Defence Industrial Preparedness Task Force no transfer of responsibilities to the user department appears likely.[7]

According to comments made by some government officials, during the late 1980s and early 1990s the implementation of IRB provisions and the regional-development aspect of ISTC's mandate were both being undermined by an assumed concentration of infrastructure and funding in one province (Quebec) so as to enable it to become "Canada's arsenal."[8] Controversy over this issue – provoked by Defence Minister Masse's repeated statements that Quebec deserved a larger slice of the procurement pie – abated considerably after Masse left his post. Nevertheless, any constitutional wrangling over Quebec's (and Canada's) future will likely continue to generate heated debates and criticisms whenever new procurement contracts are signed with Quebec-based firms for what will inevitably be considered to be political reasons.

Even apart from this particular constitutional concern, IRB requirements are likely to remain at the forefront of all major new procurement contracts. With procurement budgets continuing to be squeezed by rising unit costs at a time of declining spending, every new "major crown project" will be the target of the demands of competing political and regional interests as well as competing manufacturers. Would-be prime contractors or other major suppliers will face increasing pressure to show the wider potential economic benefits resulting from their bids, and DND will continue to pay a premium on its limited capital procurement budget in order to "justify" the costs of acquiring new or replacement equipment.[9]

In contrast to the high political profile often attained by the requirements for industrial and regional benefits, federal government subsidies to the defence sector have attracted relatively little public attention – until very recently, that is. During the early 1990s, there was growing interest in the principal federal policy instrument of this type, the Defence Industry Productivity Program. Established in 1959 as the Industry Modernization for Defence Exports Program, and evolving through at least four subsequent stages of administrative adjustment and refocusing, DIPP now faces a period of rather difficult and possibly crucial reassessment.[10] Even though it may yet escape radical surgery, DIPP has a number of lesser ailments that need remedy. We begin by discussing these lesser problems, which have disturbed industry representatives and government officials alike.

The overall level of DIPP funding available to industry has become a source of dispute on two counts: first, because in March 1990 Ottawa decided to reduce total DIPP monies as part of its efforts to resolve broader fiscal dilemmas; and second, because there exists the possibility that the subsidy program may, at some future point, become a contentious issue under either the FTA and NAFTA or, more likely, the GATT. Federal officials and industry executives have argued that DIPP funding fell from some $235 million in 1990–91 to $178 million in 1991–92 and have expressed concern about this decline.[11] Industry leaders and associations have been quick to point out that their foreign competitors often receive higher levels of government support; their predicament is exacerbated, in their view, by the provision that DIPP funds (normally provided on a fifty-fifty, or lower, shared basis) be repaid once companies have achieved projected export sales. (Contractors in the United States, by comparison, have been able to reclaim up to 100 percent of their independent research and development expenditures without similar repayment obligations.)[12] One sector in particular – aerospace – is already hard-pressed to attract capital for investment or to allocate profit margins to reinvestment, despite a good record of investment relative to other domestic manufacturing sectors. Further cuts in DIPP or other government support, it has been suggested, could precipitate an exodus of such technology-intensive companies to low-cost countries where financial support is more readily available.[13]

The argument that DIPP funding has diminished has been challenged by at least one organization, which maintains instead that expenditures in 1990 were closer to $300 million, despite government announcements of planned reductions.[14] The figures of $178 million and $300 million were actually cited by the respective sides in the same set of hearings before the Commons Subcommittee on Arms Export in October and November 1991, clearly highlighting their different interests and, perhaps, different definitions of what constitutes DIPP funds.[15] Part of the wide discrepancy may result from using as a basis for calculations budget allocations versus actual expenditures, or of including all sources of ISTC financial assistance under the rubric of DIPP. To the extent, however, that lower profits and growing pressures from parent corporations to cut reinvestment rates have reduced the demand for DIPP assistance while the complaints by industry have continued to rise, the correct figure may fall between the two. In any event, the downward trend clearly reflects developments in other areas of government expenditures.[16]

Whether DIPP subsidies might, at some future point, become an issue under either the GATT or the FTA (and NAFTA) is, to some extent, a function of their overall amounts and of the manner in which the funds are employed. In the context of the GATT, much would depend on whether the question of government industrial subsidies is approached on an individual-program basis or whether a minimum threshold is established below which challenges could not be made against a program. In the latter case, DIPP subsidies would represent only a small percentage of total industry sales and might therefore be acceptable. If a program-by-program approach is adopted, however, then DIPP's legitimacy could be questioned by overseas competitors; in that case, of course, the considerable subsidies offered to many of these overseas competitors would face much the same criticism. Stalled as the GATT negotiations had been over the more fundamental dispute regarding agricultural subsidies, the DIPP has not yet been severely pressured from this direction.

A growing policy dilemma exists concerning the support provided through DIPP subsidies to industries (particularly the aerospace sector, broadly defined to include electronics and instrumentation) that have moved increasingly into civilian-related manufacturing over the past two decades. The national-security orientation of DIPP has until now ensured its exemption from GATT's purview and, more recently, from that of the Free Trade Agreement. In testimony to the House of

Commons in 1991, however, ISTC officials readily acknowledged that by 1994 "only 20 percent of the defence and aerospace industry activity will be related to defence items and the remainder will be devoted to civilian-related items."[17] Pratt & Whitney Canada, by far the leading recipient of DIPP funds, and McDonnell Douglas were both cited as examples of companies making use of DIPP monies to invest in primarily civilian applications, while ISTC (as it was then called) was said to be "working seriously with many of the large, particularly larger, defence companies in an effort to identify potential in the civilian aerospace and other related civilian activities."[18]

The long-term goal of this policy is to make use of DIPP funding to aid companies in identifying and developing "sustainable diversified activities." As one member of Parliament has pointed out, however, "one of the problems is that … if you shifted [DIPP] into a direct subsidy to industry for non-defence products, it would become an unfair subsidy under the Free Trade Agreement."[19] Although one might argue that DIPP funding is being used for domestic purposes only in order to sustain Canadian defence production, neither the explicitly export-oriented criteria used in evaluating applications for DIPP support nor the obvious fact that DIPP funds are, at times, used by manufacturers of exclusively civilian products offers much support to such a claim. Indeed, as already noted, this is one of the issues raised by the United States, not in the context of the FTA or of the NAFTA negotiations but rather in that of the Department of Defense's review of all of its bilateral defence trade relationships.

Some other aspects of DIPP (and IRB policies) have drawn *domestic* criticism because of the manner in which the subsidies have been directed at fostering regional economic development across Canada. For example, when asked to identify the one key policy initiative causing the greatest difficulty for the defence industry, an executive of a larger company lamented that "government policies for Crown projects are devoted to the introduction of new companies into a very small market … rather than the support and strengthening of the current base that often result in federal subsidies to establish new firms to the detriment of established firms." Pursuing such a policy into the 1990s, he suggested, would "likely result in one-time projects leaving an uncompetitive industry to compete in a more difficult world market and the final elimination of whole segments of the defence base."[20]

The appropriate policy solution, according to those who take this view, is for the government – presumably, Industry Canada – to initiate "funded R&D programs leading to the establishment of new high technology products capable of being sold in the U.S.A. and international market."[21] Competition, it is argued, should be reduced and acquisition projects should be directed to existing well-proven companies in order to ensure their economic viability and continuing growth.

The question of possible subsidy challenges under GATT or under the FTA/NAFTA arises immediately in assessing this argument, but it is also questionable whether established manufacturers actually do lose out to small, new suppliers in seeking government funding. As Table A.5 reveals, R&D funding by Industry Canada and the Department of Foreign Affairs and International Trade (DFAIT) does indeed support a large number of small firms. However, Table 6.1 and Table A.5 taken together also show that by far the largest percentage of monies is obtained by a relatively few, larger manufacturers, mainly located in the metropolitan regions of Toronto and Montreal. It has been estimated that between 1969 and 1990, almost 75 percent of DIPP grants went to only twenty companies, with the leading five receiving 60 percent. Pratt & Whitney Canada dominated all other recipients throughout this period, and Table A.5 shows that this trend is continuing into the mid-1990s even as overall DIPP funding levels may be declining.[22]

To the extent that DIPP grants as a percentage of total DIPP allocations are awarded primarily to larger established manufacturers located in central Canada, it follows that both the industry's criticism of its dilution and the government's argument that its funds support economic development and reduce regional disparity are not only contradictory but inaccurate. Of course, one should not ignore the obvious point that for smaller, third-tier defence-related manufacturers, relatively much lower R&D or other DIPP grants can provide essential backing for the pursuit of business. In fact, the amounts involved have been slight indeed: beyond the top twenty DIPP recipients between 1969 and 1990, "there were more than 600 companies that combined received only 17.7 percent of programme funding."[23]

THE QUESTION OF CONVERSION

So long as the international political-security context was dominated by East-West confrontation, criticisms of government subsidization of defence production through DIPP mainly concerned the scale and direction of the funding; the program itself, and the need for a capable defence industry, usually went unchallenged, save for a few opposition groups such as Project Ploughshares, a "task force on disarmament and development" sponsored by the Canadian Council of Churches.[24] Since the end of the Cold War, however, there has emerged a greater interest in challenging the nature or "philosophy" underlying DIPP. The question whether defence manufacturers should be encouraged to convert themselves into commercial enterprises arose especially in the context of the Commons review of defence-related export policies in Canada.

Not surprisingly, much of the rhetoric on the subject of conversion was simply a part of the political posturing of opposition NDP and Liberal members in preparation for the 1993 federal election. Apart from the general popularity of proposals to cut defence budgets and programs, the promise of new business and new jobs through conversion policies had obvious electoral appeal to those directly affected by a downsizing of the defence industry and by the threat that some Canadian subsidiaries of foreign corporations might be closed by the parent companies as they sought to protect their overall corporate interests. Nevertheless, whether and how government defence-related R&D programs should be restructured so as to encourage the development of commercial technologies and products is a legitimate policy question in Ottawa, Washington, London, Paris, or even Moscow.[25] In turn, how to encourage or induce industry to pursue conversion as a realistic alternative has led those pressing for change of this type to propose that DIPP be used as a conversion-assistance fund rather than a defence export-oriented program.[26]

Leaving aside the past problems and failures encountered by defence manufacturers who have sought to compete extensively in the civilian marketplace, if the still-elementary views regarding conversion are to become a practical reality, then several difficult questions must be addressed by its proponents; the particular characteristics of the Canadian defence industrial base must also be taken into account more adequately. The crucial question, obviously, is that of cost – for retraining both management and technical staff and production employees, for extensive plant modifications and retooling, and for market research. Whether DIPP funding has declined to $178 million or remains at $300 million, the price of a national industrial conversion program would likely be much higher than either of those figures. It might not be unreasonable to assume – given earlier NDP and Liberal Party criticism of the EH-101 project, for example – that additional funds would have to be drawn from the capital portion of the defence budget, now that "attacking the overhead" has apparently been consummated.[27]

Closely behind the direct cost issue are what can be termed indirect cost concerns, which would come from at least two other industry sources. The first group consists of other domestic industries or economic interest groups also experiencing the pains of economic adjustment – the Atlantic fisheries, or industries hard-pressed by overseas competitors – who would question why defence manufacturers should be singled out for special assistance. The second group, which would grow over time, would be made up of Canadian companies now facing added competition from new, "converted" rivals subsidized by government grants. Adequate provisions, financial and otherwise, would be required in order to respond to their concerns.

Mention has already been made of the possibility of DIPP's being challenged on the grounds that its use to support civil and commercial industry is prohibited by the GATT and the FTA. Similar complaints might conceivably be levelled against a conversion-assistance subsidy program, but since such programs are being instituted or examined by a number of European governments, by the EC, and by the United States itself as part of their own post-Cold War adjustment policies, serious difficulties are unlikely to arise from this direction.

Conversion programs being developed by the larger defence industrial countries in NATO may offer justification for Canadian examination of similar policies, but they do not necessarily provide useful models. One problem immediately apparent in the discussions of conversion initiatives in Ottawa is that, too often, their proponents are not familiar with the particular character, structure, and composition of the Canadian defence industrial base, and tend instead to import their views from the United States or Europe. "Conversion" can be a very misleading term in the Canadian context, for two reasons: first, because the bulk of the defence industry is already primarily civil in its orientation; and second, because many technologies described as "defence technologies" could more accurately be called dual-use. The argument that DIPP subsidies are military overlooks the fact that the companies using these grants are in many cases civil-oriented – for example, McDonnell Douglas and the former MBB Helicopters (both entirely commercial) or even the largest DIPP recipient, Pratt & Whitney Canada. While DIPP certainly cannot be said to have brought about this concentration by itself, it does continue to be utilized by those civil aerospace companies, as well as by more heavily defence-oriented companies such as Litton Systems Canada. As noted by one observer, "diversification of product mix of defence-oriented companies has long been a DIPP priority."[28]

The emphasis placed on dual-use technology and products by many companies of the aerospace sector (again, broadly defined to include electronics and instrumentation) further complicates the question of conversion. In some instances, companies may use the same skills or sell the same products, with the label "defence" being applied because of the nature of the *recipient* rather than of what is being supplied. Indeed, opponents of Canadian defence or defence-related sales frequently use this method when describing exports.[29] Conversion, in such cases, is not a matter of retooling or retraining but rather of inducing or obliging companies to forsake domestic and international government defence contracts.[30]

What is often overlooked is that conversion has been under way in the defence industry for several years, under the more accurate, if less eye-catching, name of "diversification." Examples of the two variants currently figuring in Canadian corporate strategies were discussed earlier, but diversification should not be considered simply as a recent response to a shrinking and saturated international defence market beset by leaner domestic defence procurement prospects. Diversification in response to changing market conditions predates the end of the Cold War: the rationalization of the simulation and training subsector and the shift in the sales ratio of Canada's CAE Electronics (the world's leading aircraft simulator manufacturer) towards civil markets are notable examples of such market-driven "conversion."[31]

There is some concern that declining defence orders in foreign national markets may lead parent corporations to withdraw to their home base either by closing their Canadian subsidiaries altogether or by terminating the defence portion of their production. Rising production costs in Canada, along with the FTA and now NAFTA, add further incentives to shift the location of production through subsidiaries. Given the possibility of plant closures and downsizing, conversion funding programs may be indirectly regarded by politicians as a valuable means of attempting to maintain employment. To be sure, regional economic or employment benefits have been an important element of defence procurement in Canada, but in this instance "conversion" may simply be a convenient alternative term for "job protection." In this context, however, it will be far from easy for conversion proponents to justify special funds for defence companies when much greater job losses are taking place in other manufacturing sectors.

This is not to discredit or undermine the idea of conversion but merely to suggest the hurdles that its advocates will face in the coming years. Where true conversion may be of greater validity (as well as a more accurate label) is in the case of individual aerospace companies that remain heavily defence-dependent and of the shipbuilding and ship-repair industry, which to all intents and purposes is entirely dependent on federal defence work for its survival. Because defence-dependent aerospace companies face the most severe difficulties in their attempts to break into civilian markets, the limited funds likely to be made available if conversion becomes a reality in Canada would have a greater impact if they were targeted at these firms than if they were used to support manufacturers that are already largely oriented towards civilian markets.

The shipbuilding and ship-repair industry in Canada presents an especially difficult policy problem. Despite the award of a $500-million contract for twelve coastal-patrol and mine-countermeasure vessels to a consortium led by Fenco Engineers, the industry faces a major structural crisis as there are simply too many shipyards competing for too little domestic business, with limited export prospects. Groups such as the Canadian Maritime Industries Association press for more regular, if smaller, contracts; for a new acquisition policy that would end the practice of fixed-price contracts; and for the return of previously cancelled subsidy programs. Others, however, are advocating greater purchasing of foreign warships "off-the-shelf," which might then be outfitted in Canada to meet Ottawa's naval requirements. In the meantime, existing naval programs continue to face financial problems and long delays – the result, argue those in favour of reform, of regional political pressures for job maintenance that hinder the efficient rationalization of an uncompetitive and oversized industry.[32]

Our review of the contemporary domestic context of the Canadian defence industry reveals the array of policy issues facing those directly charged with oversight of that sector. We have not discussed the primary macroeconomic concern – that is, the exchange rate of the Canadian dollar – which, though frequently cited as a problem for an industry so dependent on exports or seeking to improve its international competitiveness, remains beyond the control of any of the departments with defence industry mandates. Similarly, we have not addressed the topic of rationalization of the government bureaucratic structure and of the mandates of departments regarding the defence industry, although we shall do so later on. First, however, and in keeping with our belief that the development and viability of defence production in Canada can only be properly understood in the context of demand- and supply-side variables at the domestic and international levels, we consider the North American policy environment by surveying the major current debates in the bilateral defence economic relationship.

REASSESSING THE
BILATERAL RELATIONSHIP:
MARKET ACCESS AND
CANADA-U.S. DEFENCE
INDUSTRIAL BASE POLICIES

The idea of seeking a formal defence economic treaty with the United States has been attracting increasing attention at Canadian defence industry seminars and conferences since the late 1980s.[33] Despite the Free Trade Agreement, Canadian defence companies must still deal with legislation aimed at protecting the U.S. defence industries and with periodic Congressional incursions into the defence market at the behest of industry subsectors (recent examples being anchor chains and sonobuoys) or individual companies.[34] The relatively frequent rotation of Pentagon personnel also means that the Canadian defence industry or the Canadian Commercial Corporation must repeatedly overcome the lack of familiarity of new procurement officers with the terms, or even the existence, of the DDSA and DPSA.

Although the possibility of referring to a binding treaty that, unlike the DDSA/DPSA, could not be amended at the whim of Congress has great appeal to many observers, a number of Canadian government officials – and some of their U.S. counterparts – regard the notion of a treaty as potentially very counterproductive. They argue that the DDSA/DPSA have proven to be a useful set of arrangements and that efforts to establish a formal agreement might only serve to bring to Congress' inevitably parochial attention a relationship better left at the non-political level.[35] In the past few years, however, the Department of Defense has been urged by Congress and the Department of Commerce to reappraise its bilateral defence trade memoranda of understanding so as to take industrial-base considerations more fully into account – not necessarily to promote greater advantages for U.S. industry but to be more critical of the actions of partner countries. The Defence Production Sharing Arrangement, as previously mentioned, has come under close scrutiny, and this has precipitated an internal Canadian defence economic review.

In seeking to determine how that defence economic review might affect the access of Canadian defence manufacturers to the U.S. market, we must consider the debate that took place during the early phases of negotiations for the North American Free Trade Agreement. That debate sheds some interesting light on the rationale for exempting defence trade issues from the earlier Free Trade Agreement with the United States, and it also suggests why no formal treaty on this matter is likely to be attained.

In surveying the Canadian agenda for matters worthy of inclusion in the NAFTA talks, a question that quickly arose was whether Canada's science and technology aspirations should be introduced in the current trade negotiations since technology was not covered in the FTA negotiations. Four elements constituted these "aspirations": access to information; access to government procurement; participation in R&D contracts and consortia; and resolution of the overlap of America's "national security" concerns and measures with its economic and commercial interests.[36]

Those who favoured the inclusion of access to technology as an agenda item in the NAFTA negotiations – a minority – had several concerns. A significant one was that there appeared to be emerging in the United States a post-Cold War tendency to shift from "pure" defence-related subsidies and procurement towards subsidies for the civilian market under the rubric of national economic competitiveness. As part of this trend, and under pressure from Congress, national-security exemptions or restrictions may be gradually expanded to include economic and industrial considerations. An institutional example, which pitted the Bush administration against Congress, was the growing involvement, in the late 1980s, of the Defence Advanced Research Projects Agency in dual-use technologies; indeed, there has been much discussion of creating a civilian counterpart to that agency.[37]

A second factor in the argument for including access to technology in NAFTA was the recognition that Canadian technology-intensive companies, which are small by u.s. standards (and in absolute terms), must compete for contracts against American firms that operate under the protection of extensive small-business set-aside provisions and the 1982 Small Business Innovation Development Act. Small-business set-asides remain central to the Canadian defence industry's complaints about u.s. protectionist legislation and practices.

Though not necessarily or directly related to the NAFTA deliberations, the more specific issue of Canadian access to u.s. defence-related, advanced-technology projects also led to questions about future market access. A number of obstacles (in addition to those mentioned earlier) exist in the case of defence technology. While the bilateral Memorandum of Understanding on Strategic Technology Exchange has provided Canadian contractors with access to American strategic technical data and led to the establishment of a "joint certification program," national-security restrictions and other obstacles continue to impede access. Canadian firms can request specified data but have no assurance that they will actually be provided; the technology exchanged must still be unclassified, whereas by their very nature advanced defence-related R&D projects contain considerable levels of classified information; and a large amount of critical defence technology is excluded under the "DoD Approved Use Only" listing that permits release of such technologies *only* to qualified u.s. contractors for bidding on, or performing, Department of Defense contracts.

Other barriers include restrictions on foreign ownership, control, and influence associated with the Committee on Foreign Investment in the United States; the exclusion of Canadian companies from DoD contract briefings involving critical technologies; and the provision that the technology being exchanged must be administered and controlled in Canada by DND, effectively excluding commercially owned and administered technology. Confronting these difficulties, Canadian defence manufacturers have been unable simply to resort to the DDSA or DPSA to assist them. To the contrary, discussions between Canadian government and industry officials have revealed extensive industry dissatisfaction with the implementation or observance of the DDSA's terms by U.S. officials, both in Congress and at the Pentagon.[38]

Adding access to technology to the NAFTA agenda ultimately found little support in the Canadian government. In general terms, attempts to use an umbrella agreement in order to overcome U.S. national-security concerns – even under the broader, non-military definition of those concerns emerging in the post-Cold War era – were considered likely to lead to greater, not lesser, Congressional protectionism. Even more, it was argued that the United States would never "allow for a mechanism to permit Canadians to challenge security classifications before some sort of tribunal ... even if the notion of national security is gradually extended to cover non-defence (i.e., economic) security."[39]

It was recognized that the issue of Canadian access to U.S. defence technology and procurement must be qualified by "reasonable expectations" – in other words, that Canadian industry would have to offer something of value to the United States in return. As was demonstrated by the negotiations between the Defense Advanced Projects Research Agency (DARPA) and the EC's ESPRIT research program, which took place without a formal government-to-government accord, collaboration can be pursued when it is mutually advantageous. Should Canadian companies and the Canadian government be prepared to invest time and money in the development of a project, it was argued that DARPA or some other U.S. government agencies and departments (including Defense and Commerce) would prove naturally amenable to negotiation. Even if the exchange proved to be of demonstrably greater value to Canada than to the United States, the expectation was that DARPA would find it a worthwhile means of gaining access to areas of noted Canadian technological expertise. Government officials in Ottawa who support this view point to the "critical technologies list" as a useful guide to DoD views on domestic R&D weaknesses and other countries' strengths.[40]

These same officials also noted, however, that if undertaken without due consideration for the limits of "reasonable expectations," Canadian efforts to pursue greater access to American technology (or simple access to individual programs) could in fact become doubly counterproductive. First, there are certain critical technologies or programs involving them to which access will simply not be granted under *any* foreseeable circumstances. And second, the very process of raising this policy issue or of seeking such access can generate irritation and decrease the support of u.s. officials who might otherwise be broadly sympathetic to the value of collaboration with Canadian defence manufacturers and with Ottawa.[41]

Three main options can be discerned in the debate over technology access and NAFTA. One is simply to leave the issue for review and negotiation at a later date within a multilateral forum (such as GATT). This can, in some ways, be considered similar to the suggestion that Canada-u.s. defence economic arrangements be decided upon indirectly through NATO's CNAD forum and the defence trade study initiative in Brussels. An agreement on a NATO defence trade code of conduct and dispute settlement mechanism, should one be reached, might also set the terms of bilateral defence trade and defence industrial base relations. A second option identified during this exercise is to regard the access issue as one that must await a more comprehensive bilateral settlement. In civilian or commercial cases, this could mean finding a resolution via the existing FTA; in defence-related cases, this would imply establishing a formal Canada-u.s. treaty. As we argued above, however, the achievement of such a treaty is highly unlikely; and even if one were signed, it might prove to be counterproductive.

The third option is to seek to establish less formal, more specific agreements on what is to be procured and how it is to be traded. Such ad hoc agreements could be pursued at different levels – intergovernmental, interdepartmental, state/provincial, and regional/municipal. Commercial agreements of this type need have no direct connection to the wider, more formal NAFTA; rather, it may suffice that NAFTA negotiators seek to ensure that the trilateral treaty did not create other impediments to the conclusion of such agreements. Such an approach would fit best with governments disinclined to adopt any initiatives smacking of industrial policy. Though the current Democratic administration in the United States and the Liberal government in Canada may not share the suspicions of their Republican and Conservative predecessors regarding industrial policy, they may yet find this option to be the most practical and achievable.

Such informal arrangements and ad hoc or project-specific agreements already exist, and they will likely continue to be the basis of bilateral defence economic relations, subject as usual to political interference and to individual interpretations. At the same time, however, that relationship is undergoing reassessment and change as a result of discontentment on both sides. That is why the potential consequences of the Canadian defence economic review should be examined carefully, since they are likely to influence the economic viability and future prospects of the domestic defence industrial base.

The review process is not likely to produce a revised, fully coordinated policy framework for dealing with defence economic issues; to do this would require the kind of convergence between departments that, as we have seen, does not exist. More probable – indeed, some elements may have already begun to emerge – are alterations in the terms of use of particular policy instruments and adjustments in the organization or mandates of many federal agencies. The mandates of such central departments as DND, IC, or DFAIT, however, are unlikely to experience any substantive changes such as interdepartmental transfers of authority.

At least some of the stigma that might have been attached to Canadian IRB requirements was eliminated by the 1986 decision to refocus these requirements from their earlier quantitative emphasis towards longer-term qualitative gains through technology transfer, investment, and future export potential as well as regional development. However, as the United States gradually expands its definition of national security to embrace aspects of economic competitiveness – a perspective already apparent in U.S.-Japanese defence trade relations – Canadian IRB requirements may again face criticism from Congress and elements of the Department of Commerce, should they be seen to generate unfair advantages for civilian industries competing against U.S. companies either within North America or in overseas markets.

If such objections were to arise over IRB provisions, Canadian officials might wish to draw attention to the comparatively much larger industry adjustment subsidies now being debated in the House of Representatives and the Senate. While such a response would be a reasonable one in the case of DIPP funding of civilian as well as defence aerospace ventures, however, it is much more difficult to justify the requirement that additional benefits accrue to Canada from a defence economic relationship that, in the eyes of the U.S. critics, already provides Canadian-based manufacturers with favoured access to their market.

Should U.S. complaints about Canadian "double-dipping" through the DPSA have an impact upon the current review of IRB policy provisions, one change that could be anticipated is an undertaking that future benefits requirements would be directed towards established defence manufacturers only, rather than towards the establishment of new companies across Canada. In that event, the reaction of defence manufacturers and the effect on the defence industrial base would depend on the level or tier of industry under consideration. Supporting established (and usually larger) companies would be welcomed by those suppliers who have been advocating just such a revision in Ottawa's IRB policy. By contrast, such a change would be detrimental to the smaller, lower-tier suppliers, among which are some of the most innovative Canadian aerospace manufacturers.

Already faced with continually rising costs and risks and with growing competition even within their specialized niche markets, smaller Canadian suppliers will be under even greater pressure to merge with, or sell to, upper-tier manufacturers – or else go out of business altogether. This process of vertical integration has already taken place in respect of several enterprises, including MEL Defence Systems, Amherst Aerospace, Ernst Leitz (Canada), and Telemus Electronics, not to mention the purchase of portions of Leigh Instruments by Spar Aerospace after Leigh ran into financial and other difficulties. Smaller, highly specialized aerospace firms will prove increasingly valuable and tempting targets for larger manufacturers seeking to ensure their future in the Canadian defence industrial base.

The shipbuilding and ship-repair industry may be the least economically secure of the defence sector, but its almost total dependence on government procurement also renders it the least vulnerable to shifts in the terms of Canada's defence economic relations, whether with the United States or with Europe.[42] By contrast, the aerospace industry cannot avoid being vulnerable to any changes in access to the U.S. market, or to U.S. demands for revisions of Canadian policies associated with the DDSA/DPSA. Just as the views and interests of American companies concerning cooperation with Japanese defence suppliers or the effects of European initiatives vary greatly depending on their size (among other factors), so too the impact of change on the Canadian aerospace industry will vary depending on whether individual firms are among upper- or lower-tier suppliers, on whether they are domestic or foreign-owned, and on whether they are heavily oriented towards defence or are among the ranks of diversified and primarily civilian manufacturers.

While U.S. pressures on the DDSA/DPSA may well force Ottawa to make difficult choices, the effects of those choices on the defence industry will be contingent upon a variety of factors. What can be said, however, is that "the state in Canada," as it "continues to attempt to set the terms and conditions of production and investment," will once again have to reconsider its "forms of favouritism and its favourites."[43] And developments in the United States are not the only factors that will lead to such a reconsideration.

OVERSEAS POLICY ISSUES: EXAMINING PRIORITIES

Two policy issues dominate discussions about how changes in the overseas international context will likely affect Canadian defence industrial base and defence trade policies in the coming years. The first issue, with which we end this chapter, is Canada's defence economic relationship and arrangements with its European NATO allies. The end of the Cold War and the movement, however halting, towards Western European political and economic integration raise questions about the future of the transatlantic defence economic relationship. To return to our analysis of Canada's transatlantic defence industrial base and trade policies in this period of change, we shall now examine the issues mired in debates in Ottawa over the country's research, development, and production (RDP) agreements, as well as over the attractiveness of its future involvement in international joint development projects (IJDPS).

The second issue, in some senses much closer to home but also broader in its possible implications, is the debate over Canada's defence equipment export policy. We adverted earlier to the deliberations of the House Subcommittee on Arms Export regarding the usefulness and appropriateness of the Defence Industry Productivity Program and the idea of conversion; in our concluding chapter we shall return to that subcommittee's principal focus.

The RDP mechanism was touted by the Working Group on Defence Products in its report to the Task Force on Europe 1992 as offering a potentially valuable policy instrument by which Ottawa could seek to address the concerns of Canadian defence companies about emerging protectionist sentiments associated with the EC's Single Market program and the IEPG's parallel defence industry initiatives.[44] We suggested earlier, however, that only limited success has been achieved through RDP agreements so far. Indeed, the RDP policy process in Ottawa has itself come under close scrutiny on the part of both government and industry, each wondering how effective it is in fostering bilateral industrial cooperation or in promoting Canadian defence exports.

The debate over the management of RDP agreements has focused on what its critics regard as the inappropriate departmental leadership in the hands of the Department of Foreign Affairs and International Trade. In this department's view, "because of its role in the management of international relations and the stimulation of defence product sales, [it] is appropriately mandated to retain the lead role and promote the interests of industry."[45] Industry, however, does not concur in this assessment, and a September 1989 report by the Aerospace Industries Association of Canada argued that "DND is probably best positioned to receive this mandate" since it was responsible for defining operational requirements and long-term defence equipment plans, for controlling defence procurement and the CRAD (internal DND R&D) budget, for representing Canada in NATO, and for separate but complementary research and technology exchange agreements with each of the RDP partners.[46] According to the association, Foreign Affairs and Industry Canada (known at the time as External Affairs and Industry, Science and Technology Canada, respectively) should hold the status of associate partners in these agreements, based on their mandates for international trade promotion and for industrial and technological development. For its part, DND continued to stress the view that "the first and foremost requirement is for a defence industry based in Canada that is capable of meeting Canada's security needs."[47]

The strength of the association's arguments and the logic of DND's perspective are partly undermined by the simple fact that defence production in Canada cannot be self-supporting even at the best of times – and these are far from the best of times from the budgetary perspective. So long as the aerospace industry looks to export markets for 70 to 80 percent of its total defence sales, DFAIT's international trade mandate cannot be ignored. And while DND understandably considers that the industry's primary task and motivation are to supply Canadian security requirements, the political and economic realities of defence procurement in Canada must inevitably intervene.[48] Under these circumstances, it is unlikely that the defence economic review could achieve a significant transfer of responsibility from Foreign Affairs to DND. In fact, the RDP pattern in Canada should be seen as a likely model for the United States itself, as Commerce increasingly injects its departmental interests (along with those of Congress) into the making of defence economic policy, at the expense of the freedom previously enjoyed by the Department of Defense.

As with the RDP agreements, the record of Canadian participation in international joint development projects offers scant evidence of success in the promotion either of international defence economic cooperation or of defence exports. One student of the RDP process has noted that "industry to industry relations are probably far more effective than government to government relations" in obtaining access to European defence programs and technologies, while an internal DND discussion paper remarked that "if a tally were to be made of the performance of NATO, participating governments and the defence industries in IJDPs, industry would emerge the clear winner."[49] The fact that in both cases these comments were made by government officials, not industry representatives, suggests that even though the relative ineffectiveness of government activities has been recognized, a solution remains only a distant possibility.

The primary challenge facing government officials as they attempt to rationalize and streamline policies on defence industry and defence trade issues – one that is readily apparent in the case of the RDP agreements – is the variety of objectives, interests, and needs that inevitably arise from a policy area that crosses domestic and international boundaries and that includes economic, industrial, political, and security matters. In Canada, the lead role over international projects is acknowledged as a DND prerogative, but the nature of these projects is such that their success (and hence their utility for Canadian defence companies) depends on other countries' interpretations of their own interests – and in particular on the United States' willingness to commit long-term funds to their support. In this context, the fate of the Nunn Amendment and the contradictions that existed even within the terms laid down by the sponsor of that measure suggest that such projects have at best a difficult future in the post-Cold War era of declining defence procurement and reassessment of national priorities.

PART THREE

Conclusion

CHAPTER EIGHT

What Kind of Defence Industry for Canada?

Beyond the issues of the efficiency of bilateral and multilateral project management and oversight arrangements, and the relative merits of domestic security and economic benefits considerations for continuing such initiatives, there is another, more fundamental policy debate – one with implications for the entire domestic defence industry – involving not only the composition and structure of the defence industrial base but also the very necessity for it. At its most dramatic level, this debate pits those who believe that Canada must, for a variety of reasons, retain a broadly based, economically viable, and technologically advanced industry capable of supporting its defence establishment against those who are flatly opposed to that policy option. Less dramatically, but of greater potential relevance for the future of Canadian defence economic policies, there is the division between the advocates of what might be called "Canada, Inc." and those who call for a reconsideration of existing policies, in particular with regard to the export of Canadian defence products. It is really this latter, less dramatic, contest that is of greater significance to our analysis, for the clash of diametrically opposed beliefs is unlikely to lead to a decision in favour of either position in the short to medium term.

As applied to the Canadian context, the term "military-industrial complex," while it has a degree of populist appeal, is used in a manner that is both simplistic and inaccurate. At the same time, even more carefully circumscribed and neutral labels attached to Canadian policy analysis cannot adequately account for the divergences of activities, interests, and goals discussed in this book. Central to any examination of these diverse aspects of the defence industrial base are the policies affecting the ability of Canadian defence producers to market their goods abroad.[1] It is nevertheless useful to have some form of short-hand description to encompass those public agencies that together develop and implement defence economic policies, especially those related to exports. We use here an alternative term suggested by one participant in the formulation of Canadian defence export policies – Canada, Inc. While suggesting the industry's export orientation, that term encompasses those government departments which are either purchasers (DND, the "user" department but also a supporter of a broad and economically sustainable DIB) or promoters of defence industry output (DFAIT, ISTC, and DGS – the latter now including the Canadian Commercial Corporation).[2]

On the need to continue to support Canadian defence exports while observing existing restrictions, the views of Canada, Inc. have been aptly summarized in the testimony of a former assistant deputy minister for trade development before the Commons Subcommittee on Arms Export in November 1991: "Within strict parameters, exports of military goods thus make a vital contribution to Canadian security, and are a legitimate and important commercial enterprise, bringing investment, technology, and high quality jobs for thousands of Canadians, in both civilian and defence sectors."[3] Other than sales to the United States, all Canadian defence exports require an export permit, and approval by the minister of Foreign Affairs is needed for all shipments

to countries that threaten Canada or its allies, that are under UN Security Council sanctions, that are engaged in or under imminent threat of hostilities, or that have a persistent record of human rights abuses (unless it can be demonstrated that there is no reasonable risk that the goods might be used against the civilian population).[4]

Representatives of Canada, Inc. insist that adequate export-policy guidelines exist within the foreign-policy framework of Canada's commitment to foster arms control, disarmament, and conflict resolution, and to promote human rights and domestic institutions. These guidelines have proven to be very flexible, however. In the view of those advocating stricter enforcement, they were interpreted too loosely by the Secretary of State for External Affairs (now minister of Foreign Affairs) during the 1980s and early 1990s, enabling Canadian defence manufacturers to sell their products to restricted countries either directly or through reexport as components of other suppliers' equipment. To justify their position, the proponents of changes in the export policy guidelines cite the "laxity" in existing restrictions and the recent move in the U.N. Security Council – galvanized by the Gulf War – to apply tighter controls on arms transfers to areas of "excessive buildup."[5]

Among the various reform proposals advanced, in particular by Project Ploughshares analysts, there have been a number of suggestions aimed at tightening the definitions of restricted countries and areas in order to make export restrictions more enforceable. Such initiatives are not without problems of their own, especially with respect to what criteria should delimit an "area of tension" or a "human-rights violating" country. The former, for example, might include the United Kingdom, given the long-standing, violent confrontation in Northern Ireland, while some observers might argue that Canada itself should be added to the list of the latter countries.[6] Moreover, without easy recourse to the courts to ensure enforcement, even a much more restrictive definition would be open to avoidance or, at minimum, reinterpretation. On the other hand, opening up the export approval process to regular legal challenges that could delay or reverse export approval would render it virtually impossible for Canadian suppliers to operate outside the u.s. and European defence markets. One immediate result could be the relocation of many companies, especially the return of Canadian subsidiaries of foreign producers to their parent corporation's home base. One compromise proposal might be to create a two-tier system of controls that differentiates between strictly military products and dual-use or primarily commercial products; under such a system, the bulk of Canadian exports would fall within the second category. To date, however, that alternative has been opposed by the advocates of new and tougher export policy guidelines.

Despite the problems inherent in reforms that could lead to more frequent legal challenges, Canadian defence manufacturers have been relatively silent on the issue. In several instances, company executives have even indicated that a clearer and more predictable export approval process might make their international marketing planning much more efficient by enabling them to avoid wasting time on export proposals unlikely to be authorized. The central desiderata for manufacturers, within reasonable limits at least, are stability, predictability, and clarity. They do have one fear – namely, that an end-user control system might be imposed on *all* defence exports, including those to the United States and to the European NATO members.

The arguments for attaching end-use clauses onto sales of Canadian defence products are twofold. First, many of the components sold to the u.s. or European NATO governments and contractors are in turn built into platforms that may then be reexported to countries on Canada's restricted list. And second, if the case of Sweden is of relevance (as reformers believe), end-use controls make it easier to detect or even suspect policy violations before the approval of export permits has been granted. End-use controls, to their proponents, do not represent an effort to apply Canadian laws and regulations "extra-territorially."[7]

But how useful is the Swedish example? Its relevance to the Canadian situation is less than transparent. To begin with, Sweden is a neutral state and not a member of an alliance, and restrictions such as those it imposes would at the very least prove to be politically contentious within NATO. (It must be said, however, that Canada has not shrunk from undertaking actions that have raised hackles among the Allies in the past, in particular when it decided in 1992 to end the stationed force commitment in Europe.) Moreover, as a direct consequence of its neutrality Sweden has historically maintained a far broader range of defence industry capabilities than Canada (including the production of its own fighter aircraft and heavy armoured vehicles) as it sought to ensure relatively autonomous supply and support for its comparatively more powerful military forces. Until very recently, Sweden's defence industry has been oriented primarily towards supplying the country's own military requirements and has not depended on export sales to maintain its economic viability. Sweden's definition of military goods has also been limited to major platforms and to "pure" military products. Finally, the Swedish defence industry is not heavily dependent on access to a single export market.

Reaction in the United States to the imposition of end-user controls on Canadian components, for example, would probably be similar to that of NATO European governments when the Reagan administration attempted to limit the ability of European defence companies to export platforms containing American technology. As a result of those actions, U.S. technology and parts have, whenever possible, been "designed out" of such new European programs as the Tornado and EFA.[8]

That last point is of more than passing relevance to the issue of end-user controls. It should be recalled that controls of this type were deliberately excluded from the purview of the NATO defence trade initiative as being too politically sensitive and therefore unlikely to be resolved. The *unilateral* imposition of controls is certainly feasible, but it would necessitate a significant revision of all existing bilateral defence technology-sharing and trade agreements, including the DDSA, DPSA, and RDP accords. In addition, it would make Canadian participation in cooperative international projects problematical, should these regain any momentum. One political repercussion would be to reinforce Congress' predilection to steer contracts to U.S. manufacturers, undermining the efforts of the NADIBO in favour of defence industrial integration and giving Canadian-based manufacturers another reason to relocate southward.[9]

Whatever the validity of the objections raised here, if the political will exists to reform export-control policy and to cushion the worst effects of such reforms – in the interests, if nothing else, of preserving jobs in advanced-technology manufacturing – then amendments to the export-control provisions are certainly possible. While this possibility is greater under the current Liberal government than it was under its Conservative predecessor, changes in government do not alter the validity of the issues and concerns discussed above. Whether or not the Chrétien government takes any concrete action in this regard, the recommendations of the subcommittee should not be expected simply to disappear from the debate over Canada's defence economic policies. As the importance of foreign markets continues to grow, future exports of defence products will almost certainly rekindle critical scrutiny of Canada's international trade in such goods.

To paraphrase loosely the words of Harvard professor Michael Porter, for the defence industry (as for other forms of economic activity), success and prosperity are created, not inherited.[10] One lesson that has become clear from our review and analysis of the problems and prospects, as well as the incentives and constraints, facing the Canadian defence industrial base in the first post-Cold War decade is that creating the conditions for success is a very complex and difficult task. Defence industry executives and government policy makers must deal with an array of pressures, ranging from changes in the international security and political-economic structures to emerging trends in the international defence market; within Canada, the domestic political and economic realities of defence procurement further complicate the choices that must be made.

Our task here, indeed our explicit objective, has not been to write a definitive guide for those charged with charting the future path of the defence industry in Canada. Rather, we have sought to identify and explicate as comprehensively and systematically as possible the leading sources of change affecting the demand for defence – in particular, for Canadian defence products – with a view to assessing the ability of the domestic DIB to continue supplying its products to national and international markets in an increasingly Darwinian environment. We have sought to focus on those issues most directly related to the defence industry, leaving to others such questions as general economic measures to improve Canadian investment in R&D and to foster economic competitiveness.[11]

The end of the Cold War, bringing with it mounting pressures to direct resources towards finding solutions to domestic economic problems, has reduced the international demand for defence equipment while simultaneously raising the domestic political salience of defence economic policies. An immediate result of this has been the decline of international cooperative research, development, and production programs, accompanied by fears of a rising tide of protectionism in both the United States and Europe.[12] Industries on either side of the Atlantic have begun the process of rationalization; though that process has advanced further in Europe, American industry must now grapple with a shrinking order base.[13] Individual companies have sought to ensure their survival and growth by forming new strategic alliances and joint ventures or by engaging in divestitures, mergers, and acquisitions; in doing so, they have begun to diversify within or even out of the defence business.[14]

Canadian defence companies have so far been partly cushioned from the more dramatic effects of declining defence budgets, thanks to the changes that have occurred in the industry since the late 1950s. Even so, domestic rationalization has taken place at all levels of the aerospace industry, with significant acquisitions by Bombardier and with the sale of many smaller, specialized electronics firms. The decisions of u.s. and European parent corporations may yet cause further movement in the top tier, and the downsizing of the lower tiers is likely to continue; as we indicated in our short series of case studies, there is no substitute for analyzing individual companies if one seeks either to predict or simply to comprehend industry trends, for corporate strategies vary widely with ownership, product mix, and degree of dependence on defence. One thing only seems evident: the process of change will continue for some time to come.

The former Conservative government's policies regarding the support of the defence industry have been criticized for "favouring specific clients while abdicating ... responsibility for the broad social consequences of economic restructuring."[15] Examining the "range of political economy instruments" at the disposal of government departments does, it is true, throw light on the "limits to liberalism" in a globalized economy, but it should not be assumed from this that there exists a coherent policy or a set of coherent and complementary objectives pertaining to the defence industrial base, either in Canada or elsewhere. The defence economic review begun under the previous government was a useful, if tentative, attempt at addressing dilemmas associated with what some analysts have called "ad hocism practiced with a vengeance,"[16] but even now it appears that the personal predilections of a defence minister may play as important a role as any other factor in setting the terms under which industrial-base decisions must be made.

What is needed, more than at any period during the Cold War, is a thorough airing of those issues raised in this book which are of critical import for the future of the defence industrial base in Canada. Arms export policy is simply one – and not necessarily the most significant – of those concerns. Far more important is how and why Canada procures equipment for its armed forces. The question whether it *should* is moot: as long as military assets are held to be useful, if not vital, for the prosecution of foreign- and defence-policy goals in Canada, then so too should the means of equipping and sustaining those assets be a primary national concern.

As this book goes to print, the Chrétien government has launched major, and arguably basal, reviews of both its foreign and its defence policy. It would be distressing if the policy directions emanating from those reviews were not complemented by the development of a well-articulated policy pertaining to defence procurement in its broadest sense. It has never been an easy task to craft policy in the area of defence acquisition, but the challenges of today, as we have tried to show in this book, are sufficiently daunting for Canada's defence industrial base that we might well conclude that, absent a national commitment to arrest or otherwise moderate the forces of defence industrial Darwinism, we may find that the answer to the question raised in the title of this chapter turns out to be, "none."

And while that outcome might be pleasing to many, it needs to be stressed that the *ends* of policy can never be completely divorced from the *means* of policy, as is apparent to anyone familiar with the current controversies associated with Canada's long-standing commitment to international peacekeeping.

Appendix

Table A.1
Value[1] of Arms Trade Within NATO, by Country, 1984–88

Recipients	Suppliers						
	United States	France	United Kingdom	Germany	Italy	Others[2]	Total
Belgium	1,600	0	0	0	0	10	1,610
Denmark	450	20	50	0	0	30	550
France	800	0	10	0	60	20	890
Germany	2,500	280	60	0	0	180	3,020
Greece	700	490	0	160	10	90	1,450
Iceland	0	5	0	0	0	0	5
Italy	1,100	0	0	0	0	20	1,120
Luxembourg	30	0	0	0	0	0	30
Netherlands	2,100	0	10	410	0	20	2,540
Norway	675	10	0	70	0	290	1,045
Portugal	210	20	0	30	0	90	350
Spain	2,100	80	30	10	190	20	2,430
Turkey	2,000	20	470	650	30	60	3,230
United Kingdom	3,300	0	0	0	0	20	3,320
Total Europe	17,565	925	630	1,330	290	850	21,590
Canada	850	0	0	0	0	60	910
United States	0	10	1,100	650	170	925	2,855
Total North America	850	10	1,100	650	170	985	3,765
Total NATO	18,415	935	1,730	1,980	460	1,835	25,355

Source: Conference of National Armaments Directors, "Report … on an Initial Investigation," annex IV.

1 In millions of current dollars.
2 Includes non-NATO suppliers.

Table A.2
Total NATO Arms Trade, 1978–88[1]

	Arms imports		Arms exports	
	Amount	*Total*	*Amount*	*Total*
	($ millions)	(Percent)	($ millions)	(Percent)
1978	2,060	0.3	11,650	1.7
1979	2,440	0.3	11,120	1.3
1980	3,200	0.3	13,740	1.4
1981	3,800	0.4	19,180	2.0
1982	4,270	0.4	18,500	2.1
1983	4,765	0.5	21,400	2.4
1984	4,570	0.4	21,420	2.3
1985	4,295	0.4	20,120	2.1
1986	3,730	0.3	17,000	1.5
1987	4,925	0.3	22,260	1.7
1988	5,695	0.4	18,540	1.3

Source: Conference of National Armaments Directors, "Report ... on an Initial Investigation," annex II.
1 Both trade within the Alliance and with the rest of the world, in millions of current dollars.

Table A.3
High-Tech and Arms Trade of NATO Countries, 1987[1]

	Trade of high-tech goods				Defence trade		Defence share in total high-tech trade	
	Exports $	Imports $	Share of exports	Share of imports	Exports $	Imports $	Share of exports	Share of imports
Belgium	7,273	8,774	9.9	12.8	30	160	0.4	1.8
Canada	7,487	15,811	10.1	20.2	160	170	2.1	1.1
Canada					1,458	967	19.4	6.1
Denmark	3,651	4,129	17.1	18.6	30	110	0.8	2.7
France	25,670	26,677	19.8	19.6	2,700	290	10.5	1.1
Germany	51,123	40,578	18.3	21.4	1,830	730	3.5	1.8
Germany					1,427	1,094	2.8	2.7
Greece	162	1,214	302	11.6	40	280	24.7	23.1
Italy	14,858	19,398	13.0	19.5	360	200	2.4	1.0
Netherlands	12,776	15,328	16.1	20.5	625	600	4.9	3.9
Norway	1,129	4,101	9.4	19.5	20	230	1.8	5.6
Norway					63	123	5.5	3.0
Portugal	824	1,896	9.1	16.8	60	20	7.2	1.0
Spain	7,059	7,969	16.4	22.0	430	979	6.1	12.3
Turkey	352	1,833	4.3	17.6	10	950	2.8	51.8
U.K.	28,956	31,100	26.0	23.2	2,100	550	7.2	1.8
U.K.					2,015	465	6.9	1.5
U.S.A.	74,437	86,408	37.7	24.0	14,300	625	19.2	0.7
U.S.A.						4,900		5.7

Source: Conference of National Armaments Directors, "Report ... on an Initial Investigation," annex III.

1 Dollar values are in millions, and share values are market share percentages. *Italics* within the table show the reported results of a questionnaire on NATO defence trade.

Table A.4
Top Twenty-Five Defence Firms in the World,[1] 1989–90

Company	1990[2]			1989[2]		Percentage of revenue in defence
	Defence revenue	Total revenue	Operating income	Total revenue	Operating income	
McDonnell Douglas Corp.	10,300[3]	16,255	18	14,589	250	63
General Electric Corp.	9,770	58,414	7,707	54,574	7,036	17
General Dynamics Corp.	8,759	10,173	(811)	10,043	584	86
British Aerospace plc	8,555	20,384	1,131	17,570	853	42
Lockheed Corp.	7,866	9,958	335	9,891	2	79
Boeing Corp.	5,862	27,595	1,385	20,276	675	21
GM Hughes Aircraft	5,860	7,820	–	7,440	–	75
Thomson-CSF	5,838	7,298	394	6,647	343	80
GEC	5,435	18,334	1,582	16,981	1,686	30
Martin Marietta Corp.	5,324	6,126	328	5,796	307	87
Raytheon Corp.	5,075[4]	9,268	7,987	8,796	7,456	55
Northrop Corp.	4,941	5,490	210	5,248	(80)	90
United Technologies Corp.	4,700[4]	21,442	751	19,532	702	22
Deutsche Aerospace[5]	4,035	8,406	–	8,541	–	48
TRW Inc.[6]	3,300	8,200	573	7,300	581	40
Panavia Aircraft GmbH	3,295	3,295	–	2,911	–	100
Mitsubishi Heavy Industries[7]	3,265	17,238	1,025	15,513	831	19
Rochwell International Corp.[8]	3,200	12,379	624	12,518	735	26
Westinghouse Electric Corp.	3,196	12,915	518	12,844	1,048	25
Litton Industries Inc.[9]	3,100	5,160	456	5,030	456	60
Aerospatiale	3,041	6,469	7,495	6,252	3,945	47
Grumman Corp.	2,600	4,041	85	3,558	67	64
Allied-Signal Inc.	2,469	12,343	462	11,942	528	20
Dassault Aviation	2,430	3,377	133	3,424	248	72
Rolls-Royce Plc	2,365	7,098	890	5,729	741	33

Source: Based on a worldwide survey of contractors, *Defence News*, 22 July 1991, 6.

– not available

1 Ranked by defence revenue.

2 All values are in million of dollars, based on exchange rates at 31 December 1990.

3 Government sales, more than 90 percent defence.

4 Government sales.

5 Deutsche Aerospace 1989 and 1990 figures not fully compatible due to reorganization. Deutsche Airbus not included.

6 Includes government sponsered R&D.

7 Contract awards by Japan's Defence Agency. Japanese firms are not allowed to export defence equipment.

8 Year ending 30 September.

9 Year ending 31 July.

Table A.5

Contributions Made to Defence Industry Firms by ISTC[1] and External Affairs, 1988/89–1990/91

Company	1988–89	1989–90	1990–91
Alberta			
EDO Canada Ltd.	229,531		
Amptech Corp.	334,867		187,467
Hiltap Fittings Ltd.	164,014		
Applied Metal & Plastic Technology Corp.	212,714		
Pyramet Industries Ltd.		165,347	
Global Thermoelectric Power Systems Ltd.		183,978	164,953
			[f]268,050
General Systems Research Ltd.	436,809	330,714	
Standen's Ltd.		378,760	607,083
Total DIPP	1,377,935	1,058,799	959,503
All			1,227,553
British Columbia			
MacDonald Dettwiler & Associates Ltd.	3,729,009	1,984,037	1,396,798
	[d]332,968	[e]1,024,000	[f]199,764
	[e]3,090,550		
Ballard Battery Systems Corp.	131,264		401,865
R A C E Technologies Inc.	159,553	143,697	212,441
Crystar Research Inc.			647,353
International Submarine Engineering Ltd.	609,850	227,420	
EBCO Industries Ltd.	1,668,293		
B & I Manufacturing Ltd.	127,500	140,337	
Seastar Instruments Ltd.	113,548		
Cominco Ltd.	151,260	[f]599,000	
Chemac Industries Inc.			424,997
AR Technologies Inc.		189,762	
Glenayre Electronics Ltd.	316,785	348,733	210,010
		[P]125,230	[P]453,175
Johnson Matthey Electronics Ltd.			1,279,681
Total DIPP	7,007,062	3,033,986	4,573,145
All	10,430,580	4,782,216	5,226,084
France			
European Space Agency	415,074	[i]3,986,574	122,422
	[l]4,500,000	[j]901,436	[j]1,448,698
	[m]1,400,000	[k]12,294,059	[k]2,685,000
		[l]6,914,293	[k]2,420,000
		[m]908,648	[l]7,092,000
		[n]1,387,174	[m]1,172,000
			[n]1,420,002
			[r]1,545,000
			[s]188,127
			[t]907,000
			[u]993,175
Total	6,315,074	26,392,184	19,993,424

Company	1988–89	1989–90	1990–91
Manitoba			
Precise-to-Form Casting Inc.	404,256		
Bristol Aerospace Ltd.	150,506		
Boeing Canada Technology Ltd.	423,326	996,971	
Franklin Enterprises Ltd.	293,820		
Spiroll Kipp Kelly (1984) Ltd.	295,149		
Inventronics Ltd.			245,123
Total DIPP	1,567,057	996,971	245,123
New Brunswick			
Arvin Special Machinery Ltd.			498,380
York Structural Steel Ltd.			337,957
Total DIPP			836,337
Nova Scotia			
Metocean Data Systems Ltd.	201,480		
Hermes Electronics Ltd.	1,613,771	765,887	1,467,709
Atlantic Defence Industries Ltd.	537,859		
I M P Group Ltd.	1,017,448		431,832
Advanced Materials Engineering Centre	300,526	895,616 [h]897,945	
Total DIPP	3,671,084	1,661,503	1,899,541
All		2,559,448	
Ontario			
Laser Machining Centre Inc.		185,959	
Linamar Machine Ltd.		377,578	3,013,785
LIKRO Precision Ltd.		220,000	
LMH Machine & Tool Co. Ltd.		222,000	
Tenneco Canada Inc.	631,635 [b]1,400,000	411,365	
TDMJ Machine & Tool Co. Ltd			250,841
TD Precision Ltd.			141,000
Liburdi Engineering Ltd.	134,509	[c]265,811	[c]232,431
Telemus Electronic Systems Inc	155,163	315,069	
Leigh Instruments Ltd.	1,100,000	3,326,778	
Invar Manufacturing Ltd.	2,091,494		
Indal Technologies Inc.	1,286,061	2,288,439	
The Queensway Machine Products Ltd.	491,030	364,432	
Hughes Leitz Optical Technologies Ltd.			225,929
Honeywell Ltd.	135,203	187,381	
Toronto Fastener Industries Inc		121,288	
Thomson & Nielsen Electronics Ltd.			113,956
International Custom Products			100,227
Litton Data Images			232,853
The Electrofuel Manufacturing Co.	266,632		184,033
KFW Canada	485,093		241,281
John T. Hepburn Ltd.	505,163 [e]452,941	406,223 [a]183,855	[a]271,048

Company	1988–89	1989–90	1990–91
Jannock Inc.	155,990		
J & S Tyler Precision Products Inc.		195,000	
Kondor United Aircraft Parts Ltd.	174,000	276,398	155,892
Swissway Machining Ltd.	168,278	282,796	
Prior Data Sciences Ltd.	487,500	211,238	890,136
Prototype Circuits Inc.		346,028	471,431
Pylon Electronic Development Co. Ltd.	245,042	102,859	
Price & Knott Manufacturing Co. Ltd.	504,408		
Spar Aerospace Ltd. (2 locations)	693,360	1,041,297	1,004,961
		916,024	4,492,672
Original Machine Tools Inc.		480,000	
Sparton of Canada Ltd.	2,173,952	779,087	532,231
Polysystem Machinery Mfg Inc.	187,500		
R C Metal Fabricators Ltd.	130,790		
Racal Filter Technologies Ltd.		537,337	133,426
Romax Tool Corp.			191,000
Ro-Star Precision Inc.	168,600		
Sanders Canada Inc.	219,845		
Silcofab Division Robco Inc.	123,018		
Reil Industrial Enterprises Ltd		368,777	
Rainford Corp.		198,700	
Raytheon Canada Ltd.	409,453	677,869	606,216
	e2,172,694	e2,187,095	e940,211
Space-Flite Technologies Inc.	165,430		
Optech Inc.	270,471		1,010,399
Novatronics Inc.		115,889	
MBM Tool & Machine Co. Ltd.	292,500		
McDonco Machine Ltd.	202,910	118,635	
McDonnell Douglas Canada Ltd	23,843,861	7,656,139	
MBB Helicopter Canada Ltd.	2,436,237	1,200,628	1,442,901
Magna Electronics	123,483		
Lucas Aerospace Inc.		238,765	364,919
M A Electronics Canada Ltd.	505,119		
M E L Defence Systems Ltd.	120,300	175,536	
Hawker Siddeley Canada Inc.	o3,153,226		229,626
	e4,002,817		e129,750
Menasco Aerospace Ltd.	4,838,938	2,730,060	2,499,672
N.W. Clayton Co. Ltd.		258,275	
National Auto Radiator Mfg. Co. Ltd.		274,096	670,904
Newbridge Networks Corp.	P1,985,284	P2,962,216	167,526
			P5,000,000
Murata Erie North America Ltd	208,408	622,386	
Mitel Corp.			572,815
			b503,276
			e1,998,725
Merco Industries Ltd.		304,900	
Strite Industries Ltd.		518,089	
Mitchell-McPherson Machining Ltd.	140,000		365,000

Company	1988–89	1989–90	1990–91
Litton Systems Canada Ltd.	8,008,675	7,122,947	20,049,116
	ᶜ202,326	ᶜ148,677	ᶜ132,686
	ᵈ176,320		
Senstar Corp.		447,695	717,278
Chicopee Manufacturing Ltd.	406,683		277,500
College Tool and Die Ltd.		304,195	
Com Dev Ltd.	1,103,614	1,758,467	671,764
	ᶜ196,482		
Champion Road Machinery Ltd.	1,139,300	803,450	
	ᵉ4,809,290	ᵉ1,449,992	
		ᶠ110,375	
Centra Industries Inc.			151,645
Canstar Communications	1,516,470		1,202,463
Vac-Aero International Inc.	245,908	364,174	245,000
Cayuga Automatic Machining (1985) Ltd.		242,798	
Compar Connectors Division of DGW Electronics			115,091
Computing Devices Co.	1,052,118	3,342,894	4,767,770
Data Images Inc.	278,311	338,478	
Dellcom Industries Inc	152,195	145,097	
Devtek Corp.	447,438		
Dalsa Inc.		133,240	737,441
Cyclone Manufacturing Inc.		203,000	483,840
Coordinate Tool Ltd.	182,500	138,784	
VAC Developments Ltd.		293,474	
Havlik Technologies Inc.	247,904		492,629
Vadeko International Inc.			183,431
Canadian Astronautics Ltd.	1,210,631	1,837,856	ᶜ230,828
	ᶜ203,684	ᶜ303,299	
B C Instruments Inc.	295,018		
BM Hi-Tech Inc.		108,151	
VRA Precision Inc.			109,811
ATS Automation Tooling Systems Inc.		348,508	
Anderson Metal Ind. Inc.	350,807		
AAstra Advanced Ceramics Inc.		102,025	
333111 Ontario Ltd.		116,375	***168,625
Almax Industries	179,897		
Bell-Northern Research Ltd.	1,175,259	1,286,589	1,377,208
Boeing of Canada Ltd.	3,176,682	52,342,524	·2,104,041
Cametoid Ltd.	454,076		111,537
Campagna Engineering Inc.	328,793		
Canada Wire and Cable Ltd.		1,657,573	ᶜ749,987
		ᵉ5,384,994	ᵉ116,501
Calmos Systems Inc.	191,716		
	ᶜ118,192		
	ʰ1,019,086		
Varian Canada Microwave Products			380,168
Venture Tool Co (Windsor) Ltd	227,700		
C-Tech Ltd.		235,658	
DEW Engineering and Development Ltd.		176,600	312,962

Company	1988–89	1989–90	1990–91
Crossbow Electronics Inc.	206,600	210,240	
Diemaco Inc.	865,222	483,086	130,663
Fullerton Sherwood Engineering Ltd.	173,609	135,625	
Futuretek Manufacturing Inc.		204,059	
Fleet Aerospace Corp.			173,548
Fell-Fab Products Ltd.	136,484	134,364	174,160
Fag Bearings Ltd.	221,989	915,540	6,457,477
Fathom Oceanology Ltd.	290,059		
GM Associates			345,622
Gamma Foundries Ltd.	106,001		
Gruhle Mfg. Ltd.	175,285		
Guildline Instruments Ltd.		162,836	
Haley Industries Ltd.		187,091	541,505
Geometrix Ltd.		271,700	
Gennum Corp.	932,995	418,645	p344,638
	c172,000	p139,879	
Garrett Canada	7,655,980	6,580,771	3,159,799
General Electric Canada Inc.	a258,441		
Factory 2000 Inc.	137,000		
Fleet Industries	257,424		
DY-4 Systems Inc.	1,407,628	1,229,773	1,758,078
Dowty Canada Ltd.	2,562,459	4,410,9921	4,274,759
Digital Dynamics Ltd.		179,026	
Donlee Precision	397,072		
Eagletronic Industries Inc.		320,000	477,701
EMCON Emanation Control Ltd		337,554	
Diemaster Tool Inc.	789,872	162,519	
Ernst Leitz Canada Ltd.	242,131	283,525	
Excentrotech Precision Inc.			273,323
Dowty Canada Electronics Ltd.	111,090		b2,293,688
E S Fox Ltd.	306,073		
Ursel Systems Ltd.	278,036		
Total DIPP	85,896,080	119,531,218	82,731,587
All	106,218,863	132,667,411	95,675,356

Quebec

Company	1988–89	1989–90	1990–91
Wilson Machine Co. Ltd.	196,992	258,530	
TW Manufacturing Inc.		453,105	
113778 Canada Ltd.	330,096	141,756	
Shellcast Foundries Inc.	100,802		
Tourage de Précision Airborne Ltée		607,465	
Sider-Tech Ltée	277,255	113,510	
SMI Industries Canada Ltd.	215,047		
Société d'outillage MR Ltée			185,060
Technologie Rasakto 2416–5391 Québec Inc.	357,137		
U D T Industries Inc.	820,529		165,233
Spar Aérospatiale Ltée.	10,143,796	9,761,369	3,437,035
	c655,074	c2,075,792	c458,749
	f219,861		g339,072

Company	1988–89	1989–90	1990–91
Tesamatec Inc.		439,208	200,805
Stone Marine Canadienne Ltée.		424,746	430,254
Stedfast Inc.			316,268
Usinage Multiprécision Inc.	122,450		457,903
Velan Inc.	121,751		160,249
Textron Canada Ltd.		6,458,904	
Virtual Prototypes Inc.	336,049	244,568	233,044
Vide et Traitement Canada Inc.		400,000	499,405
Vestshell Inc.	375,215		
Tecrad Inc.	156,604	[c]127,137	
	[b]113,250		
	[g]113,250		
Vittforge Inc.	153,245		
K & K Tool Ltd.	111,699		
Entreprises Roger Gentner Inc.		147,529	343,097
Elimétal Inc.	313,300		
Corporation d'usage Métro	297,500	170,888	759,678
Caoutchoucs Acton Ltée			114,072
FRE Composites Inc.		197,626	721,584
			[a]486,224
General Electric Canada Inc.		[a]213,651	
Industries Trident Inc.	337,446		
Hochelaga Aerospace Inc.		314,654	201,805
Héroux Inc.	924,918	[a]259,272	1,761,854
	[a]294,700		[a]421,497
Harrington Tool & Die Inc.			352,500
Canadian Marconi Co.	8,350,827	10,189,650	14,031,744
	[c]113,961	[c]104,076	
	[c]167,724		
CAE Electronics Ltd.	6,184,373	5,547,917	5,167,380
		[g]101,681	[g]1,312,248
Ballistech Systems Inc.		113,902	
Avcorp Industries Inc.	175,270		*312,918
Alta Precision Inc.	411,782		
Aérospatiale Hemmingford Inc.		197,150	
Bell Helicopter Textron	679,243		4,747,679
Bendix Avelex Inc.	1,233,054	537,389	1,587,971
		[g]256,282	[g]229,151
CVDS Inc.			122,685
C R L Technologies Inc.			304,067
C P S Industries Inc.	499,185		
Bombardier Inc.	42,590,053	58,641,442	32,471,407
	[a]972,407	[c]182,996	[q]1,778,676
	[c]302,255	[c]765,630	[c]558,622
	[c]2,136,828		
Joly Engineering Ltd.		347,811	480,482
KK Machine Products Inc.		136,801	277,551
Pratt & Whitney Canada	60,175,554	71,454,948	45,405,699
		[c]174,665	

Company	1988–89	1989–90	1990–91
Placage Tecnickrome Inc.			157,492
Performance L T Inc.	215,000	243,150	
Pega Aerospatiale Inc.		215,360	
RCA Inc.		140,198	**672,896
		ª233,809	
Remtec Inc.	105,424	265,613	
Securitex Systems Inc.		605,538	
S I D O Ltée	197,050		
Rolls-Royce (Canada) Ltd.		ª710,917	
Ressorts Cascades Inc.	106,537		
Outillages Avitec Inc.		186,204	
Oerlikon Aerospace Inc.	769,646		2,289,034
Les Industries Aérospatiales Mécair Inc.			237,845
Les Industries C A T Inc.	120,000		
Les Entreprises A W S M Ltee.	258,722		
Leesta Industries Ltd.		172,500	533,416
Les Industries Patenaude Inc.	270,797		
Les Industries Unigear Inc.	286,942		
Mitec Electronics Ltd.[2]	292,254	381,298	301,325
		ꞌ150,567	ꞌ176,201
Mesotec Inc.	218,793	386,862	
Mecaero Canada Inc.	204,824	173,813	
Les Trempeurs d'acier du Québec Inc.	109,354		
Aero Machining Ltd.		498,649	148,113
Total DIPP	139,146,515	170,570,053	119,589,550
All	144,235,825	175,926,528	125,349,990
Saskatchewan			
SED Systems Inc.		ᵇ153,602	536,290
Total DIPP			536,290
All		153,602	
Canadian total DIPP	501,118,058	296,852,530	211,371,076
ALL	529,953,669	318,144,975	230,996,274

Source: Government of Canada. *Public Accounts*, vol. 2, part 2, "Additional Information and Analyses."
   Ottawa: Canadian Government Publishing Centre.

NOTES

1   In 1988/89 ISTC did not exist. Regional Industrial Expansion and Science and Technology contributions are listed instead.

2   Mitec Electronics Ltd. and Mitec Intergrated Circuits Ltd. are known as Mitec Manufacturing Ltd. and all three names are used. DIPP funding uses Mitec Electronics and funds to develop, acquire and exploit technology use the other two names.

*   DIPP contribution given to Canadian Aircraft Products, a division of Avcorp.

**   DIPP contribution given to Electro Optics, a division of RCA.

***   DIPP contribution given to Koss Machine & Tool Co., a division of 333111 Ontario Ltd.

FUNDING SOURCES

No superscript: Contributions under the Defence Industry Productivity Program.

a   Contributions under the Industrial and Regional Development Act.
b   Contributions under sub-agreements made pursuant to Economic and Regional Development Agreements/General Development Agreements with provinces.
c   Contributions to Canadian firms to develop, acquire and exploit technology.
d   Contributions to promote the development of Canadian export sales.
e   Development Assistance.
f   Incentives to support industrial co-operation programmes and projects.
g   Grants to Quebec for Science and Technology.
h   Contributions under Technology Outreach and Technology Opportunities in Europe Programs.
i   Contribution to the Large Satellite Program.
j   Contribution to the Payload and Spacecraft Development and Experimentation Program.
k   Contribution to Remote Sensing.
l   Contribution to the general budget
m   Contribution to the Earth Observation Preparatory Program.
n   Contribution to the Hermes Program.
o   Contribution to a specific firm.
p   Contributions under Microelectronics & Systems Development Program.
q   Contribution to enterprise development.
r   Contribution to the Olympus Program.
s   Contribution to the Advanced Systems and Technology Program.
t   Contribution to the Data Relay and Technology Mission.
u   Contribution to the Polar Orbit Earth Observation Mission.

Notes

PREFACE

1 For a critical appraisal of the role and influence of domestic economic and social policy concerns in Canadian procurement decisions, see Byers, "Canadian Defence and Defence Procurement." A variety of studies of defence procurement in Canada are presented in *Canada's Defence Industrial Base.*

CHAPTER ONE

1 According to one author, domestic politics and transnational contacts in western Europe and the Soviet Union helped shape the Soviet leadership's views during the treaty negotiations. See Risse-Kappen, "Did 'Peace Through Strength' End the Cold War?" See also Deudney and Ikenberry, "Who Won the Cold War?"; and Gaddis, "How Relevant Was U.S. Strategy?" A short discussion of the varying European responses to the treaty may be found in Haglund, *Alliance Within the Alliance?*, esp. 4–7 and 104–6.
2 Kaiser, "Germany's Unification."
3 The immediate political aftermath of the coup attempt is ably documented in Mandelbaum, "Coup de Grace."
4 The "power transition" literature is vast, the most widely discussed recent work being Kennedy's *The Rise and Fall of the Great Powers.* A cautionary perspective on the rush to celebrate the dissolution of military dangers in Europe comes from General John R. Galvin, at the time SACEUR (Supreme Allied Commander Europe), quoted in Corddry, "Reducing U.S. Forces in Europe." A broader but also cautionary view is presented in Halliday, "Look Back in Danger."

5 Gilpin, *War and Change*, esp. chap. 5. See also Carr, *Twenty Years' Crisis*. For a useful review of recent writings on "hegemonic stability" and the related matter of a postulated U.S. "decline," see Lagon, "'Not Too Tart'."

6 Deudney and Ikenberry, "International Sources of Soviet Change," 90.

7 Although "hegemonic war" remains a remote prospect, the rise of conflict both within and near the former Soviet Union is an ominous trend, with uncertain implications for the West. See Schmemann, "Russia and Its Nasty Neighborhood Brawls"; Rogov, "International Security and the Collapse of the Soviet Union"; and Goble, "Russia and Its Neighbors."

8 See Shevtsova, "The August Coup and the Soviet Collapse"; Snyder, "Nationalism and Instability"; Goble, "Ethnicity and National Conflict"; Maynes, "Containing Ethnic Conflict"; and Shehadi, "Ethnic Self-determination."

9 Meyer, "How the Threat (and the Coup) Collapsed"; Blacker, "Collapse of Soviet Power"; Pipes, "Soviet Union Adrift"; Herspring, "State of the Soviet Military"; Donnelly, "Evolutionary Problems"; and MacFarlane, "Collapse of the Soviet Union."

10 In the 1990 National Military Strategy report, U.S. Army General Colin Powell, chairman of the Joint Chiefs of Staff, wrote that the "decline of the Soviet threat has fundamentally changed the concept of threat analysis as a basis for force structure planning"; reported in Matthews, "Soviet Demise."

11 In "Thinking About Nuclear Weapons," D. Cox examines the effects of the attempted Soviet coup on U.S.-Soviet arms control initiatives. The proliferation issue is discussed further in Fetter, "Ballistic Missiles," though not specifically with reference to the disintegration of the Soviet Union. For a discussion of what can be done with the nuclear arsenal of the former Soviet Union, see Miller, "Western Diplomacy"; Dizard, "Two Pairs of U.S. Fuel Cycle Companies"; Steyn and Meade, "Potential Impact of Arms Reduction"; and von Hippel, "Control and Disposition of Nuclear-Weapons Materials."

12 President George Bush's September 1991 announcement of unilateral nuclear weapons reductions offers support for the view that American planners had accepted such a conclusion. See Leopold, "Cutbacks Signal End to U.S. Strategic Modernization." See also Gray, "Strategic Sense, Strategic Nonsense": "The prospect of a nuclear World War III has all but vanished" (p. 13).

13 Mandate for Negotiation on Conventional Armed Forces in Europe, quoted in Anthony, Courades Allebeck, and Wulf, *West European Arms Production*, 18.

14 See for example, Adams and Briley, "Conventional Convergence"; and Rogov, "Changing Defense Posture."

15 *Guide to Canadian Policies*, 24.

16 "Statement on the Resolution of Problems Concerning the CFE Treaty," issued by the North Atlantic Council, in *NATO Review* 39 (June 1991): 27.

17 Hitchens and Leopold, "Pressure Grows For Republics to Adhere to CFE"; Hitchens, "Germany Pushes CFE Plan"; and Leopold, "European Arms Summit." See also Rogov, "Military Reform."

18 The successful transfer of the roughly 6,500 tactical nuclear warheads spread across the other former Soviet republics back to Russia appears to have taken place without any major difficulties. See Leopold, "War-head Transfer." It is worth adding that, in any case, non-ratification of the CFE Treaty by the new republics, while it would concern NATO members, "would not radically alter NATO's new threat environment ... its net effect in Europe will largely be to postpone the emergence of a possible CFE II regime, for which one could argue most Europeans are not ready anyway"; Fortmann, "NATO Defense Planning," 47.

19 De Bardeleben, "Madly Off in All Directions." Though his pessimism should not be exaggerated, Mearsheimer, in "Back to the Future," is the principal exponent of the view that the new European order will be much more dangerous, since it is multipolar, than that of the bipolar Cold War era.

20 Mandelbaum, "Coup de Grace," 175–7; Goble, "Ethnicity and National Conflict." For one instance, see Rubin, "Fragmentation."

21 The label is ours, not Mearsheimer's. Nevertheless, the latter's article has triggered some vigorous rebuttals. In particular, see Van Evera, "Primed for Peace"; and Kupchan and Kupchan, "Concerts, Collective Security, and the Future of Europe." A comprehensive review of "the greatest *peaceful* political change ever to occur in the international system" can be found in Buzan et al., *European Security Order.*

22 On the 1989 Summit in Brussels, see Wegener, "Management of Change"; and North Atlantic Council, "A Comprehensive Concept of Arms Control"; on the Turnberry meeting, see North Atlantic Council, "Ministerial Meeting." The chief result of the London Summit is the "London Declaration on a Transformed North Atlantic Alliance, 5–6 July 1990." For the November 1991 Rome Summit proceedings, see the "Rome Declaration on Peace and Cooperation," and "The Alliance's Strategic Concept," both in *Transformation of an Alliance.*

23 On 1 November 1993 the Maastricht Treaty entered into force, establishing the European Union. The EU has three pillars: 1) the European Communities (comprising the European Community [EC], earlier

known as the European Economic Community [EEC]; the European
Coal and Steel Community [ECSC]; and the European Atomic Energy
Community [EURATOM]); 2) intergovernmental cooperation on foreign
and security policies; and 3) intergovernmental cooperation on justice
and home affairs. Depending on the context, we shall refer throughout
this text both to the EU and the EC. For a discussion, see U.K. Foreign
and Commonwealth Office, "Institutions," 1.

24 NATO support for CSCE is documented in the "London Declaration," 6–7.
For a more recent statement, however, see NATO, "Interlocking Institu-
tions." At the 31st Munich Conference on Security Policy, Willem van
Eekelen, secretary general of the WEU, remarked that NATO's summit the
previous month constituted a "peaceful revolution" insofar as Alliance-
WEU links were concerned; author's notes, Munich, 6 February 1994.

25 Fortmann, "NATO Defense Planning," 56.

26 Driscoll, "European Security."

27 T.-D. Young, "Reforming NATO's Command and Control Structures."

28 Wörner, "Speech," 8.

29 Flanagan, "NATO and Central and Eastern Europe"; Shea, "NATO's Eastern Dimension"; and Simon, "Does Eastern Europe Belong in NATO?"

30 See interview with Gen. Vigleik Eide, chairman, NATO Military Committee, in Hitchens, "One on One."

31 For a skeptical view of the utility of nuclear weapons, see Frye, "Zero
Ballistic Missiles."

32 C. Miller, "NATO Unveils Rapid Reaction Corps."

33 The changes in command structure are described in NATO, "NATO's
New Force Structures."

34 See Mortimer, "European Security"; Gambles, "European Security Integration"; and Schmidt, "Evolution of European Security Structures."

35 Glaser, "Why NATO Is Still Best." On the difficulties that continue to
bedevil EC attempts to establish a cohesive and authoritative foreign policy, see Kremp, "EC's Foreign and Security Policies"; and *Die EG auf dem
Weg zu einer Gemeinsamen Aussen- und Sicherheitspolitik.* The problems and
weakness of CSCE are ably summarized in George, "Lofty Goals"; and
Hitchens, "CSCE Ministers." The fundamental goals and objectives, as
well as the structures and institutions, of the CSCE are documented in
the Joint Declaration and the Charter of Paris for a New Europe. See
"The CSCE Summit." As well, see Canada, Secretary of State for External Affairs, "CSCE Helsinki Document 1992."

36 Gomeau and Kern, "How Little Is Enough?"; Holzer, Munro, and Muradian, "Aspin Cuts to Redefine Military."

37 Letter to the authors from David Cooper, executive policy coordinator
to the Assistant Secretary General for Defence Support, International
Staff, NATO, Brussels, 21 June 1991. A more complete discussion of the

history, rationale, and workings of the CAPS can be found in Cooper and Bishop, "NATO's Conventional Armaments Planning System."

38 D. Cooper, "Allied Arms Cooperation." For a similar case, put forward by one of the most widely recognized exponents of armaments cooperation in NATO, see Callaghan, *Pooling Allied and American Resources*. See also Daniell, "Security and Economy."

39 E.J. Healey, "Conference of National Armaments Directors." See also Hitchens, "NATO to Mesh Arms Trade Rules." On the CDI, see Harris, "Trends in Alliance Conventional Defense Initiatives."

40 "PAPS is meant to be a tool available as required for conducting programmes on a systematic basis and should not be regarded as a set of formal and mandatory steps in the implementation of CNAD projects"; Conference of National Armaments Directors, *Handbook*, 2.

41 Interview, NATO International Staff, December 1991. During the 1990–91 CAPS cycle, nations reported on 482 separate armaments targets, which then were divided into "functional" and "equipment" areas for analysis. As a result, some eighty-one recommendations for action were presented for CNAD approval and implementation. See D. Cooper, "Allied Arms Cooperation," 34.

42 Interview, NATO International Staff, December 1991.

43 National delegations at NATO have worked to neutralize the "stronger" vision of the CAPS that was being advanced by members of the International Staff. As of late 1993, their efforts appeared to be effectively leading the change in emphasis towards the "weaker" and politically unobtrusive information exchange form; interviews, NATO, January and December 1991, and September 1993.

44 See Haglund, "Changing Concepts"; and Klepak, "Changing Realities."

45 See Stuart, "NATO's Future"; and *NATO's Eastern Dilemmas*.

46 These were: in the Gulf War, under the command of U.S. General Schwartzkopf; in Turkey, under NATO command; in the Persian Gulf, as naval units under WEU command; in Turkey and Iraq, to assist the Kurdish refugees; in Israel, as U.S. and Dutch troops manning Patriot batteries; and in Zaire, with American airlifting of Belgian and French troops; reported in Stützle, "NATO Commander Galvin."

47 Coulon, "L'ONU veut une armée permanente"; and Berdal, "Whither UN Peacekeeping?"

48 This argument is put forward in Russett and Sutterlin, "The U.N. in a New World Order." The authors conclude (p. 83) that the degree of U.S. predominance in the planning and execution of the Gulf War "will likely limit the willingness of Council members to follow a similar procedure in the future," and that "some U.N. capacity to carry out these functions on a permanent basis" would be desirable. See also Weiss and Hayes Holgate, "Opportunities and Obstacles."

49 Amre Moussa, permanent representative of Egypt to the United
Nations, quoted in "What Kind of World?"

50 For a discussion of potential new tasks for the U.S. armed forces, see
Owen, "Job Hunting." For a similar discussion regarding Canada, see
Pugliese, "Canadian Warriors."

51 More significant perhaps may be contracts to engage in "clean-up" activities following military base closures, but companies are proving
extremely hesitant to take on such work because of possible implications for legal liabilities that might emerge.

52 U.S. General Accounting Office, NATO: A Changing Alliance; Lunn, "Reassessment."

53 Finnegan, "Pentagon Cancels 13 Weapons." The plan envisaged reducing the Navy's battle force ships from 545 to 451; Air Force tactical
fighter wings from thirty-six to twenty-six; and Army divisions from
twenty-eight to eighteen. See Sokolsky, "After the 'Maritime Strategy'."

54 See Baker, "DoD Weighs More Force Cuts."

55 Figures represent DoD outlays requests. See Baker, "DoD Weighs More
Force Cuts"; and Finnegan, "U.S. Defense Cut Spurs Threats by Democrats."

56 Quoted in Finnegan, "DoD Request Awaits Trial by Fire."

57 "2–War Military Budget Goes to Congress," International Herald Tribune.

58 Statement by the British Secretary of State for Defence, Tom King,
"Options for Change," 25 July 1990, Hansard 248 CD 92/3, Job 1–19;
Miller and Witt, "Britain's White Paper." For background discussions on
U.K. Defence policy, see Sabin, "British Strategic Priorities"; and Mager,
"Continental Commitment."

59 See de Briganti, "Germany Reverses Plan"; and Hitchens, "German
Cuts." The Bundeswehr plan for 1993 would cut 43.7 billion Deutsche
marks (US$27.6 billion, at 1992 rates) from proposed defence spend-
ing over the 1993–2005 period. There is good reason to believe that
even deeper cuts are in the offing, however. See Fisher, "Kohl to Order
a Sharp Cut"; and "No Rest for Rühe," The Economist.

60 Legge, "NATO's New Strategy."

61 Added to these capabilities are improved surveillance facilities and
greater emphasis on advanced conventional weapons in order to
increase the effectiveness of reduced force levels. See Lowe, "European
Defence Industry."

62 Leopold, "EIA: Electronics to Thrive Despite Defense Budget Cuts."

63 There is some controversy about the effectiveness of all advanced-technology weapons used in the Gulf War. Particular attention has focused
on the performance record of the Patriot air-defence system. See Stein
and Postol, "Patriot Experience"; more generally, see Cohen, "Mystique
of U.S. Air Power."

CHAPTER TWO

1 A good review of the state of international security studies as a disci-
   pline can be found in Nye, "Contribution of Strategic Studies." See also
   Nye and Lynn-Jones, "International Security Studies"; and Chipman,
   "Future of Strategic Studies." An earlier text examining the interaction
   of economic and security issues is *Economic Issues and National Security*. A
   useful recent discussion can be found in Kapstein, *Political Economy of
   National Security*.

2 "Competitive interdependence" is explored more fully in Destler and
   Nacht, "Beyond Mutual Recrimination"; the authors take the notion
   from Bergsten, *America in the World Economy*, chap. 8. The concept refers
   to the continuing pursuit of economic benefits in international relations while seeking to mute economic conflict. The concept of "divisive
   competition" was suggested during interviews held at NATO Headquarters, Brussels, January 1991. At that time, several officials stated their
   concern that with the decline of the Soviet military threat, "there has
   been a notable reduction in the urgency to harmonize the economics
   of defence production with security policy," raising fears of a U.S.-Euro-
   pean "commercial/economic competition" and trade confrontation.

3 Hitchens, "Arms Chiefs of NATO."

4 Gilpin, *Political Economy of International Relations*, 81.

5 The classic exposition on the so-called "free rider" problem remains
   Olson and Zeckhauser, "Economic Theory of Alliances." The rationaliza-
   tion, standardization, and interoperability issue is ably discussed in
   Hagen, "Twisting Arms"; and in Hartley, *Economics of Defence Policy*, chap.
   7. A recent summary of the burden-sharing debate is found in White,
   "NATO in the 1990s."

6 Kapstein, *The Political Economy of National Security*, xv.

7 Hawes, "Assessing the World Economy." See also Spero, *The Politics of
   International Economic Relations*.

8 Kindleberger, *The World in Depression*, 305.

9 The following figures are taken from Hawes, "Assessing the World Economy," 163 (Table 1).

10 Hawes, "NATO in a Post-Hegemonic World."

11 A broader historical review of integration theory is provided in Pent-
    land, "Integration, Interdependence and Institutions." More directly
    related to the EC initiative is Pentland, "Europe 1992 and the Canadian
    Response." It may be worth noting that although the Single European
    Act was passed in December 1985, it did not legally come into force
    until July 1987. Hence, readers may find references to either year in lit-
    erature dealing with the act and with EC92.

12 N.M. Healey, "EC92," 25.

13 Ibid., 23. An insightful, if overly anecdotal, consideration of these issues is found in Pitts, *Storming the Fortress*; and in Strategic Business Research Group, *Europe 1991*.

14 See for example, Preeg, "The U.S. Leadership Role in World Trade"; Turenne Sjolander, "Managing International Trade"; and Wolfe, "The World in a Grain of Wheat."

15 Hyland, "The Case for Pragmatism." This was written before the U.S.-EC compromise of late 1993, but the point remains valid.

16 N.M. Healey, "EC92," 27–8.

17 See for example, van den Muyzenberg and Spickernell, "Restructuring in the Defence Industry." Conditions within individual national defence markets are described in Street, *Defence Bulletin*.

18 Latham and Slack, "The Evolving European Defence Sector," 3.

19 Ibid., 3.

20 In *Economics of Defence Policy* (p. 63), Hartley applies public-choice analysis since "this approach shows that choices about defence are made in political markets." For a useful collection of studies stressing the political dimension of national defence procurement policies, see *The Defence Industrial Base and the West*. This perspective also informs the approach taken in Kapstein, *Political Economy of National Security*, chap. 1, and 208–12.

21 *Canadian Defence Industry Guide*, 31.

22 On the history of the autarky/efficiency dilemma, see Moravcsik, "Arms and Autarky." The transfer of responsibilities – and of personnel – from the IEPG to the Western European Union and the new WEAG was agreed to by national defence ministers on 4 December 1992. The transition period is still under way as this is written in early 1994. For the sake of clarity, we will retain reference to the IEPG in the following discussion of what were IEPG initiatives. Regarding the transferral, see Walker and Gummett, "Nationalism, Internationalism and the European Defence Market."

23 The Culver-Nunn Amendment to the Department of Defense Appropriation Authorization Act of 1975 "encouraged" European governments to accelerate their attempts to achieve equipment standardization in NATO; for details see Hagen, "Twisting Arms," 19–23.

24 It was suggested during interviews that these political differences had rendered the action plan's objectives increasingly obsolete as other institutions – most notably the EC – continued their own initiatives; interviews, Brussels, December 1991.

25 IEPG, *Copenhagen Communiqué* and *Policy Document*.

26 Interview, London, January 1991; the interviewee also pointed out that the quality of these bulletins is uneven between members, with some smaller countries not producing them at all.

27 IEPG, *Policy Document*, 3, par. 12.

28 The comment, from an unnamed top French industry official, is cited in de Briganti, "IEPG Moves to Open Markets." European governments differ considerably in their support of *juste retour* and in their desire to see it enshrined in policy declarations; interviews, Brussels and London, January and December 1991.

29 IEPG, *Policy Document*, 4.

30 *Towards a Stronger Europe*, vol. 2, 41. The IEPG's concerns here are strikingly similar to those expressed in the May 1990 report of the Office of Technology Assessment, an analytical arm of the U.S. Congress. The OTA report noted that the "loss of technological supremacy may be an unavoidable long-term cost of maintaining strong security alliances. It might also be the price of gaining access to foreign defense technology in the future"; OTA, *Arming Our Allies*, 3. While the latter argument retains some validity, the former has come under critical scrutiny in the post-Cold War era, as we illustrate in our discussion of the American debate over defence economic policy.

31 IEPG, *Policy Document*, 1, par. 3; and *Copenhagen Communiqué*, 4 (our emphasis). Latham and Slack, in "Evolving European Defence Sector" note several possible interpretations of the term "reciprocity" (pp. 59–61): for North American governments, the preference would be national treatment reciprocity (two-way national treatment, with each country's firms being treated as domestic producers in the other's market), and the worst-case scenario would be mirror-image reciprocity (with mutual restrictions remaining in place until both sides' regulations are standardized). So far, IEPG members appear to be divided among themselves over the issue, though U.S. officials in NATO do not perceive any overall intention to block American companies from participating in European markets; interviews, Brussels, January 1991.

32 Philippe Roger, directorate of international relations, quoted in de Briganti, "IEPG Moves to Open Markets," 3. Roger commented at that time that "there will be no question of a European preference" in defence procurement; the divisions within and between IEPG member countries over such questions were amply illustrated when, less than six months later, French Defence Minister Pierre Joxe promised greater French government support for domestic defence industries and called for a European preference in defence procurement "so that continental manufacturers may benefit more from European contracts." See de Briganti, "Joxe Promotes European Preference."

33 On the notion of a "two-way street," see Hagen, "Twisting Arms," 64–8. See also a paper written by the chief executive officer of Deutsche Aerospace, who argues that "in over forty years of the Atlantic Alliance we have never truly succeeded in building a transatlantic two-way street in the armament sector"; Schrempp, "Security and Economy," 10.

34 With a 1990 budget of US$135 million, EUCLID clearly did not approach the scale of the U.S. Defense Advanced Research Projects Agency (DARPA), which had a $1.5 billion budget for FY1991. See Hobbs, "Research and Development in NATO."

35 A recent discussion of security challenges and institutional responses in Europe will be found in Mahncke, "Parameters of European Security."

36 In *European Community*, Pinder provides a helpful introduction to the various governance bodies of the EU.

37 Rupp, "Progress Towards a More United Europe," 1. See also Anderson, "Western Europe and the Gulf War."

38 See Wallace, "What Europe for Which Europeans?"

39 "The Deal Is Done," 51–2. The French position has been supported especially by Germany, while Italy and the Netherlands back Britain in favouring stronger ties to NATO and the United States on security matters. See Hitchens, "Tri-Nation Statement"; and Hitchens, "Europe Sharpens WEU Teeth."

40 See Nonnenmacher, "Breakthrough in Maastricht." See also Fortmann and Haglund, "Europe, NATO and the ESDI Debate."

41 France obtained President Bush's agreement that he would not object to the establishment of a formal link between the WEU and the EC, with the former executing EC decisions; in return, Defence Minister Joxe announced his government's intention to increase its participation in NATO's military affairs through attending meetings of the Military Committee and the Defence Planning Committee. See Tiersky, "France in the New Europe," 140–2.

42 The key paragraph, 1(b), of article 223 reads as follows: "Any Member State may take such measures as it considers necessary for the protection of the essential interests of its security which are connected with the production of or trade in arms, munitions and war material; such measures shall not adversely affect the conditions of competition in the common market regarding products which are not intended for specifically military purposes."

43 Rupp, "Progress Towards a More United Europe," 4.

44 Latham and Slack, "Europe's Evolving Defence Sector," 17.

45 See Steinberg, *Transformation*, 61.

46 On the article 223 dispute, see Story, "La Communauté européenne et la défense de l'Europe"; and Lello and Richardson, "Draft Report on Challenges to Transatlantic Co-operation."

47 Steinberg, *Transformation*, 63, fn. 79. It must be remembered that even though the Maastricht agreement indicated that the WEU was to operate as the "defence arm" of the EU, the two remain separate institutions (though both are headquartered in Brussels). Indeed, there remains a

degree of rivalry between the EU and WEU over jurisdiction in defence
industry issues; interview, Brussels, September 1993.

48 Although Delors' initiative concerning EC aid for European industry
did not specifically name its target sectors, defence and aerospace are
regarded as probable candidates for a part of the US$4.5 billion pro-
posal under two separate programs – worker retraining and R&D (especially to support defence industry conversion plans). See Hitchens,
"Delors Proposes EC Contribute Funds to European Industry." Under
a special aid program called PÉRIFRA (*régions périphériques et activités
fragiles*), launched in 1991, the European Parliament set aside approximately $63.5 million for FY1992 to assist regions facing economic hard-
ship as a result of defence industry cuts or base closings. The aid is in
the form of matching funds (i.e., it does not go directly to defence
companies or the military). See Hitchens, "EC to Aid Communities."

49 Rupp, "Progress Towards a More United Europe," 4. Rupp notes that as
the civil market integration process continues, "it will become increasingly difficult for the IEPG to shelter defence industrial interests from
the overall industrial development in the European Community." European Community goals for the commercial aerospace industry are summarized in Commission of the European Communities, *Competitive
European Aeronautical Industry.*

50 Moodie, "Defense Implications," 24; and Hitchens, "EC Officials Seek to
Boost Defense Competition."

51 Moodie, "Defense Implications," 23–4.

52 The impact of IEPG and EU actions on transatlantic relations need not
be the result of deliberate intent on the part of the Europeans: "From
the U.S. perspective, the motivation for European action does not
matter if the impact is the same: exclusion of U.S. firms from European
defence markets, even for the relative short term"; Moodie, "Defense
Implications," 18.

53 Interviews, Brussels, December 1991.

54 The existence of a de facto industrial policy, a point frequently made by
interviewees in Europe, also is recognized within the United States: "To
a great extent, U.S. government policy already shapes and controls the
structure of the defense industries, the international arrangements they
may engage in, and their access both to domestic and foreign defense
markets"; OTA, *Arming Our Allies,* 29. The "school" of strategic trade theorists and advocates includes Senator Jeff Bingaman, chairman of the
Armed Services Subcommittee on Defense Industries. See Kapstein,
Political Economy of National Security, 195. A useful review of works of this
school can be found in Richardson, "Political Economy of Strategic
Trade Policy." Richardson notes that the "analysis and evaluation of

trade and industrial policy in 'strategic' environments ... are neither a passing fashion nor an academic fancy. Real policy decisions are being undertaken around the world in this light" (p. 134). See also Nasar, "Risky Allure," 4:1.

55 Friedberg, "End of Autonomy," 85.

56 Kapstein, *Political Economy of National Security*, 196. For estimated u.s. defence industry layoffs through to the mid-1990s, see Finnegan, "Industry Faces Unprecedented Workforce Cuts"; Edgar, "Security, Competitiveness, and International Cooperation"; Sims, "For Weapons Makers"; and Saunders, "Defence Jobs Under Fire."

57 Discussed in Silverberg, "Proposed Defense Production Act"; and Silverberg, "Compromise Defense Production Act."

58 President-elect Clinton, addressing his supporters in Little Rock late on the night of his victory, proclaimed his election to be a "clarion call for our country to face the challenges of the end of the Cold War," and pledged to address the "conversion of our economy from a defense to a domestic economic giant"; quoted in Horvitz, "Clinton, Reassuring the Allies, Affirms 'Continuity' of American Foreign Policy."

59 ota, *Arming Our Allies*, 3. Dependence on foreign sources of defence-related equipment and technologies has become an increasingly important issue, particularly since the Gulf War but also partly as a response to the earlier linkages made by Congressional critics of international collaboration development programs. See, for example, *Bolstering Defense Industrial Competitiveness; Industrial Base*; and Miskel, "Thin Ice." For reviews of the dib/foreign dependence issue that are more critical of "alarmist" and interventionist prescriptions, see Moran, "Globalization of America's Defense Industries"; and Ratner and Thomas, "Defence Industrial Base."

60 Cited in Mastanduno, "Do Relative Gains Matter?" 74.

61 Ibid., 84–93; Edgar and Haglund, "Japanese Defence Industrialisation"; and Haglund, "'Techno-Nationalism'."

62 Rhodes, "Japanese-United States Relationship." See also Behr, "u.s. Is Prepared to See Trade Relations Worsen"; and Behr, "A Message for Japan."

63 Friedberg, "End of Autonomy," 85.

64 The involvement of the Commerce Department and the u.s. Trade Representative, as well as Congress, in making revisions to the original DoD memorandum of understanding on the fsx program "constituted a departure from previous practice. Increasingly, Japanese defence industrialists and some nationalistic government officials now support a policy of kokusanka, or dib autonomy." See Baker, "Japanese Defense Firms."

65 ota, *Arming Our Allies*, 3.

66 The U.S.-U.K. Harrier aircraft and Trident submarine projects might be considered as such examples; these, however, have been bilateral agreements only, and they have not fostered multinational follow-up programs. American commentators frequently cite the F-16 coproduction agreement with Belgium, the Netherlands, Denmark, and Norway as an excellent example of successful U.S.-European collaboration; but European officials in the large defence industrial countries strongly disagree, with one British industry executive commenting that "this particular programme appears to be too much a benefit match for the U.S. industry and economy without equal technological rewards for Europe"; quoted in Edgar, "MRCA/Tornado," 76.

67 Silverberg, "EEC Import Plan."

68 Quoted in Moodie, "Defense Implications," 22.

69 Baker's remarks, made at a meeting of NATO foreign ministers in December 1990, led one official there to comment that "trade has never been an issue at NATO meetings before, and the Americans were clearly issuing a warning by bringing it to us"; reported in *Defence Newsletter*, 6 December 1990. The warnings issued by Vice President Quayle and several Republican senators at a conference in Munich stirred a controversy that made headlines in European and North American newspapers. See, for example, Fisher, "U.S. Officials."

70 Moodie and Fischmann, "Alliance Armaments Cooperation," 33.

71 Pentagon and State Department interviews, Washington, September 1990.

72 Two of the best-known studies on the role and influence of Congress in the foreign economic policymaking process are Destler, *American Trade Politics*; and Pastor, *Congress and the Making of U.S. Foreign Economic Policy*. Pastor's text, published in 1980, obviously does not consider the increased capabilities and resources or the changes in membership and organization that have occurred in Congress since the early 1980s. Our study leans more towards Destler's view that changes in Congress and in the nature of the issues with which foreign economic policy must deal – that is, the growing domestic economic impact of international interdependence – are placing great strains on the policy process and its orientation. See also Baldwin, *Trade Policy in a Changing World Economy*, chap. 12; and Vernon and Spar, *Beyond Globalism*. For a short study that sets out some of the possible linkages between the defence economic domain and the debates referred to above, see Edgar, "Congress and American Defence 'Trade' Policy."

73 See Polsky, "U.S. Industry"; and Baker, "Officials Label Industrial Base Study Shortsighted."

74 Mastanduno, "Do Relative Gains Matter?" 113.

75 Hyland, "Case for Pragmatism," esp. 38–43.

76 Taft, "Prospects for a NATO Defense Trade Agreement." American officials at NATO have noted that the label "defence GATT" subsequently proved problematical for other NATO members; the CNAD study does, however, include one section on the lessons to be learned from the GATT; interviews, Brussels, December 1991.

77 Fursdon, *European Defence Community*, 45.

78 Correspondence from a Canadian official at NATO, Brussels, January 1990.

79 The unit was titled a "study group" rather than a "task force" to emphasize its informal nature, the latter title implying too strongly that there was a recognized task to be performed. Its first written output was a preliminary draft ("Report on NATO Defence Trade"), tabled on 21 January 1991, followed by the first official version in March (CNAD, "Initial Investigation"). The group's members comprised representatives from Canada, Denmark, France, Germany, Italy, the Netherlands, Norway, Portugal, Spain, the United Kingdom, and the United States; Belgium did not sit officially although it attended as an observer; it subsequently joined the group.

80 The work plan also features a concentration upon: 1) key areas affecting defence trade among the allies; 2) extension of cross-purchasing; and 3) harmonization of military requirements. See CNAD, "Group on NATO Defence Trade."

81 Interviews, Brussels, December 1991. Difficulties regarding the feasibility and comprehensiveness of the data collection exercise are discussed in NATO, Director, Economics Directorate, *Expert Teams on the Improvement of Statistics*. If such data collection proves either impossible or largely meaningless, of course, it would make measurement of the development of a more open market extremely difficult. See NATO, Chairman, Expert Team on Defence Trade Statistics, *Defence Trade Statistics*, annex, par. 9.

82 The CNAD report noted that "although some nations in the informal group believed that the issue of third country sales may have bearings on intra-Alliance defence trade, it was agreed that the discussion of its political implications went beyond the scope of the study"; CNAD, "Report on an Initial Investigation," 2. American end-user or re-export regulations have long been a contentious issue with European governments; they are one reason why the latter would often prefer to "design out" U.S. components in projects such as the Tornado and European Fighter Aircraft. See Latham, "Conflict and Competition," 98. At the same time, both the United Kingdom and France objected to having NATO as a forum for the discussion of arms export policies to "third countries"; interview, Brussels, December 1991.

83 The United States initially objected to what it saw as a tendency to focus only on legislative "buy national" restrictions and to ignore the wide variety of other, equally restrictive but informal (i.e., not legislative) practices and procedures. This would have depicted the United States as being a "severely restrictive" market. The 21 June 1991 report identified *eleven* general categories of obstacles to NATO defence trade; CNAD, "Report," 17–19; interviews, Brussels, January 1991.

84 Hitchens, "France, Allies Differ."

85 Interviews, Brussels, December 1991. The legal status and level of national signatory of the proposed code of conduct thus remain to be properly settled, though the former issue is partially resolved in that the code would describe a "political and moral commitment" by NATO governments, without legal status for the immediate future. See NATO, Defence Procurement Policy Officer, *Issues Relating to the Development of a Code of Conduct*, 2, par. 6 and 7.

86 The suggestion of a "three-tiered" armaments market is made in Moravcsik, "European Armaments Industry." Moravcsik argues the case for "free and open competition" for smaller components and lower-technology systems, balanced competing consortia for medium sized and major subsystems, and collaboration on design and selection of dual production sources for platforms. See also Holt, "NATO Defence Production."

87 Hitchens, "France, Allies Differ," 3.

88 "NATO Code of Conduct in Defence Trade," 3.

89 Rogers, "Europeans in the USA," 1214.

90 NATO, note by Belgian NADREP (representative of national armaments directors). The NADREP suggests that countries that are not "developing defence industrial" nations be divided into "large," "medium," and "small" categories, depending on their ability to develop and produce a range of complete weapons systems and defence equipment. Obviously, Belgium would be considered a "small" country.

91 Interviews, Brussels, January and December 1991.

92 Interviews, Brussels, December 1991. All European delegations, including even those most supportive of the initial proposals made by former Ambassador Taft, are sceptical about the ability of the U.S. mission to NATO to press its case with Congress.

93 U.S. officials at NATO have pointed out that if U.S. trade restrictions were embodied in Department of Defense regulations rather than legislation, if national security waiver authorizations were attached – as they are in bilateral memoranda of understanding – and if the Nunn-Quayle amendments for IJDPs could be involved, then executive actions could be taken to help foster transatlantic defence trade, even without necessarily seeking the approval of Congress and the repeal of its protectionist

legislation; interviews, Brussels, December 1991. European disingenuity arises when national procurement officials argue that "right now, nothing prevents U.S. industry from bidding for European contracts. We had hoped that the same attitude would prevail in the United States, but this is not the case; in fact, it's even forbidden by law," without acknowledging the numerous nonlegislative requirements, practices, and procedures that do serve to restrict North American access to those markets; Maj. Gen. Guillaume Van Dient, quoted in de Briganti, "U.S. Trade Stance."

94 The "first-order attitudinal and structural obstacles" include respectively, American concerns that resource pooling will erode national technological competitiveness, and the inability of European governments fully to eliminate unnecessary R&D or defence industrial capability duplication, as well as the absence of an overarching structure to link European and North American "pools" of DIB capabilities. These are related to issues of sovereignty, divergent macroeconomic budget and resource policies, and other questions in the realm of national policy (which therefore require solutions of formal political treaty status). "Second-order attitudinal problems," which most often are the reported topics of dispute, include, for example, the linkage of non-military requirements to collaborative projects (such as *juste retour* and offsets); and out-of-phase equipment replacement schedules or funding plans (i.e., issues that have solutions in new bureaucratic procedures). See Callaghan, *Pooling Allied and American Resources*, 3–9.

95 Callaghan, "NATO at Forty."

96 Kapstein, "International Collaboration."

97 Even a watered-down code, at the time of writing, remained blocked by a disagreement over the inclusion of end-use restrictions. In particular, Turkey rejects such restrictions on its freedom to employ military equipment, while Germany insists on such restrictions. Though unspoken within NATO, the concern is over the possibility that Turkey will use its military against Kurdish extremists within its borders. In the absence of agreement by all of the sixteen members, the CNAD will not adopt the code, and uncertainty remains over how long the impasse may continue; interviews, NATO, Brussels, September 1993.

CHAPTER THREE

1 Interviews, Brussels, December 1991. The issue of the feasibility of collecting accurate and comprehensive defence trade data is discussed in NATO, Director, Economics Directorate, "Expert Team on the Improvement of Statistics."

2 The data in the text and in the appendix tables are NATO figures derived from information collected by the U.S. Arms Control and Disarmament Agency. They refer to arms transfers of conventional military equipment, including "tactical guided missiles and rockets, military aircraft, naval vessels, armoured and non-armoured military vehicles, communications and electronic equipment, artillery, infantry weapons, small arms and ammunition" and dual-use equipment that has been identified as military in purpose. For a more complete definitional discussion, see CNAD, "Report," annex I, 1.

3 Ibid., 9. Table 4 of the CNAD report gives average annual equipment expenditures between 1984 and 1988 of $39.16 billion for NATO Europe and $77 billion for the United States; see table 4, annex V, 47.

4 High-technology trade is taken to mean "the OECD category of goods manufactured by high technology industries requiring a high R&D intensity"; ibid., 9.

5 Ibid., 15. For a variety of studies that serve to illustrate this fundamental point regarding the defence procurement process, see *The Defence Industrial Base and the West.*

6 Holt, "NATO Defence Production," 3.

7 Ibid.

8 See Callaghan, *Pooling Allied and American Resources,* 23.

9 Augustine's comments are cited in ibid., 31–2; and in Yates, "Market Forces," 59.

10 On the Arrow cancellation, see Stewart, *Shutting Down the National Dream;* Dow, *The Arrow;* Shaw, *There Never Was an Arrow;* and Peden, *Fall of an Arrow.*

11 Hartley, *Economics of Defence Policy,* 144.

12 Walker, "Defence," 375.

13 Ibid., 378.

14 The idea of a "Japan model" of defence industrialization is discussed in more detail in Edgar and Haglund, "Japanese Defence Industrialisation."

15 The issue of foreign dependence has generated a wide variety of recommendations and responses. For a small sample of this diversity, see OTA, *Arming Our Allies;* Moran, "Globalization"; and Ratner and Thomas, "Defence Industrial Base."

16 A careful and critical analysis of the notion of minimum efficient scale (MES) is provided in Hartley, *Economics of Defence Policy,* 97–103.

17 Steinberg, *Transformation,* 13.

18 New competitors in the global arms market, particularly in the lower and middle ranges of technology, include Brazil, Israel, South Korea, and the People's Republic of China; see Bajusz and Louscher, *Arms*

Sales, 9–12. For a comprehensive survey of global arms-production trends, see *Arms Industry Limited.*

19 Steinberg, *Transformation,* 29. On the plight of Dassault, see Moravcsik, "1992 and the Future of the European Armaments Industry," 5.

20 Witt, "Plessey Runs Out of Room."

21 See Miller and Witt, "Ferranti Purchase."

22 GEC's possible interest in British Aerospace Dynamics is reported in Witt, "Britain's General Electric."

23 See van den Muyzenberg and Spickernell, "Restructuring in the Defence Industry"; and *A Single European Arms Industry?,* 52–4.

24 Van den Muyzenberg and Spickernell, "Restructuring in the Defence Industry," 6.

25 Steinberg, *Transformation,* 13, 29.

26 The SIPRI report assumes cuts in European defence spending of 3 to 5 percent a year. The report also suggests that a second CFE agreement would impose large NATO force reductions; currently the prospects for such an agreement remain dim because of political uncertainties in Eastern Europe and the CIS. The SIPRI findings are reported in "West's Arms Industry Faces Slump." See also Walker, "Defence," 378.

27 As quoted in "West's Arms Industry Faces Slump," 11.

28 "Horizontal integration" of common product lines, by fostering larger production runs, reducing R&D duplication, and eliminating competitors, can offer the greatest economic benefits; "sectoral consolidation" involves a broader grouping of industry activities beyond individual product lines, thus offering potential R&D synergies in closely related technologies; "complementary grouping" is the broadest approach and ranges from groupings of complementary activities, to diversified conglomerates. This approach can help to enhance opportunities for systems integration work or simply offer a stronger financial hedge against losses in any one individual business or product line. Examples of each strategy, respectively, are: GEC's acquisition of Marconi and of Ferranti Defence Systems; the consolidation of a broad range of electronics capabilities in the United Kingdom under GEC, and in France under Thomson-CSF; and finally, DASA in Germany and British Aerospace in the United Kingdom. See Steinberg, *Transformation,* 77–80.

29 These problems have arisen with regard to the proposed sale of the missile and aerospace divisions of LTV, Dallas, to the French company Thomson-CSF. See Silverberg, "LTV Sale Stirs Little French Interest"; and Silverberg, "DoD Will Guard LTV Technology."

30 Steinberg, *Transformation,* 84–96. See also Walker and Gummett, "Britain and the European Armaments Market."

31 Further consideration of these problems may be found in Latham and Slack, "European Defence Sector," 37–8.

32 "Structural trends," involving the nature of corporate organization and relationship with other manufacturers, contrast with "substantive trends," which include diversification, use of versatile (dual-use) technologies, and emphasis on systems integration capabilities. See Steinberg, *Transformation*, 105.

33 The example of the European Fighter Aircraft consortium is cited by some commentators as an instance demonstrating how "transnational industrial structures in the defence field can acquire great political leverage, causing government to order weapons systems and allocate contracts against their better judgement." See Walker and Gummett, "Britain and the European Armaments Market," 441.

34 Steinberg, *Transformation*, 106.

35 Ibid., 107.

36 Reported in Silverberg, "Atwood Rebuts Industry Concerns."

37 Finnegan, "Upswing in Aerospace."

38 Daniell, "Security and Economy," 11.

39 See R. Daly, presentation to the conference on "Reconstitution."

40 Finnegan, "Upswing in Aerospace."

41 Aspin, "Tomorrow's Defense," 3.

42 On the notion of reconstitution, see U.S. Department of Defense, "Primer on Reconstitution Policy"; and *Reconstituting America's Defense.* Criticisms and comments on the new acquisition policy are highlighted in Silverberg, "Atwood Rebuts Industry Concerns."

43 Figures reported in Finnegan, "Industry Faces Unprecedented Workforce Cuts." A more recent study from the Defense Budget Project research group similarly predicted possible job losses of up to 814,000 in civilian defence-related positions. See Finnegan, "1 in 4 Defense-Related Jobs." The financial difficulties facing U.S. companies are highlighted in Finnegan, "U.S. Firms' Profit Erosion." See also Sims, "For Weapons Makers"; and Saunders, "Defence Jobs Under Fire."

44 See Sullivan, presentation to the conference on "Reconstitution."

45 See Callan, presentation to the conference on "Reconstitution." See also Pietrucha, "Contractors Cautiously Diversify"; and Finnegan, "Defense Stocks."

46 McDonnell Douglas' core competencies in its tactical air arm have been identified as: i) product definition and concept exploration; ii) avionics and subsystem integration; iii) manufacture; iv) final assembly and test; v) simulation; vi) product support; and vii) program and supply management. Together these go throughout the life-cycle of a system or platform, although elements i)-iv) inclusive contain the major parts of a program. See Sullivan, presentation to the conference on "Reconstitution."

47 Limited examples of efforts to move into non-defence markets are cited in Polsky, "Diversity, Profits Guide Firms' Guns-to-Butter Conversion."

On the general theme of defence conversion, see Gansler, "Transforming the U.S. Defence Industrial Base."

48 Discussed in Finnegan, "Analysts Praise Olin-Alliant Merger."

49 Polsky, "Hughes' Missile."

50 Reported in Polsky, "Continued Upswing."

51 OTA, *Arming Our Allies*, 28.

52 Ibid., 33.

53 See Baker, "Officials Label Industrial Base Study Shortsighted."

54 Aspin's proposals consist of four major elements: selective upgrading,
selective low-rate procurements, "rollover plus" (involving prototyping,
improvement of manufacturing technology, and operational testing);
and "silver bullet procurements" of advanced technology weapons systems. See Aspin, "Tomorrow's Defense"; and Silverberg, "Aspin Outlines Plan." On industry criticisms of the lack of support from the Bush
administration, see Polsky, "U.S. Industry."

55 Van den Muzenberg and Spickernell, "Restructuring in the Defence
Industry," 2.

56 OTA, *Arming Our Allies*, 23–4.

57 CNAD, "Report," annex IX, 2.

CHAPTER FOUR

1 Pugliese, "Canadian Lawmakers Fret"; Harbron, "Hard Economic
Times?"

2 Masse suffered in part from a legacy of recent decisions, not all of which
were taken during his tenure, that seemed to some to support the claim
that Quebec was receiving more than its "share" of defence procurement.
See, for one such decision, Campbell and Pal, "The CF-18 Affair." On the
debates at that time regarding the controversial EH-101 purchase, see C.
Young, "Campbell's Controversial Helicopters"; Lynch, "Hanging Helicopters on Campbell"; and Werier, "Helicopter Purchase."

3 For a judicious balancing of both external and domestic determinants
of Canadian defence (including defence industrial) policy, see Middlemiss and Sokolsky, *Canadian Defence*.

4 Kirton, "Consequences of Integration"; McLin, *Canada's Changing
Defense Policy*, esp. chap. 4 and 7; Avery, "Canadian Defence Policy"; Van
Steenburg, "Canadian-American Defence Economic Cooperation"; and
Middlemiss, "Road from Hyde Park."

5 Defence Industrial Preparedness Task Force, *Expanding the North American
Defence Industrial Base*, 61 (hereafter referred to as the "DIPTF Report").

6 Department of National Defence, "Defence Production Sharing," 13.
The text of the Hyde Park Declaration is reproduced and discussed in
greater detail in Yost, *Industrial Mobilization*, 20–1.

7 In addition, the declaration was promoted as the economic analogue of Ogdensburg, which had earlier linked each country's industrial preparedness interests and established a model upon which later agreements could be based; see DIPTF Report, 63.

8 DIPTF Report, 67–8.

9 See Haglund, "Canadian Strategic Minerals."

10 By 1956, Canada had made available some 600 aircraft to the European allies, under mutual aid. See Rempel, "Canada's Troop Deployments," 216.

11 DIPTF Report, 78–83; on the DPSA, see Yost, *Industrial Mobilization*, 24–5, 82–3.

12 The "rough balance" provision is discussed in Yost, *Industrial Mobilization*, 25.

13 DIPTF Report, 84. Canadian defence R&D was to be supported in part by new funds set up under the Defence Industry Productivity Program (DIPP) in 1959 at the same time as the DPSA (although it did not assume its current abbreviated title of DIPP until 1969); see Epps, "Defence Industry Productivity Program," 6.

14 *Canadian Defence Industry Guide, 1991*, 7.

15 Danford W. Middlemiss, quoted in DIPTF Report, 89.

16 This concern was raised by several attendees and speakers at the *Financial Post* conferences on "The Canadian Defence Industry: Building for the Future" (Ottawa, 24–25 October 1990) and on "Canada's Defence Industry: The Post-Gulf Chopping Block" (Ottawa, 24 October 1991).

17 *Canadian Defence Industry Guide, 1992*, 8. For a short but valuable review of defence policy during this period, see Middlemiss and Sokolsky, *Canadian Defence*, 31–45.

18 *Canadian Defence Industry Guide, 1991*, 9.

19 *Canadian Defence Industry Guide, 1992*, 10–11.

20 Boyd, "Canadian Defence Procurement," 139.

21 Details of the April 1989 budget revision are provided in the *Canadian Defence Industry Guide, 1992*, 14–17. The more recent February 1992 budget and announcements regarding the Defence Capital Acquisition Program are included in the latest defence policy statement, *Canadian Defence Policy*.

22 Pugliese, "Canada Unveils $1.5 Billion Procurement Program."

23 See, for this trend, Byers, "Canadian Security and Defence," 35.

24 Boyd, "Canadian Defence Procurement," 14.

25 Tucker, *Canadian Foreign Policy*, 153. Tucker examines the LRPA competition and industrial benefits issues in some detail in chapter 5. A useful review of industrial benefits policy from the early 1970s to the late 1980s is found in Scott, "Canada's Defence Industrial Base," 12–22. See also the discussion in Fox, "Politics of Procurement."

26 Galigan and Herring, "Defence Industrial Impact," 1.

27 Quoted in *Canadian Defence Industry Guide, 1992*, 11.

28 See "NADIB Manifesto." The full NADIBO documentation, in the form of an introductory pamphlet and three accompanying booklets, also offers a historical background to the creation of the organization; see Department of National Defence, *NADIBO*. As well, consult Thomas, "Expanding the North American Defence Industrial Base."

29 Claggett, "Government-Industry Duet."

30 Ibid., 6; see also Wall, "Defence and Industrial Policy."

31 Calder and Furtado, "Canadian Defence Policy," 12. See also, though it does not discuss the defence industrial base in any detail, Doern, Maslove, and Prince, *Public Budgeting*, esp. chap. 9.

32 DND, "Impact of 1992 Federal Budget." Note, of course, that these are reductions in projected spending in future fiscal years rather than actual cuts in current spending levels. Prior to the election of the federal Liberal government, modest increases in actual defence spending were planned until FY1997. This does not, however, take into account the effect of inflation or "defence inflation" and says little about expenditures on new capital equipment programs.

33 DND, "National Defence: Budget Impact"; DND, "Budget Briefing."

34 Not included here, but discussed in the next two chapters, are those other actors either in the policy-making process or somehow involved closely in its interpretation and implementation, including industry associations (e.g., Canadian Defence Preparedness Association, Forum for Industrial Participation, Aerospace Industries Association, Canadian Maritime Industries Association, Conference of Defence Associations), and regional or municipal organizations such as the Ontario Ministry of Industry, Trade and Technology, and the Ottawa-Carleton Economic Development Corporation.

35 Note that changes to this structure are ongoing as federal departments are reorganized, with changes in EAITC (now DFAIT) the most obvious example; despite such changes, the table nonetheless offers a good illustration of the complexity of the federal bureaucracy dealing with defence industry issues in Canada. Depending upon the particular concern, other federal government departments and agencies with roles to play in defence-industry related policies include Energy, Mines and Resources; Transport Canada; and Emergency Preparedness Canada (especially EPC as a result of the 1987 Emergency Legislation). See Cannizzo, "Federal Government."

36 IRBs, proposed by industry in response to a government Request for Proposal (RFP), are expected to be contractible and measurable, occasioned by a particular procurement, and occurring only following the

issue of the RFP; see Allen, "Industrial and Regional Benefits Policy"; and Woods, "Defence Procurement Issues and Challenges."

37 Treddenick, "Regional Impacts," 155; Government of Canada, *Making Sense Out of Dollars*, 25–6.
38 See Government of Canada, *Canada-U.S. Free Trade Agreement*.
39 Allen, "Industrial and Regional Benefits Policy," 7.
40 These competing criteria are highlighted in Treddenick, "Regional Impacts," 154.
41 Interview, Industry, Science and Technology Canada, Ottawa, 4 November 1990.
42 Ibid. Also see E.J. Healey, "DND and IB Policy."
43 Quoted in Dooner, "Canadian Defence Production," 2.
44 Treddenick, "Regional Impacts," 154–7.
45 Allen, "Industrial and Regional Benefits Policy," 6; also Scott, "Canada's Defence Industrial Base," 17.
46 Procurements with a value between $2 million and $100 million, however, must still be vetted by a Procurement Review Committee consisting of representatives from the central agencies, policy departments, and main operating departments, with the objective of obtaining benefits similar to those sought through the MCPs.
47 Cannizzo, "Federal Government," 41. A thorough, though dated, study of the ADATS procurement can be found in Fox, "Politics of Procurement." For a critical review, see Boehnert and Howie, "ADATS: A Wise Choice?"
48 Fox points out that the domestic Canadian market for the ADATS was expected to be approximately 5 percent of the eventual world market for the system, which was seen as therefore offering Canadian industry the chance to participate early in a project with a potentially vast market; see Fox, "Politics of Procurement," 179.
49 The new Canadian content policy is explained in a recent series of booklets published as *Procurement Policy: The Way We Do Business*. On the place of the defence industry in Ottawa's Prosperity Initiative aimed at improving government-industry cooperation, see Ray Sturgeon, presentation to the 1990 *Financial Post* conference.
50 On the Defence Industrial Preparedness Task Force, see Department of National Defence, "Defence Industrial Preparedness: A Foundation For Defence." See also the presentation of Brian Schumacher, Associate Deputy Minister, Trade Development and Chief Trade Commissioner, EAITC, to the 1990 *Financial Post* conference. One of the objectives of the Prosperity Initiative is to tackle this problem by establishing a "one-stop shopping" environment for exporters, including defence manufacturers. There is no implied goal of creating the degree of government/

industry collaboration extant in, for example, the United Kingdom and France. The objective also may clash with proposals to amend the regulations affecting defence exports, discussed in chapter 6.

51 For insight into the size and makeup of the Canadian DIB, see *Canada's Aerospace Industry*; Government of Ontario, *Aerospace/Defence Directory*; Shadwick, "Focus on Defence Industries in Ottawa"; Coulon, "Dossier sur l'industrie de défense au Québec"; Treddenick, "Economic Significance"; and Middlemiss, "Canada and Defence Industrial Preparedness."

52 For an article stressing the size and power of a Canadian military-industrial complex, see York, "Rejecting the Peace Dividend." York cites "political scientists" who estimate that the Canadian military lobby could have as many as three million members; if true, this would mean about 12 percent of the country's total population belongs to this "lobby." For a similar, though much more nuanced, restatement of this theme, see Langille, "Developing a Complex," 19.

53 See Wall, "Economic Impact," esp. 5–16; and Caron, "Economic Impact."

54 Interviews, ISTC, Ottawa, 4 November 1990. When it obtained the systems integration contract for the CPF program, Paramax Electronics was a wholly owned subsidiary of Unisys Corporation, being run through Unisys Defence Systems. Oerlikon Aerospace, which was established in Saint-Jean- sur-Richelieu when its parent company won the CF-LLAD contract competition, remains a wholly owned subsidiary of Oerlikon Buehrle Holding Ltd. It is interesting to note that both of these companies, which were brought to Canada as a consequence of DND contracts and associated IRB demands, are now in very vulnerable positions as defence opportunities decline and existing contracts (the EH-101 especially) are cancelled.

55 By the end of the 1980s, Ontario and Quebec together accounted for some 91 percent of total employment in the aerospace industry and for 92 percent of employment in the defence electronics sector. The proportion is considerably lower for the shipbuilding and ship-repair industry, at about 36 percent.

56 For a comprehensive listing, see *Canadian Defence Products Guide*.

57 Industry executives also make similar comments regarding the need to adapt to new processes or techniques in order to remain internationally competitive.

58 Canadian-owned aerospace firms in the top ten, after the de Havilland sale, are de Havilland, CAE Electronics, Canadair Group of Bombardier, and Spar Aerospace. Foreign-owned companies are Bell Helicopter Canada (U.S.); Litton Systems Canada (U.S.); MBB Helicopter Canada (Germany); McDonnell Douglas Canada (U.S.); Oerlikon Aerospace (Switzerland); and Pratt & Whitney Canada (U.S.). See ISTC, *Aerospace*.

59 The CPF project is reviewed in greater detail in Middlemiss and Sokolsky, *Canadian Defence*, 197–207. For background information on naval
procurement, see Middlemiss, "Economic Considerations"; Davis,
"Naval Procurement"; and Davis, "Defence Supply Naval Shipbuilding
Panel."

CHAPTER FIVE

1 Wall, "Defence and Industrial Policy," 27–8.
2 Middlemiss, "Canadian Defence Funding," 13.
3 An excellent review and analysis of defence spending is found in Treddenick, "Defence Budget."
4 Government of Canada, *Making Sense Out of Dollars*, 34; DND, "Budget
Briefing."
5 For one such argument, see York, "Rejecting the Peace Dividend."
6 These figures are taken from Middlemiss, "Canadian Defence Funding,"
14–15. The 1.5–percent estimate is ours, and reflects an assumption
about likely GDP growth and defence-spending reductions over the next
few years.
7 DND, "Opening Remarks," 1 (hereafter cited as "Collenette Remarks").
8 Government of Canada figures, reported in York, "Rejecting the Peace
Dividend." Also, *Making Sense Out of Dollars*, 14.
9 DND, *Canadian Defence Policy*, 14. A valuable critical analysis of Canadian
defence funding approaches since the 1960s may be found in Middlemiss, "Paying for National Defence." Arguments against the view that
any particular ratio is critical may be found in Treddenick, "Defence
Budget," 9.
10 Middlemiss, "Canadian Defence Funding," 15–16; DND, "Budget Briefing."
11 Middlemiss, "Canadian Defence Funding," 16. The argument, of course,
is widely recognized and was supposed to have been addressed by the
1987 Defence White Paper.
12 DND, *Canadian Defence Policy*, 12. Debate continues over whether the
LLAD program should be cancelled following the decision to withdraw
all Canadian forces from Europe, since this also eliminates the principal operational role and theatre for the new system. Critics argue that,
with maintenance costs included, cancellation now would save money
in the long term despite the costs of breaking the contract with Oerlikon Aerospace. Supporters point out that twenty of thirty-six ADATS
have already been delivered, that contract cancellation entails high compensation costs, and that the ADATS can easily be stored for use in
future contingencies (such as more vigorous military peace enforcement in the former Yugoslavia).

13 DND, *Canadian Defence Policy*, 12–13. Discussing the estimated \$2.7 billion capital procurement budget set for FY1992–93, the DND chief of supply commented that DND would have to focus on "essential" requirements and capabilities only; "desirable" equipment would have a low priority. See Sturgeon, presentation to the 1990 *Financial Post* conference. This approach was reaffirmed by DND officials in a briefing session on the February 1994 budget.

14 One government official we spoke with suggested that Canada should put less emphasis on "science" (the "R" of R&D) and focus more upon the greater benefits to be obtained from investing in product development. Export sales, essential for Canadian manufacturers, are not achieved through investing in "enabling technologies" that have very limited immediate results; interview, Ottawa, 15 August 1991. DND officials state that, because financial resources are limited, DND simply cannot assist manufacturers, and these companies must therefore turn to new business opportunities in exports, other federal government contracts, or even outside the defence sector altogether.

15 Middlemiss, "Canadian Defence Funding," 19.

16 This argument is made in DND, *Canadian Defence Policy*, 14–15; until recently, there had existed a gulf between such official rhetoric and the political will of the government to implement its own stated policy preferences.

17 On the advisory panel and the carefully delayed base-closure review process, see York, "Report Proposes New Process"; "A New Strategy of Deception," *Ottawa Citizen*; and "Pork and Bases," *Globe and Mail*. The likely effect of this lengthy process is considered in Pugliese, "Base Closure Delays." Opposition to base closures is reported in Cox, "Group Challenges Decision."

18 "Collenette Remarks," 2–3.

19 Middlemiss, "Canadian Defence Funding," 19. The topic of premiums and "value for the defence dollar" in this sense has begun to come under close scrutiny of late, but there is still very little systematic analysis available.

20 See Pugliese, "Canada Unveils \$1.8 Billion Procurement Program."

21 On the LSVW contract details, see Department of National Defence, "\$200 Million Contract." In total, 2,750 trucks were scheduled for delivery between August 1993 and March 1995. The April 1992 policy statement indicates that while some new projects are possible (e.g., modernizing existing 105-mm howitzers), "for the next few years, the principal equipment capabilities of the Land Force will be found in the existing inventory"; DND, *Canadian Defence Policy*, 25.

22 Freeman, "Bell, GM Win Defence Deals."

23 "Comment," *Wednesday Report* 6 (29 April 1992): 2.

24 Conversations with a number of government officials in Ottawa confirm
the current low morale of many of those involved in various aspects of
defence procurement and DIB-related activities. For a sampling of
reporting on Masse's comments, see Gunter, "Making Federalism Pay";
Fleming, "Masse Serves Only Quebec"; Rohmer, "Giving Quebecers the
Facts"; and Harper, "Defence Minister – or Quebec Minister?" A more
sympathetic review of Masse's efforts can be found in Watson, "Quebec's Defence Industrial Base." See also Vastel, "L'armée des autres."

25 See "Comment," *Wednesday Report* (pp. 1–3), for a fuller account of the
selection process and the history of the helicopter competition. A view
opposite to that conveyed in the several articles mentioned above may
be found in Mooney, "There's No Political Plot."

26 The debate is set out briefly in Pugliese, "Canada Reviews Last EH-101
Bid." By the late winter of 1993, the EH-101 had taken on an interest-
ing political complexion, as opposition (and even some Conservative)
figures sought to tarnish the image of the front-runner in the race to
replace Brian Mulroney as the head of the Conservative party, Kim
Campbell, who happened to be Minister of National Defence. See York,
"Military Helicopters"; York, "Copter Contract"; "Kim Campbell and
Her Helicopters," *Globe and Mail*; Mooney, "Paramax Defends EH-101
Helicopter Sale"; and Ward, "Critics of New Helicopters Like Them."

27 For the remainder of the decade at least, the CF-18 will remain in service and attrition will be dealt with by using aircraft returning from
Europe to supplement the Canada-based fleet. A mid-life update, including upgrading sensors and avionics systems, was proposed in the April
1992 defence policy statement; CND, *Canadian Defence Policy*, 28.

28 "In the absence of the ambitious naval modernization programme outlined in the 1987 White Paper, the recoupment of that investment
[that is, in regenerating the domestic shipbuilding and systems integration capability] becomes much more problematic – as does the survival
of all of the major shipbuilding and naval systems engineering players
associated with CPF and TRUMP"; *Canadian Defence Industry Guide, 1992*,
24.

29 Pugliese, "Canadian Shipbuilders."

30 The idea of purchasing new naval vessels off-the-shelf, with Canadian
companies then installing systems for specific Canadian Navy requirements, has been advanced by retired Rear Admiral Fred Crickard, as
reported in Pugliese, "Canadian Shipbuilding Industry." A successful
sale of frigates to Saudi Arabia might prove a temporary salve, but even
so it could not resolve the basic dilemma – too much capacity for too
little demand – facing the shipbuilding industry in Canada.

31 As of this writing, regular forces stood at 74,800; DND, "Reduction Plan
for Military Personnel," 1.

32 Figures taken from U.S. Government, *Budget, FY 1992*, part 7, historical tables, 30–6.

33 Silverberg, "Defense Industry"; Gomeau, "The Pentagon's Future Plans."

34 Munro, "U.S. Cuts Spur Sonobuoy Firms." On the small but steadily recurring Canadian market for sonobuoys, see DND, *National Defence Estimates*, part III – for example, 1990–91, 80; 1991–92, 80; and 1992–93, 91.

35 See, for Congressional involvement in the USN's *Seawolf* submarine, Ross, "Defense Industry of Connecticut."

36 The OTA study estimated U.S. defence industry employment would fall from 2,900,000 to between 2,280,000 and 2,370,000 from 1991 to 1995 under the current planned reductions. If faster-paced reductions occurred, the study suggested a figure of between 1,980,000 and 2,080,000 by 1995, and 1,500,000 by 2001. While these figures are only estimates, they illustrate the potentially massive scale of job losses that Congress has in mind when it examines DIB and defence trade policy issues. For further details, see OTA, *After the Cold War*, 19.

37 In 1990 America's aerospace industry employed 1.3 million people; by the end of 1993, employment had shrunk to 900,000. See Daniell, "Security and Economy," 12.

38 Reported in Finnegan, "U.S. House OKs $1 Billion."

39 Rep. Martin Frost, quoted in Finnegan, "House Democrats Eye Plan." See also Todd, "On the Defensive."

40 The history of the DDSA/DPSA is examined fully in Middlemiss, "Road From Hyde Park."

41 Between 1959 and 1990, the total deficit to Canada in bilateral defence trade was approximately $4 billion, on exports of $36.4 billion. However, government officials argue, first, that without these trade arrangements to assist Canadian companies this deficit would have been far larger; and second, that the deficit was cyclical, not structural or inevitable – the temporary outcome of Canadian procurements of major platforms (especially the CF-18). Hence, a sizable Pentagon contract for LAVs or the ADATS LLAD system, for example, could reverse this trend. On the first point, and the trade figures, see Brian Schumacher, Associate Deputy Minister, Trade Development and Chief Trade Commissioner, EAITC, "Presentation to the Subcommittee of the Standing Committee on External Affairs and International Trade," 7 November 1991. The second point was raised during interviews with ISTC officials, Ottawa, November 1990.

42 See *NADIBO Papers*.

43 The memoranda of understanding with France, Italy, and the Netherlands have already been amended and reviewed, taking into account the pressures on the Office of Foreign Contracting (DoD) for greater

emphasis on defence-related cooperation and less on defence trade balances. See U.S. Government, General Accounting Office, *European Initiatives*, 43–4. In a speech in late 1990, a senior EAITC officer noted of the U.S. Defense Management Review that its 1,500 or so recommendations regarding acquisition and logistics management practices possessed "no consideration of the requirements of the North American defence economic base, no consideration of the implications for second sources, and no consideration of the ramifications for DND as a NORAD and NATO partner"; see Sandor, "Notes for a Speech," 10.

44 The general content of the U.S. review document, its background, and its major weaknesses or biases were conveyed to the authors during interviews with several Canadian and U.S. officials, particularly from ISTC, EAITC, and the Pentagon, between late 1990 and early 1992. On constraints against access to the U.S. market, see, for example, EAITC, Defence Programs Bureau, *Canadian Industry and the United States Defence Market*, 5–8; and EAITC, Defence Programs Bureau, *Defence Export Shippers' Guide*, esp. 5–9.

45 The more optimistic appraisal of the review process came mainly from the Canadian Embassy in Washington; interview, September 1990, and subsequent correspondence. The "Gibson Report" itself was ultimately rejected, and a new report was commissioned by the Pentagon. This second report was accepted by both Washington and Ottawa in October 1992. See Schumacher, presentation to the 1990 *Financial Post* conference.

46 DND, internal discussion paper, April 1991, 9.

47 Ryan, "Defence Sales in the USA."

48 One trade official had noted that the "biggest barrier to this market is not protectionism or even budget cuts, but rather our collective inability to invest the effort to find out how the system works."

49 Computing Devices Company, which provides the fire control systems for the U.S. M1 and M1A1 MBTs and the British Challenger 2, is seeking to cushion the worst effect of falling MBT production by applying its technology to light armoured vehicles; see *Canadian Defence Industry Guide, 1991*, 26.

50 Interview with ISTC official, Ottawa, February 1992.

51 A valuable attempt to quantify Canadian defence trade with Europe is found in Fergusson, "Canadian Defence Trade and Europe." A less stringent methodology is applied to Canada's international defence-related exports in Regehr, *Arms Canada*.

52 Aerospace Industries Association of Canada, *RDP Task Force Report*, 1 (emphasis in the original).

53 It is interesting to note the marked difference of opinion on this particular project, and on the RDP agreements broadly, between External

Affairs officials and the conclusions reached in the AIAC report. The
CL-289, it might also be noted, was an anomaly in that it was developed
for a foreign military requirement – that is, not as a joint defence need
of the three participants. See AIAC, *RDP Task Force Report*, 7.

54 As of September 1989, no projects had emerged as a result of Canada's
RDP agreements with Belgium, Denmark, Italy, the Netherlands, Sweden, Norway, or the United Kingdom; the Canadair CL-289 was the
only joint project from the RDP with Germany (signed in 1964); neither the CL-289 nor the ERYX antitank missile projects with France
were considered as formal RDP activities. See AIAC, *RDP Task Force
Report*, 11–14. The quotation concerning the CL-289 was obtained from
Canadian government correspondence regarding the AIAC report.

55 The critical remark is taken from p. 2 of the AIAC report; the more positive evaluation is found in a Defence Programs Bureau (EAITC) discussion paper attached as annex 2 to the AIAC report.

56 At least prior to national defence budget cuts made since the end of
1990, some of these opportunities were identified to be: with Germany,
intrusion detection, security equipment, helicopter recovery systems,
mine countermeasures and surveillance systems; with Italy, aircraft simulators, communication and navigation equipment; with France, the
CL-215 and electronic components; and with the United Kingdom, ASW
equipment, aircraft simulators, and MBT fire control computers. See
Sandor, "Notes for a Speech," 15–16.

57 See Hitchens, "Taft: NATO Must Remove Barriers to Defense Trade."

58 In *Arms Canada*, Regehr attempts to document the reexport of Canadian defence-related products originally provided for U.S. equipment,
as well as direct Canadian export sales.

CHAPTER SIX

1 The U.S. figures are estimates made by the Center for Strategic and
International Studies in Washington and are cited in Skibbie, presenta-
tion to the 1990 *Financial Post* conference. See also Sims, "For Weapons
Makers." The decline in the number of Canadian suppliers was dis-
cussed at the 1990 *Financial Post* conference in the presentation by
Michael O'Brien, editor of *The Wednesday Report*. See also York, "Ottawa
Lacks Defence Conversion Plan."

2 Among the companies that disappeared in these various ways are: Leigh
Instruments, after thirty years of operating as a relatively small, innovative defence electronics company (note, however, that part of Leigh has
been bought by Spar Aerospace); Amherst Aerospace (now IMP Aerospace Components); MEL Defence Systems, purchased by Lockheed Canada; and Ernst Leitz (Canada), now operating as Hughes Leitz Optical

Technologies. See *Canadian Defence Industry Guide, 1992*, 20. The failure
of Leigh Instruments took place during uncertainties over its ownership, though problems with fulfilling its contracts played some role in
the collapse; see, for example, Davies, "Crash at Leigh"; and Blackwell,
"Defence Firm Goes Under."

3 Other casualties of the adjustment process include Telemus Electronic
Systems, SED Systems, and Honeywell Canada's Advanced Technology
Centre, which had been the firm's "Canadian value-added" contribution to domestic research and development facilities; interview, Ottawa,
28 January 1990.

4 On more than one occasion during research for this study, company
executives were unwilling to answer questions, partly because of concerns about revealing sensitive information that might assist competitors. We are particularly grateful, therefore, to those who felt they
could assist with both general and specific information; some are noted
in the references that follow, but others requested that their discussions
be non-attributable, and we have respected their desire.

5 See ISTC, *Aerospace and Defence-Related Industries*. Job reductions at Pratt
& Whitney are reported in "Financial Focus," *Defense News*, 20 April
1992, 25.

6 For Pratt & Whitney DIPP grants between 1988–89 and 1990–91, see
Appendix Table A.5. Of course, if the objectives and nature of the DIPP
funds are altered dramatically by the new Liberal government, this circumstance may also change.

7 Concerning the thwarting of the original sale of de Havilland to the
consortium of Aérospatiale and Alenia, see Pugliese, "EC Blocks
Merger." The details of the final agreement are discussed in Mittelstaedt, "$640-million Deal."

8 See Romain, "Deal Moves Bombardier."

9 "Bombardier Praises Boeing," *Globe and Mail*.

10 On Winegard's statement, see Pugliese, "EC Blocks Merger"; the support of the aerospace industry by the federal government, including
the provision of export assistance through the Export Development Corporation, is examined critically in Laux, "Limits to Liberalism."

11 Pugliese, "Bombardier, Ontario Purchase de Havilland." McDonnell
Douglas and de Havilland, both located in southern Ontario, are
regarded as the "critical foundations of this sector and any erosion of
their capabilities could have a significant negative impact on the rest of
the companies in the province" as a result of their letting of subcon-
tracts to tier-two and tier-three companies. See Ing, "Focus on Defence
Industries."

12 Romain, "Deal Moves Bombardier."

13 Presentation to the 1991 *Financial Post* conference.

14 See *Canada's Aerospace Industry, 1990–1991*, 50.

15 Reported in Howard, "Helicopter Fight."

16 The authors are indebted to a number of government officials for discussions on this subject. In this instance, these discussions – held in Kingston in November 1993 – took place in private (and hence non-attributable) conversation.

17 Niemy, presentation to the 1990 *Financial Post* conference.

18 Details of each company's products and markets are given in the 1991–92 edition of *Canada's Aerospace Industry*, with the caveat that Bombardier has since purchased de Havilland.

19 The discussion of Paramax is based on the presentation given by Paul Manson, then senior vice president, Paramax Electronics, at the McDermid-St Lawrence seminar on "Aerospace and Defence: Investment Considerations for the Nineties," Toronto, 26 November 1990, though it has been updated to take account of subsequent events. Later references are noted as appropriate.

20 See Pugliese, "Paramax Insists Spin-Off by Unisys Will Have Little Impact on Business." The company's Canadian branch now operates as Paramax Systems Canada.

21 Export sales in 1990 for Paramax Electronics totalled $30 million, the result of a U.S. Navy contract to develop an airborne computer system: reported in ibid.

22 Paramax and the other Canadian companies involved in the EH-101 were slated to supply approximately 50 percent of the total content of the EH-101s used in Canada, and 10 percent of an international export market estmated, perhaps optimistically, at some 750 additional helicopters worldwide. See Howard, "Helicopter Fight."

23 Manson, presentation to the McDermid-St Lawrence seminar.

24 This is made clear in reading transcripts of the presentations of industry executives to successive *Financial Post* conferences on the Canadian defence industry; in one rather ironic instance, an industry executive spoke of the problems his company faced in training its top personnel to adopt a more commercial-oriented outlook. One year later, that executive had been released by his company!

25 While retaining its capabilities in commercial and military avionics (i.e., land, sea, and air navigation), Honeywell put up for sale its electro-optics, covert operations, munitions, and marine systems divisions. A Honeywell spokesman noted that the decision to divest was taken prior to the collapse of the Soviet threat in Europe and was a response to *market* not political trends; interview, Ottawa, 18 January 1990.

26 An instance of mission-driven equipment concerns is the current debate about the worthiness of the M113 tracked armoured personnel carrier, and the wheeled Cougar fire-support vehicle, both in service with Canadian

units in Bosnia-Herzegovina on humanitarian-relief missions. See Koring, "Vintage Vehicles"; and Koring, "Equipment 'Appropriate'."

27 Manson, presentation to the McDermid-St Lawrence seminar.

28 For an insightful argument that the "weak competitive position of Canadian technology-based firms makes it imperative that our managers investigate the benefits to be derived from becoming involved in industry R and D alliances," see Litvak, "Industry R and D Alliances."

29 See Enchin, "Spending Cuts."

30 See, for insight into the controversy, Nixon, "Defence Exports."

31 The two caveats attached to this observation are, first, that while defence-dependent companies have only a limited ability to change the structure and composition of the industrial base by diversification, the collapse of a company such as Leigh Instruments can obviously have a significant impact. This might be called change resulting from the failure of corporate strategy rather than from the strategy itself. The second caveat is that although the primarily civil companies have greater freedom to pursue strategies, government policies must also be taken into account in considering the effects on the defence industrial base as a whole.

32 Both Canadian Marconi and Litton Systems Canada export between 80 and 85 percent of their production; both, however, are also heavily dependent on defence markets for their total sales. See the presentation to the 1991 *Financial Post* conference by John Simons, president and chief executive officer, Canadian Marconi Company; and that by Art Schwartz, marketing manager (naval systems), Litton Systems Canada, to the McDermid-St Lawrence seminar.

33 Niemy, presentation to the 1991 *Financial Post* conference.

CHAPTER SEVEN

1 Laux, "Limits to Liberalism," 114–15. Though Laux's article was prepared at the beginning of this decade and referred to the Conservative government, her observations remain apt in the present context.

2 Possibly equally useful would be a division into micro-economic, macro-economic, and international economic policy contexts, as undertaken in the largely American-oriented text by Kapstein, *Political Economy of National Security*. Kapstein includes defence industrial base and procurement issues under the category of "micro" issues; defence economic relations are categorized as international concerns; and defence spending and budgeting are regarded as macro-economic policy matters. Since most discussions by Canadian academics, government officials, and industry representatives focus on particular markets or regions, however, we have consciously sought to retain the use of similar analytical divisions in our work.

3 Lecraw, "Industrial Policy," 3. For a recent useful summary of the definition and implications of the term, see the special report on "Industrial Policy Revisited," *International Economic Insights*; see also Nasar, "Risky Allure."

4 In addition to Lecraw, see also Brenner and Courville, "Industrial Strategy." Brenner and Courville argue that the common theme in the literature on industrial strategy "is the view that the goal of industrial strategy should be the promotion of entrepreneurship and innovations" (p. 61). Laux indirectly highlights a different view, arguing that in its support of the Canadian defence industry Ottawa has ignored its responsibility for the social consequences of economic adjustment and restructuring; "Limits to Liberalism," 135.

5 A useful discussion of the need for "adjustment" policies, set in the context of Canadian public policy (including defence policy), will be found in Doern, Maslove, and Prince, *Public Budgeting*, 141–2.

6 Concern over the continuing failure of the federal government to address the issue of adequate support for DND, and the latter's decision not to question the 1991 budget, led to the resignation in April 1991 of Vice-Admiral Charles M. Thomas and to a now-celebrated exchange of letters between Thomas and General A.J.G.D. de Chastelain, Chief of the Defence Staff. Since then, Thomas has become an outspoken critic of government decisions on defence procurement.

7 Scott, "Canada's Defence Industrial Base," 11–12.

8 Interviews, Ottawa, February 1992.

9 A highly critical review of this tendency, in the context of naval procurement, can be found in Watson, "Building Frigates."

10 For a valuable brief analysis and introduction, see Epps, "Defence Industry Productivity Program."

11 Figures given by Robert Little, Assistant Deputy Minister Personnel, Finance and Administration, in House of Commons, *Minutes of Proceedings*, issue no. 2, 7 November 1991, 2:10.

12 Epps, "Defence Industry Productivity Program," 7–8, argues that DIPP repayments have not matched total grants and that repayment terms are lax.

13 The president of the Aerospace Industries Association of Canada stated bluntly that "take away DIPP and you will seriously endanger the competitiveness of Canadian companies and force them to consider migrating to jurisdictions which understand the wealth creation ability of high technology firms and which do not hesitate to invest in them"; quoted in ibid., 5.

14 Ken Epps, Program Associate, Project Ploughshares, in House of Commons, *Minutes of Proceedings*, issue no. 1, 31 October 1991, 1:16.

15 The differences could be explained by the inclusion of some of the types of funds listed at the end of Appendix Table A.5 as DIPP funds rather than as separate sources. Even these explanations make it difficult adequately to account for the difference between the ISTC figure of $178 million and the Ploughshares estimate of $300 million.

16 Industry executives' expressions of concern over the decline in DIPP funding support cannot merely be dismissed as exaggeration or some more Machiavellian misinformation effort; however, ISTC reports also note that with the decline in U.S. Department of Defense R&D budgets, "the main impact of these events on operations of Canadian subsidiaries has been to create pressure to lower reinvestment in R&D and capital acquisitions," which in turn would lower the demand for matching DIPP grants. See ISTC, *Defence Electronics*.

17 Little, in House of Commons, *Minutes of Proceedings*, issue no. 2, 7 November 1991, 2:9.

18 Ibid., 2:17.

19 Lloyd Axworthy, M.P., in House of Commons, *Minutes of Proceedings*, issue no. 3, 21 November 1991, 3:22. Though the free-trade agreement allows exceptions for national security reasons, there are some grounds for arguing that the DIPP funds subsidize exports rather than domestic market products, and that they are used for civil rather than military purposes. The status of such subsidies under the agreement (or the GATT) would be much less certain.

20 Written correspondence from industry executive, 15 March 1990.

21 Correspondence. In interviews with ISTC officials over the period 1990–2, two themes were heard repeatedly: first, that there was a strong trend towards ISTC's becoming increasingly involved in R&D policy issues; and second, that government emphasis should be placed on encouraging product development rather than basic research and research into "enabling technologies." This especially was seen as necessary for companies working in the electronics sector.

22 Analysis for the period 1969–90 is provided in Epps, "Defence Industry Productivity Program," esp. 4–6.

23 Ibid., 4.

24 Project Ploughshares' position is that the DIPP "supports a commercial military or military-related industry aimed at an export market" and should on these grounds be abolished. See ibid., 1.

25 See *Defense Conversion*; and J. Cooper, "Transforming Russia's Defense Industrial Base."

26 The idea of conversion is placed within the broader context of a major reorientation in Canadian defence and defence-industrial-base policies in Regehr, *Arms Canada*, chap. 9. For the experience of the United

States with conversion, see Adelman and Augustine, "Defense Conversion"; Gansler, "Transforming the US Defence Industrial Base"; and L. Daly, "But Can They Make Cars?" The Liberal position on this question was announced in April 1992, and restated in March 1993. See "Liberals Announce Defence Conversion Policy."

27 The phrase "attacking the overhead" appears in DND, "National Defence: Budget Impact," 4.

28 Little, in House of Commons, *Minutes of Proceedings*, issue no. 2, 7 November 1991, 2:16.

29 See Regehr, *Arms Canada*; see also the discussion in House of Commons, *Minutes of Proceedings*, issue no. 3, 13–17. In the view of the main interest group opposing such exports (Project Ploughshares), "military goods are defined by their end use. Therefore, if a military institution is ordering a piece of equipment, it becomes military equipment." This means of counting includes not only major equipment categories, but also "light bulbs on ships" if they are "part of the whole ship's package." See the discussion with Epps in House of Commons, *Minutes of Proceedings*, issue no. 9, 1:25.

30 See ibid., 1:25–7.

31 During the late 1980s, a growth in demand for commercial flight simulators shifted CAE further towards the civil side, "but this has not been a conscious CAE policy, just a response to market demands in this particular time frame"; telephone interview with CAE executive, 7 February 1990.

32 On the difficulties facing the companies (Litton Systems Canada and Marine Industries) involved in the TRUMP program and Saint John Shipbuilding, prime contractor for the CPF program, see Pugliese, "Canada to Take Over Troubled Refit of Destroyers"; and Watson, "Building Frigates."

33 Industry suggestions for bringing the DDSA/DPSA to formal treaty-level status were put forward, for example, by Jean-Jacques Blais in his presentation to the 1991 Financial Post conference. Blais suggested that leverage in negotiations might be obtained by linking these talks to the renewal of the NORAD agreement. The most vocal proponent of a defence trade treaty remains Thomas A. Callaghan, Jr. See, for example, "The Once and Future North American Defence Market."

34 Following the award to Canadian Marconi of a contract to undertake R&D pertaining to military radios, Congress passed the Bayh Amendment to the Defence Appropriations Act, which stated that no Department of Defense funds could be used for R&D projects outside the United States if there existed an American company able to undertake the project at lower cost. For discussion of other problems of this type, see Sandor, "Notes for a Speech," 9–13.

35 Interviews, Washington, September 1990; Ottawa, January 1990 and March 1991.

36 Industry, Science and Technology Canada, memorandum, 21 August 1991.

37 The battle between President Bush and Congress over DARPA's role in supporting programs such as Sematech culminated in the firing of the Agency director, Craig Fields, in April 1990; see Reilly, "Dark Days."

38 Outlined in an internal ISTC discussion paper, 20 October 1989.

39 ISTC, memorandum, 20 August 1991.

40 See U.S. Department of Defense, *Critical Technologies Plan.* A DND official noted that Canadian and U.S. officials had been working for several months in the NADIBO to identify areas of potential technological cooperation and the barriers to such cooperation; possible areas included electro-optics, infrared sensors, and metal matrix composites; interview, Ottawa, August 1991.

41 Interviews, Ottawa, August 1991.

42 Note, however, that several specialized suppliers have been affected by protectionist actions favouring American companies providing U.S. Navy contracts.

43 Laux, "Limits to Liberalism," 135.

44 EAITC, *Task Force on Europe 1992*, 28.

45 "Defence Programs Bureau Involvement in RDP Activities," reproduced in Aerospace Industries Association of Canada, *RDP Task Force*, annex 2, 3.

46 Ibid., 36.

47 DND, memorandum, 15 March 1991.

48 During interviews, an EAITC official commented that while DND has input into policy and R&D, its bias as the procuring department did not necessarily steer the defence industry onto the best possible course; interview, Ottawa, February 1992. It is well to recall the widely reported spat in June 1987 when Monique Vézina, Minister of the Department of Supply and Services (now the Department of Government Services), argued that defence spending must be used to stimulate regional development in Canada, even at the cost of increasing the price of equipment for DND. Vézina described then-Minister of National Defence, Perrin Beatty, as being "too young to understand ... the national interest"; quoted in *Canada's Defence Industrial Base*, fn. 10, 11.

49 The first quotation is from a memorandum of 15 March 1991; the second is taken from an internal DND discussion paper, April 1991, 17.

CHAPTER EIGHT

1 A useful discussion of what constitutes the defence industrial base can be found in Treddenick, "Economic Significance." See also Pepall and Shapiro, "Military-Industrial Complex."

2 That description was suggested during interviews in Ottawa, February 1992.

3 Brian Schumacher, presentation to the Subcommittee on Arms Export of the Standing Committee on External Affairs and International Trade, 7 November 1991, 1.

4 Quoted in ibid., 2. See also Government of Canada, *Export of Military Goods.*

5 Testimony of Ernie Regehr in House of Commons, *Minutes of Proceedings,* issue no. 3, 3:5. But for a corrective to this view, see Tychonick, "Canada and the Arms Trade."

6 This point was raised by Warren Allmand, M.P. for Notre-Dame-de-Grâce; see House of Commons, *Minutes of Proceedings,* issue no. 3, 3:12.

7 Regehr, ibid., 3:7. For a review of Canada's role in the export of military goods, see Purver, "Contemporary Armaments Trade."

8 For a discussion of the Swedish defence industrial base, and the significance of Sweden's policy of non-alliance in peacetime and armed neutrality in wartime, as well as its periodic violations of its own export policy guidelines, see Hawes, "Swedish Defence Industrial Base." Sweden is currently considering rule changes "aimed at increasing arms exports and making defense companies more attractive as prospective cross-border partners." See Hitchens, "Sweden, Norway to Ease Export Rules." Sweden is also considering a yearly increase of 1.5 percent in its defence procurement budget, as well as an annual increase in its total military budget, over the next five years. See Hitchens, "Sweden Bucks the Trend." It is especially worth noting that Sweden's definition of "war matériel" on which it has imposed end-user controls has been very narrow, focussing only on products such as tanks and artillery; radars, electronics, and even some armoured vehicles do not fall within this definition.

9 Both Norway and Sweden are currently debating their export control guidelines in view of the increasing importance of exports and of international industry cooperation for the survival of their manufacturers. See Hitchens, "Sweden, Norway to Ease Export Rules." Ironically, suggestions at the hearings of the Subcommittee on Arms Export would have Canada take the opposite path to the very example (Sweden) cited in support of stricter controls on recipient countries.

10 See Thain, "War Without Bullets."

11 See, for example, National Advisory Board on Science and Technology, *Innovation and National Prosperity.*

12 Hitchens and Silverberg, "U.S. Trade Stance."

13 For the recent travails of one such company, see Finnegan, "Business Woes."

14 Finnegan, "U.S. Girds for Wave of Mergers."

15 Laux, "Limits to Liberalism," 135. During the run-up to the 1993 federal election, a recurring theme of the Liberals was that the Conservative government had abdicated responsibility to develop a "conversion" policy for the country's defence industry. See York, "Thousands of Jobs"; and McCarthy, "Adapt Defence Industry or Lose Jobs."

16 Quoted in Trebilcock, *Political Economy of Economic Adjustment*, 43.

Bibliography

Adams, Peter, and Harold Briley. "Conventional Convergence in Vienna." *Defense News* (13 March 1989): 1, 35.

Adelman, Kenneth L., and Norman R. Augustine. "Defense Conversion: Bulldozing the Management." *Foreign Affairs* 71 (Spring 1992): 26–47.

Aerospace Industries Association of Canada. *RDP Task Force Report: A Study of the Bilateral Research, Development and Production Agreements.* Ottawa: AIAC 1989.

After the Cold War: Canada Among Nations 1990–91, edited by Fen Osler Hampson and Christopher J. Maule. Ottawa: Carleton University Press 1991.

Allen, T.S. "Industrial and Regional Benefits Policy." *Capital Briefing* 13 (February 1992): 6.

Anderson, Scott. "Western Europe and the Gulf War." In *Toward Political Union*, 151–64.

"A New Strategy of Deception." *Ottawa Citizen* (3 June 1992): A12.

Anthony, Ian; Agnes Courades Allebeck; and Herbert Wulf. *West European Arms Production: Structural Changes in the New Political Environment.* Stockholm: SIPRI 1990.

Arms Industry Limited, edited by Herbert Wulf. Oxford, U.K.: SIPRI/Oxford University Press 1993.

A Single European Arms Industry? European Defence Industries in the 1990s, edited by Jane Davis Drown, Clifford Drown, and Kelly Campbell. London: Brassey's 1990.

Aspin, Les. "Tomorrow's Defense from Today's Industrial Base: Finding the Right Resource Strategy for a New Era," 12 February 1992. Cited in Les Aspin, Chairman, U.S. House of Representatives Committee on Armed Services, "A Resource Strategy for the United States." Washington, 11 February 1992.

Avery, Donald. "Canadian Defence Policy and Economic Relations with the United States, 1939–1988: An Overview." In *Economic and Strategic Issues in U.S. Foreign Policy*, 121–44.

Baker, Caleb. "DoD Weighs More Force Cuts Amid Congressional Pressure." *Defense News* (11 November 1991): 18, 36.
- "Japanese Defense Firms Expect Robust Decade." *Defense News* (18 February 1991): 16.
- "Officials Label Industrial Base Study Shortsighted." *Defense News* (2 December 1991).
Bajusz, William D., and David J. Louscher. *Arms Sales and the U.S. Economy: The Impact of Restricting Military Exports.* Boulder: Westview 1988.
Baldwin, Robert E. *Trade Policy in a Changing World Economy.* London: Harvester-Wheatsheaf 1988.
Behr, Peter. "A Message for Japan: Clinton Wants Results." *International Herald Tribune* (10 February 1994): 1, 4.
- "U.S. Is Prepared to See Trade Relations Worsen." *International Herald Tribune* (8 February 1993): 1, 5.
Berdal, Mats R. "Whither UN Peacekeeping?" *Adelphi Paper* 281. London: International Institute for Strategic Studies 1993.
Bergsten, C. Fred. *America in the World Economy: A Strategy for the 1990s.* Washington: Institute for International Economics 1983.
Blacker, Coit D. "The Collapse of Soviet Power in Europe." *Foreign Affairs* 70 (America and the World 1990/91): 88–102.
Blackwell, Richard. "Defence Firm Goes Under." *Financial Post* (16 April 1990): 1.
Boehnert, G.C., and D.I. Howie. "ADATS: A Wise Choice?" *Forum* 3 (1988): 14–20.
Bolstering Defense Industrial Competitiveness: Preserving Our Heritage, Securing Our Future, Report to the Secretary of Defense by the Under-Secretary of Defense (Acquisition). Washington 1988.
"Bombardier Praises Boeing for de Havilland Makeover." *Globe and Mail* (23 January 1992): B1.
Boyd, Frank L. Jr. "The Politics of Canadian Defence Procurement: The New Fighter Aircraft Decision." In *Canada's Defence Industrial Base.*
Brenner, Reuven, and Léon Courville. "Industrial Strategy: Inferring What It Really Is." In *Economics of Industrial Policy,* 47–83.
Budget of the US Government, FY 1992, part 7, historical tables. Washington: U.S. Government Printing Office 1991.
Building a New Global Order: Emerging Trends in International Security, edited by David B. Dewitt, David G. Haglund, and John J. Kirton. Toronto: Oxford University Press 1993.
Buzan, Barry, et al. *The European Security Order Recast: Scenarios for the Post-Cold War Era.* London: Pinter 1990.
Byers, R.B. "Canadian Defence and Defence Procurement: Implications for Economic Policy." In *Selected Problems in Formulating Foreign Economic Policy,* 131–95.

– "Canadian Security and Defence: The Legacy and the Challenges." *Adelphi Paper* 214. London: International Institute for Strategic Studies 1986.

Calder, Kenneth J., and Francis Furtado. "Canadian Defence Policy in the 1990s: International and Domestic Determinants." *Canadian Defence Quarterly* 21 (August 1991).

Callaghan, Thomas A. Jr. "NATO at Forty Needs a Two-Pillar Treaty." *NATO Review* 37 (August 1989): 21–6.

– *Pooling Allied and American Resources to Produce a Credible, Collective Conventional Deterrent*. Report prepared for the U.S. Department of Defense. Washington 1988.

– "The Once and Future North American Defence Market." Speech to a luncheon meeting of the Canadian Defence Preparedness Association and the Conference of Defence Associations Institute, Ottawa, 9 October 1990.

Callan, Byron (Prudential Bache Securities). Presentation to the conference on "Reconstitution: Force Structure and Industrial Strategy." John M. Olin Institute for Strategic Studies, Harvard University, Boston, 7–8 May 1992.

Campbell, Robert M., and Leslie A. Pal. "The CF-18 Affair." In *Real Worlds of Canadian Politics*, 19–52.

Canada, Government of. *Making Sense Out of Dollars, 1993–1994 Edition*. Ottawa: Department of National Defence 1993.

– *The Canada-U.S. Free Trade Agreement*. Ottawa: Department of External Affairs 1988.

– Department of National Defence. "Budget Briefing," by David Collenette. Ottawa, 22 February 1994.

– Department of National Defence. "National Defence: Budget Impact," by David Collenette. Ottawa, 22 February 1994.

– Department of National Defence. "Opening Remarks for the Honourable David Collenette, P.C., M.P., Minister of National Defence, for a News Conference." Ottawa, 22 February 1994.

– Department of National Defence. *Canadian Defence Policy.* Ottawa 1992.

– Department of National Defence. *Challenge and Commitment: A Defence Policy for Canada*. Ottawa: Minister of Supply and Services 1987.

– Department of National Defence. "Defence Production Sharing." Discussion paper. Ottawa, 18 March 1988.

– Department of National Defence. "Impact of 1992 Federal Budget on Defence Policy and Programmes." Backgrounder documentation, Ottawa, February 1992.

– Department of National Defence. *NADIBO*. Ottawa 1987.

– Department of National Defence. *National Defence Estimates*. Part III, "Expenditure Plan". Ottawa, various years.

– Department of National Defence. "Reduction Plan for Military Personnel." Backgrounder. Ottawa, February 1994.

- Department of National Defence. "$200 Million Contract Signed with British Columbia's Star Truck Company." News release. Ottawa, 20 March 1992.
- Department of National Defence, Defence Industrial Preparedness Task Force. "Defence Industrial Preparedness: A Foundation For Defence." Ottawa, November 1987.
- Department of National Defence, Defence Industrial Preparedness Task Force. *The Environment for Expanding the North American Defence Industrial Base.* Ottawa, June 1987.
- External Affairs and International Trade Canada. *Canadian Defence Products Guide.* Ottawa, annually.
- External Affairs and International Trade Canada. *Export of Military Goods from Canada: Third Annual Report, 1992.* Ottawa 1993.
- External Affairs and International Trade Canada. *Task Force on Europe 1992: Report of the Working Group on Defence Products.* Ottawa 1989.
- External Affairs and International Trade Canada, Defence Programs Bureau. *Canadian Industry and the United States Defence Market.* Ottawa 1987.
- External Affairs and International Trade Canada, Defence Programs Bureau. *Defence Export Shippers' Guide: United States-Canada Defence Production Sharing Arrangements.* Ottawa [undated].
- House of Commons. *Minutes of Proceedings and Evidence of the Subcommittee on Arms Export of the Standing Committee on External Affairs and International Trade.* Ottawa: Supply and Services Canada 1991.
- Industry, Science and Technology Canada. *Aerospace: Industry Profile.* Ottawa 1992.
- Industry, Science and Technology Canada. *Aerospace and Defence-Related Industries: Statistical Survey Report 1990.* Ottawa: Supply and Services Canada, 1991.
- Industry, Science and Technology Canada. *Defence Electronics, Industry Profile.* Ottawa 1992.
- Secretary of State for External Affairs. "CSCE Helsinki Document 1992: The Challenges of Change." Ottawa, October 1992.
Canada's Aerospace Industry: A Capability Guide. Toronto: Maclean Hunter, annually.
Canada's Defence Industrial Base: The Political Economy of Preparedness and Procurement, edited by David G. Haglund. Kingston, Ont.: Ronald P. Frye 1988.
Canada's International Security Policy, edited by David B. Dewitt and David Leyton-Brown. Toronto: Prentice-Hall Canada 1994.
Canadian Defence Industry Guide, 1991. Toronto: Baxter Publishing 1992.
Canadian Defence Industry Guide, 1992. Toronto: Baxter Publishing 1992.
Canadian Institute of International Peace and Security, *The Guide to Canadian Defence Policies on Arms control, Disarmament, Defence and Conflict Resolution, 1991* (Ottawa: the Institute, 1991).
Can America Remain Committed? U.S. Security Horizons in the 1990s, edited by David G. Haglund. Boulder: Westview 1992.

Cannizzo, Cynthia A. "The Federal Government and Defence Industrial Preparedness." *Canadian Defence Quarterly* 18 (June 1989): 38–43.

Caron, Serge. "The Economic Impact of Canadian Defence Expenditures." Report no. 23. Centre for Studies in Defence Resources Management, Kingston, Ont., January 1994.

Carr, Edward H. *The Twenty Years' Crisis, 1919–1939.* London: Macmillan 1939.

Chipman, John. "The Future of Strategic Studies: Beyond Even Grand Strategy." *Survival* 34 (Spring 1992): 109–31.

Claggett, W.L. "Government-Industry Duet." *Forum* 3 (1988): 4–6.

CNAD: see North Atlantic Council, Conference of National Armaments Directors.

Cohen, Eliot A. "The Mystique of U.S. Air Power." *Foreign Affairs* 73 (January/February 1994): 109–24.

"Collinette Remarks": see Canada, Department of National Defence, "Opening Remarks."

"Comment." *Wednesday Report* 6 (29 April 1992): 2.

Commission of the European Communities. *A Competitive European Aeronautical Industry,* SEC(40) 1456 final, Brussels, 23 July 1990.

Conference of National Armaments Directors: see North Atlantic Council.

Cooper, David. "Allied Arms Cooperation: Need for a Transatlantic Political Strategy." *NATO Review* 39 (October 1991): 32–5.

Cooper, David, and Jim Bishop. "NATO's Conventional Armaments Planning System: 'The CAPS'." Briefing to the Logistics in NATO symposium, Luxembourg, 16/17 January 1991.

Cooper, Julian. "Transforming Russia's Defence Industrial Base." *Survival* 35 (Winter 1993–94): 147–62.

Corddry, Charles W. "Reducing U.S. Forces in Europe: How Much Is Enough?" *Baltimore Sun* (15 March 1992): C5.

Coulon, Jocelyn. "Dossier sur l'industrie de défense au Québec." *Canadian Defence Quarterly* 21 (December 1991): S3–S14.

– "L'ONU veut une armée permanente pour soutenir ses missions de maintien de la paix." *Le Devoir* (9 October 1992): B7.

Cox, David. "Thinking About Nuclear Weapons After the Coup." *Peace and Security* 6 (Winter 1991/92): 12–13.

Cox, Kevin. "Group Challenges Decision to Close Moncton Base." *Globe and Mail* (12 November 1992): A4.

"CSCE Summit (The), Paris, 19–21 November 1990." *NATO Review* 38 (December 1990): 26–31.

Daly, Les. "But Can They Make Cars?" *New York Times Magazine* (30 January 1994): 26–7.

Daly, Richard (Director, Marketing Operations, Raytheon Corp.). Presentation to the conference on "Reconstitution: Force Structure and Industrial

Strategy." John M. Olin Institute for Strategic Studies, Harvard University, Boston, 7–8 May 1992.

Daniell, Robert F. "Security and Economy: An American Perspective." Paper presented to the 31st Munich Conference on Security Policy, Munich, 5 February 1994.

Davies, Charles. "The Crash at Leigh." *Canadian Business* (July 1990): 28–34.

Davis, S. Mathwin. "Naval Procurement, 1950 to 1965." In *Canada's Defence Industrial Base*, 97–117.

– "The Defence Supply Naval Shipbuilding Panel, 1955–1965." *Northern Mariner* 2 (October 1992): 1–14.

"Deal Is Done (The)." *Economist* (14 December 1991): 51–2.

De Bardeleben, Joan. "Madly Off in All Directions." *Peace and Security* 6 (Winter 1991/92): 2–4.

de Briganti, Giovanni. "Germany Reverses Plan to Reduce Defense Spending." *Defense News* (15 July 1991): 4, 29.

– "IEPG Moves to Open Markets." *Defense News* (26 November 1990): 3, 29.

– "Joxe Promotes European Preference for Weapons Procurement." *Defense News* (24 June 1991): 36.

– "U.S. Trade Stance Irks Europeans." *Defense News* (13 January 1992): 28.

Defense Conversion: Achieving U.S.-Russian Cooperation for an Orderly Build-down and Economic Renewal, Fall 1992 Gateway Seminar Report. Middlebury, Vt.: Geonomics Institute 1992.

Defence Industrial Base and the West (The), edited by David G. Haglund. London: Routledge 1989.

Defence Industrial Preparedness Task Force: see Canada, Department of National Defence.

Department of National Defence: see Canada, Department of National Defence.

Destler, I.M. *American Trade Politics: System Under Stress*. New York: Twentieth Century Fund 1986.

Destler, I. M., and Michael Nacht. "Beyond Mutual Recrimination: Building a Solid U.S.-Japan Relationship in the 1990s." *International Security* 15 (Winter 1990/91): 114–19.

Deudney, Daniel, and G. John Ikenberry. "The International Sources of Soviet Change." *International Security* 16 (Winter 1991–92): 90.

– "Who Won the Cold War?" *Foreign Policy* 87 (Summer 1992): 123–38.

Die EG auf dem Weg zu einer Gemeinsamen Aussen- und Sicherheitspolitik, edited by Oliver Thränert. Bonn: Friedrich Ebert Stiftung 1992).

Dizard III, Wilson. "Two Pairs of U.S. Fuel Cycle Companies Talk with Moscow on Buying Weapons HEU." *Nuclear Fuel* (20 July 1992): 11–12.

DND: see Canada, Department of National Defence.

Doern, G. Bruce; Allan M. Maslove; and Michael J. Prince. *Public Budgeting in Canada: Politics, Economics, and Management*. Ottawa: Carleton University Press 1991.

Donnelly, Christopher. "Evolutionary Problems in the Former Soviet Armed Forces." *Survival* 34 (Autumn 1991): 28–42.

Dooner, Terrence J. "Canadian Defence Production: For Military Objectives or as an Economic Instrument?" Research report submitted for the course on National Security Management, National Defense University, Washington, 22 December 1989.

Dow, James. *The Arrow.* Toronto: James Lorimer 1979.

Driscoll, R.F. "European Security: Theoretical and Historical Lessons for Emerging Structures." *European Security* 2 (Spring 1993): 15–22.

EAITC: see Canada, External Affairs and International Trade Canada.

Economic and Strategic Issues in U.S. Foreign Policy, edited by Carl-Ludwig Holtfrerich. Berlin: Walter de Gruyter 1988.

Economic Issues and National Security, edited by Klaus Knorr and Frank N. Trager. Lawrence, Kansas: Regents Press 1977.

Economics of Industrial Policy and Strategy, edited by Donald G. McFetridge, Royal Commission on the Economic Union and Development Prospects for Canada, vol. 5. Toronto: University of Toronto Press 1986.

Edgar, Alistair D. "Congress and American Defence 'Trade' Policy, 1972–92: Testing Arguments on American Foreign Economic Policy." Paper presented to the annual general meeting of the Canadian Political Science Association, Ottawa, June 1993.

– "The MRCA/Tornado: The Politics and Economics of Collaborative Procurement." In *Defence Industrial Base and the West.*

– "Security, Competitiveness, and International Cooperation in U.S. Defense Industrial Base Policy." In *Can America Remain Committed?*, 247–74.

Edgar, Alistair D., and David G. Haglund. "Japanese Defence Industrialisation." In *Japan's Military Renaissance?*, 137–63.

Enchin, Harvey. "Spending Cuts Put Sovereignty at Risk." *Globe and Mail* (27 November 1990): B15.

Epps, Ken. "The Defence Industry Productivity Program: Contributions 1969 through 1990." Working paper no. 91–2, Project Ploughshares, Waterloo, Ont., July 1991.

External Affairs and International Trade Canada: see Canada, External Affairs and International Trade Canada.

Fergusson, James. "Canadian Defence Trade and Europe: Methodological Concerns and Empirical Evidence." Research report no. 4, National Defence College, Centre for Studies in Defence Resources Management, Kingston, Ont. 1990.

Fetter, Steve. "Ballistic Missiles and Weapons of Mass Destruction: What Is the Threat? What Should Be Done?" *International Security* 16 (Summer 1991): 5–42.

Fifty Years of Canada-United States Defense Cooperation: The Road from Ogdensburg, edited by Joel J. Sokolsky and Joseph T. Jockel. Lewiston, N.Y.: Edwin Mellen 1992.

"Financial Focus." *Defense News* (20 April 1992): 25.

Financial Post. Conference on "The Canadian Defence Industry: Building for the Future." Ottawa, 24–25 October 1990.

– Conference on "Canada's Defence Industry: The Post-Gulf Chopping Block." Ottawa, 24 October 1991.

– Conference on "The Canadian Defence Industry." Ottawa, 12 November 1992.

Finnegan, Philip. "Analysts: Defense Stocks Will Surpass Market in '94." *Defense News* (10 January 1994): 10.

– "Analysts Praise Olin-Alliant Merger." *Defense News* (4 May 1992): 33.

– "Business Woes Rock McDonnell." *Defense News* (7 December 1992): 1, 42.

– "DoD Request Awaits Trial by Fire." *Defense News* (3 February 1992): 6.

– "House Democrats Eye Plan to Help Industry Diversify." *Defense News* (18 May 1992): 4.

– "Industry Faces Unprecedented Workforce Cuts." *Defense News* (20 August 1990): 3.

– "1 in 4 Defense-Related Jobs to Vanish by 1996, Study Says." *Defense News* (26 August 1991).

– "Pentagon Cancels 13 Weapons." *Defense News* (4 February 1991): 1, 30.

– "Upswing in Aerospace May Not Last, Analysts Warn." *Defense News* (27 April 1992): 40.

– "U.S. Defense Cut Spurs Threats by Democrats." *Defense News* (10 January 1994): 3.

– "U.S. Firms' Profit Erosion Outpaces Europe." *Defense News* (16 September 1991): 3.

– "U.S. Girds for Wave of Mergers." *Defense News* (30 November 1992): 1, 20.

– "U.S. House OKS $1 Billion to Ease Pain of Defense Cuts." *Defense News* (8 June 1992): 42.

Fisher, Marc. "Kohl to Order a Sharp Cut in Germany's Armed Forces." *International Herald Tribune* (8 February 1993): 1.

– "U.S. Officials Take Tough New Line On Europe." *International Herald Tribune* (10 February 1992): 1.

Flanagan, Stephen J. "NATO and Central and Eastern Europe: From Liaison to Security Partnership." *Washington Quarterly* 15 (Spring 1992): 141–51.

Fleming, Harry. "Masse Serves Only Quebec." *Halifax Daily News* (6 May 1992): 16.

Fortmann, Michel. "NATO Defense Planning in a Post-CFE Environment: Assessing the Alliance Strategy Review (1990–1991)." In *Homeward Bound?*

Fortmann, Michel, and David G. Haglund. "Europe, NATO and the ESDI Debate: In Quest of an Identity." In *From Euphoria to Hysteria*, 21–44.

Fox, William B. "The Politics of Procurement: The Low Level Air Defence Decision of 1986." In *Canada's Defence Industrial Base*, 159–85.

Freeman, Allan. "Bell, GM Win Defence Deals." *Globe and Mail* (8 April 1992): B15.

Friedberg, Aaron L. "The End of Autonomy: The United States after Five Decades." *Daedalus* 120 (Fall 1991).

From Euphoria to Hysteria: Western European Security after the Cold War, edited by David G. Haglund. Boulder: Westview 1993.

Frye, Alton. "Zero Ballistic Missiles." *Foreign Policy* 88 (Fall 1992), 3–20.

Fursdon, Edward. *The European Defence Community: A History.* London: Macmillan 1980.

Gaddis, John Lewis. "How Relevant Was U.S. Strategy in Winning the Cold War?" Carlisle, Penn.: Strategic Studies Institute, U.S. Army War College, March 1992.

Galigan, C.G., and P.G. Herring. "Defence Industrial Impact: 'Offsets' and Exports." Report no. 13. Centre for Studies in Defence Resources Management, Kingston, Ont. 1986.

Gambles, Ian. "European Security Integration in the 1990s." *Chaillot Papers* 3. Paris: WEU Institute for Security Studies, Western European Union, November 1991.

Gansler, Jacques S. "Transforming the U.S. Defence Industrial Base." *Survival* 35 (Winter 1993/94): 130–46.

George, Bruce. "Lofty Goals Still Elude CSCE." *Defense News* (3 February 1991): 24.

Gilpin, Robert. *The Political Economy of International Relations.* Princeton: Princeton University Press 1987.

– *War and Change in World Politics.* Cambridge: Cambridge University Press 1981.

Glaser, Charles L. "Why NATO Is Still Best." *International Security* 18 (Summer 1993): 5–50.

Goble, Paul A. "Ethnicity and National Conflict in Soviet Politics." In *The 'Soviet Threat' Revisited,* 31–9.

– "Russia and Its Neighbors." *Foreign Policy* 90 (Spring 1993), 79–88.

Gomeau, Edward M. "The Pentagon's Future Plans: Reductions of Great Magnitude." *Defense Media Review* 6 (February 1993): 1–3.

Gomeau, Edward M., and Heinz A.J. Kern. "How Little Is Enough? U.S. Grand Strategy in Limbo." *Defense Media Review* 6 (May 1992): 1–2.

Gray, Colin S. "Strategic Sense, Strategic Nonsense." *National Interest* 29 (Fall 1992).

Guide to Canadian Policies on Arms Control, Disarmament, Defence and Conflict Resolution 1991 (The). Ottawa: Canadian Institute for International Peace and Security 1991.

Guns and Butter: Defence and the Canadian Economy. Toronto: Canadian Institute of Strategic Studies 1984.

Gunter, Lorne. "Making Federalism Pay and Pay..." *British Columbia Report* (4 May 1992): 12.

Hagen, Lawrence S. "Twisting Arms: Political, Military and Economic Aspects of Arms Co-operation in the Atlantic Alliance." *National Security Series,* 3.

Kingston: Queen's University Centre for International Relations 1980, 35–44.

Haglund, David G. *Alliance Within the Alliance? Franco-German Military Cooperation and the European Pillar of Defense.* Boulder: Westview 1991.

– "Canadian Strategic Minerals and U.S. Military Potential: National Security Implications of Bilateral Mineral Trade." In *The New Geopolitics of Minerals*, 159–88.

– "Changing Concepts and Trends in International Security." In *Canada's International Security Policy.*

Haglund, David G., with Marc L. Busch. "'Techno-Nationalism' and the Contemporary Debate over the American Defence Industrial Base." In *Defence Industrial Base and the West*, 234–77.

Halliday, Fred. "Look Back in Danger." *New Statesman and Society* (30 December 1991): 4–5.

Harbron, John D. "Hard Economic Times? Why Not Export Warships?" *Globe and Mail* (26 October 1992): A25.

Harper, Tim. "Defence Minister – or Quebec Minister?" *Whig-Standard* [Kingston] (20 April 1992): 3.

Harris, Bruce A. "Trends in Alliance Conventional Defense Initiatives: Implications for North American and European Security." In *U.S.-Canada Security Relationship*, 41–64.

Hartley, Keith. *The Economics of Defence Policy.* London: Brassey's 1991.

Hawes, Michael K. "Assessing the World Economy: The Rise and Fall of Bretton Woods." In *World Politics.*

– "NATO in a Post-Hegemonic World: The Political Economy of Alliance Relations." In *North American Perspectives on European Security.*

– "The Swedish Defence Industrial Base: Implications for the Economy." In *Defence Industrial Base and the West*, 163–88.

Healey, Eldon J. "DND and IB Policy: A Perspective." A speech to the Canadian Industrial Benefits Association, Winter 1990 Program, Ottawa, 14 February 1990.

– "The Conference of National Armaments Directors: NATO's Forum for Armaments Cooperation." *Canadian Defence Quarterly* 19 (February 1990): 25.

Healey, Nigel M. "EC92 The Coming of Fortress Europe?" *Business Quarterly* 55 (Spring 1991): 25.

Herspring, Dale. "The State of the Soviet Military." In *The 'Soviet Threat' Revisited*, 21–9.

Hitchens, Theresa. "Arms Chiefs of NATO Fail to Set Trade Code." *Defense News* (26 October 1992): 12.

– "CSCE Ministers to Review Post-Cold War Role." DEFENSE NEWS (27 January 1992): 6.

– "Delors Proposes EC Contribute Funds to European Industry." *Defense News* (17 February 1992): 42.

- "EC to Aid Communities Crippled by Reductions in Defense." *Defense News* (27 January 1992): 35.
- "EC Officials Seek to Boost Defense Competition." *Defense News* (30 March 1992): 10.
- "Europe Sharpens WEU Teeth." *Defense News* (18 November 1991): 4.
- "France, Allies Differ on NATO Weapon Trade Issue." *Defense News* (20 April 1991): 3.
- "German Cuts Hit Army the Hardest." *Defense News* (20 January 1991): 4, 28.
- "Germany Pushes CFE Plan for East." *Defense News* (24 February 1992): 52.
- "NATO to Mesh Arms Trade Rules." *Defense News* (19 October 1992): 4, 45.
- "One on One." *Defense News* (29 April 1991): 30.
- "Sweden Bucks the Trend, Expects Budget Increase." *Defense News* (27 January 1992): 14.
- "Sweden, Norway to Ease Export Rules." *Defense News* (27 January 1992): 8.
- "Taft: NATO Must Remove Barriers to Defense Trade." *Defense News* (29 June 1992): 4.
- "Tri-Nation Statement Underscores EC Divisions on Security." *Defense News* (14 October 1991): 8.

Hitchens, Theresa, and George Leopold. "Pressure Grows For Republics to Adhere to CFE." *Defense News* (13 January 1992): 1, 29.

Hitchens, Theresa, and David Silverberg. "U.S. Trade Stance Irks Europeans." *Defense News* (5 April 1993): 1, 44.

Hobbs, David. "Research and Development in NATO: The European View." *NATO's Sixteen Nations* (December 1989–January 1990): 30–1.

Holt, J.A. "NATO Defence Production: The Need for a More Open Market Approach." Discussion paper. Brussels, NATO, November 1990.

Holzer, Robert; Neil Munro; and Vago Muradian. "Aspin Cuts to Redefine Military." *Defense News* (8 February 1993): 1, 50.

Homeward Bound? Allied Forces in the New Germany, edited by David G. Haglund and Olaf Mager. Boulder: Westview 1992.

Horvitz, Paul F. "Clinton, Reassuring the Allies, Affirms 'Continuity' of American Foreign Policy." *International Herald Tribune* (5 November 1992): 1, 6.

Howard, Ross. "Helicopter Fight Heats Up in Ottawa." *Globe and Mail* (4 July 1992): A1.

Hyland, William G. "The Case for Pragmatism." *Foreign Affairs* 71 (America and the World 1991/92).

Independent European Programme Group. *Copenhagen Communiqué,* IEPG/MIN/D-14, 16 November 1989.

- *Policy Document on the European Defence Equipment Market,* 16 November 1990.

Industrial Base: Significance of DoD's Foreign Dependence. Report to the Chairman, Subcommittee on Technology and National Security, Joint Economic Committee, U.S. Congress, GAO/NSIAD-91–93. Washington: U.S. General Accounting Office, January 1991.

"Industrial Policy Revisited." *International Economic Insights* 4 (March/April 1993): 2–23.

Industry, Science and Technology Canada: see Canada, Industry, Science and Technology Canada.

Ing, Stanley. "Focus on Defence Industries in Southern Ontario." *Canadian Defence Quarterly* 21 (February 1991): S12.

ISTC: see Canada, Industry, Science and Technology Canada.

Japan's Military Renaissance? edited by Ron Matthews and Keisuke Matsuyama. London: Macmillan 1993.

Kaiser, Karl. "Germany's Unification." *Foreign Affairs* 70 ("America and the World, 1990/91"): 178–205.

Kapstein, Ethan B. "International Collaboration in Armaments Production: A Second-Best Solution." *Political Science Quarterly* 106 (Winter 1991–92): 657–75.

– *The Political Economy of National Security: A Global Perspective.* Columbia, S.C.: University of South Carolina Press 1992.

Kennedy, Paul. *The Rise and Fall of the Great Powers: Economic Change and Military Conflict from 1500 to 2000.* New York: Random House 1987.

"Kim Campbell and Her Helicopters" (editorial), *Globe and Mail* (11 March 1993): A16.

Kindleberger, Charles P. *The World in Depression, 1929–1939.* Berkeley: University of California Press 1986.

Kirton, John J. "The Consequences of Integration: The Case of the Defence Production Sharing Agreements." Occasional paper no. 21, School of International Affairs, Carleton University, Ottawa 1972.

Klepak, H.P. "Changing Realities and Perceptions of Military Threat." In *Canada's International Security Policy.*

Koring, Paul. "Equipment 'Appropriate' Military Assured Cabinet." *Globe and Mail,* A6.

– "Vintage Vehicles Drive Up Risk." *Globe and Mail* (22 March 1993): A1.

Kremp, Herbert. "EC's Foreign and Security Policies Are Found Wanting." *German Tribune* (8 September 1991): 1–2.

Kupchan, Charles A., and Clifford A. Kupchan. "Concerts, Collective Security, and the Future of Europe." *International Security* 16 (Summer 1991): 114–61.

Lagon, Mark P. "'Not Too Tart, Not Too Sweet': The Centrist Position on U.S. Decline." *Security Studies* 1 (Autumn 1991): 163–71.

Langille, Peter. "Developing a Complex." *Peace Magazine* (April/May 1988).

Latham, Andrew. "Conflict and Competition over the NATO Defence Industrial Base: The Case of the European Fighter Aircraft." In *Defence Industrial Base and the West.*

Latham, Andrew, and Michael Slack. "The Evolving European Defence Sector: Implications for Europe and North America." research report no. 3,

Centre for Studies in Defence Resources Management, Kingston, Ont., Fall 1990.

Laux, Jeanne Kirk. "Limits to Liberalism." *International Journal* 46 (Winter 1990/91): 113–36.

Lecraw, Donald J. "Industrial Policy in the United States: A Survey." In *Economics of Industrial Policy and Strategy.*

Legge, Michael. "The Making of NATO's New Strategy." *NATO Review* 39 (December 1991): 9–14.

Lello, José, and Bill Richardson. "Draft Report on Challenges to Transatlantic Co-operation." North Atlantic Assembly, Defence and Security Committee, Subcommittee on Defence Cooperation. Brussels, October 1989).

Leopold, George. "Cutbacks Signal End to U.S. Strategic Modernization." *Defense News* (3 February 1992): 6.

– "EIA: Electronics to Thrive Despite Defense Budget Cuts." *Defense News* (26 October 1992): 8.

– "European Arms Summit to Include Regional Crises Look." *Defense News* (21 September 1992): 10.

– "Warhead Transfer to Russia is Ahead of Schedule." *Defense News* (2 March 1991): 6.

"Liberals Announce Defence Conversion Policy." Office of the Leader of the Opposition, House of Commons, Ottawa, 26 March 1993.

Litvak, Isaiah. "Industry R and D Alliances: A Key to Competitive Survival." *Business Quarterly* 55 (Summer 1990): 61–4.

Lowe, Brian. "European Defence Industry in the 1990's." Presentation for the Defence Manufacturers' Association, U.K., 1991.

Lunn, Simon. "A Reassessment of European Security." In *What is European Security after the Cold War?*

Lynch, Charles. "Hanging Helicopters on Campbell All Part of Canadian Tradition." *Ottawa Citizen* (14 March 1993): B2.

MacFarlane, S. Neil. "The Collapse of the Soviet Union and Its Implications for the North Atlantic Security Community." In *From Euphoria to Hysteria,* 305–25.

Mager, Olaf. "The Continental Commitment: Britain's Forces in Germany." In *Homeward Bound?,* 167–87.

Mahncke, Dieter. "Parameters of European Security." *Chaillot Papers* 10. Paris: Institute for Security Studies, Western European Union, September 1993.

Mandelbaum, Michael. "Coup de Grace: The End of the Soviet Union." *Foreign Affairs* 71 ("America and the World 1991/92"): 164–83.

Manson, Paul (senior vice president, Paramax Electronics). Presentation at the McDermid St. Lawrence seminar on "Aerospace and Defence: Investment Considerations for the Nineties." Toronto, 26 November 1990.

Mastanduno, Michael. "Do Relative Gains Matter? America's Response to Japanese Industrial Policy." *International Security* 16 (Summer 1991).

Matthews, William. "Soviet Demise Leaves Pentagon Wondering Who Is the Foe." *Defense News* (24 February 1992): 34.

Maynes, Charles William. "Containing Ethnic Conflict." *Foreign Policy* 90 (Spring 1993): 3–21.

McCarthy, Shawn. "Adapt Defence Industry or Lose Jobs, Liberals Say." *Toronto Star* (27 March 1993): A10.

McLin, Jon B. *Canada's Changing Defense Policy, 1957–1963: The Problems of a Middle Power in Alliance.* Baltimore: Johns Hopkins Press 1967.

Mearsheimer, John J. "Back to the Future: Instability in Europe After the Cold War." *International Security* 15 (Summer 1991): 5–56.

Meyer, Stephen M. "How the Threat (and the Coup) Collapsed: The Politicization of the Soviet Military." *International Security* 16 (Winter 1991/92): 5–38

Middlemiss, Danford W. "Canada and Defence Industrial Preparedness: A Return to Basics?" *International Journal* 42 (Autumn 1987): 707–30.

– "Canadian Defence Funding: Heading Towards Crisis?" *Canadian Defence Quarterly* 21 (October 1991).

– "Economic Considerations in the Development of the Canadian Navy since 1945." In *The RCN in Transition*, 254–78.

– "Paying for National Defence: The Pitfalls of Formula Funding." *Canadian Defence Quarterly* 12 (Winter 1982/83): 24–9.

– "The Road from Hyde Park: Canada-U.S. Defense Economic Cooperation." In *Fifty Years of Canada-United States Defense Cooperation*, 175–206.

Middlemiss Danford W., and Joel J. Sokolsky. *Canadian Defence: Decisions and Determinants.* Toronto: Harcourt Brace Jovanovich Canada 1989.

Miller, Charles. "NATO Unveils Rapid Reaction Corps." *Defense News* (5 October 1992): 12.

Miller, Charles, and Michael J. Witt. "Britain's White Paper Urges Broad Cuts." *Defense News* (15 July 1991): 3, 22.

– "Ferranti Purchase Makes GEC Europe's No. 2 Electronics Firm." *Defense News* (29 January 1990): 44.

Miller, Steven E. "Western Diplomacy and the Soviet Nuclear Legacy." *Survival* 34 (Autumn 1992): 3–27.

"Ministerial Meeting of the North Atlantic Council at Turnberry, UK, 7–8 June 1990." *NATO Review* 38 (June 1990): 28–30.

Miskel, James. "Thin Ice: Single Sources in the Domestic Industrial Base." *Strategic Review* (Winter 1990): 46–53.

Mittelstaedt, Martin. "$640–million Deal Made to Rescue de Havilland." *Globe and Mail* (23 January 1992): 1.

Moodie, Michael. "Defense Implications of Europe 92." *Significant Issues Series* 12. Washington: Center for Strategic and International Studies 1990.

Moodie, Michael L., and Brenton C. Fischmann. "Alliance Armaments Cooperation: Toward a NATO Industrial Base." In *Defence Industrial Base and the West.*

Mooney, Paul. "Paramax Defends EH-101 Helicopter Sale." *Gazette* [Montreal] (5 March 1993): D3.

– "There's No Political Plot to Funnel Defence Bids to Quebec, Experts Say." *Gazette* [Montreal] (5 May 1992): B5.

Moran, Theodore H. "The Globalization of America's Defense Industries: Managing the Threat of Foreign Dependence." *International Security* 15 (Summer 1990): 57–99.

Moravcsik, Andrew. "Arms and Autarky in Modern European History." *Daedalus* 120 (Fall 1991): 23–45.

– "1992 and the Future of the European Armaments Industry." working paper no. 1, RP-90–001, John M. Olin Institute for Strategic Studies, Harvard University, Cambridge, Mass., September 1989.

– "The European Armaments Industry at the Crossroads." *Survival* 32 (January–February 1990): 65–86.

Mortimer, Edward. "European Security After the Cold War." *Adelphi Paper* 271. London: IISS/Brassey's, Summer 1992.

Munro, Neil. "U.S. Cuts Spur Sonobuoy Firms to Look Overseas." *Defense News* (8 June 1992): 8.

"NADIB Manifesto." *Forum* 3 (1988): 4–6.

NADIBO Papers, 12–76/1988. Ottawa: Supply and Services Canada 1988.

Nasar, Sylvia. "The Risky Allure of 'Strategic Trade'." *New York Times* (28 February 1993): 4:1.

National Advisory Board on Science and Technology, Science and Technology. *Innovation and National Prosperity: The Need for Canada to Change Course.* Ottawa: NABSAT 1991.

NATO's Eastern Dilemmas, edited by David G. Haglund, S. Neil MacFarlane, and Joel J. Sokolsky. Boulder: Westview 1994.

New Geopolitics of Minerals (The): Canada and International Resource Trade, edited by David G. Haglund. Vancouver: University of British Columbia Press 1989.

Niemy, Walter (Vice-President and General Manager of the Military Aircraft Division, Bombardier, Canadair). Presentation to the *Financial Post* conference on "The Canadian Defence Industry," 1990.

Nixon, C.R. "Defence Exports." *National Network News* 2 (15 January 1993): 6–7 ff.

Nonnenmacher, Günther. "Breakthrough in Maastricht." *La Scala* (January–February 1992): 10–13.

"No Rest for Rühe." *Economist* (13 February 1993): 50.

North American Perspectives on European Security, edited by Michael K. Hawes and Joel J. Sokolsky. Lewiston, N.Y.: Edwin Mellen 1990.

North Atlantic Council. "A Comprehensive Concept of Arms Control and Disarmament, Adapted by Heads of State and Government at the Meeting of the North Atlantic Council in Brussels on 29th and 30th May 1989." *NATO Review* 37 (June 1989): 22–7.

– Conference of National Armaments Directors. "Group on NATO Defence Trade: Work Plan." AC/259 (NDT)D/2 (Final), North Atlantic Council, Brussels, 25 October 1991.
– Conference of National Armaments Directors. *Handbook on the Phased Armaments Programming System (PAPS)*. Vol. 1, "PAPS Framework and Procedures," AAP-20. Brussels: NATO International Staff, February 1989.
– Conference of National Armaments Directors. "Initial Investigation of the Feasibility of Improving the Conditions of Defence Trade Between NATO Allies." AC/250–D/1437, North Atlantic Council, Brussels, 12 March 1991.
– Conference of National Armaments Directors. "Report ... on an Initial Investigation of the Feasibility of Improving the Conditions of Defence Trade Between the Allies." C-M (91) 47. Brussels, 21 June 1991.
– "Ministerial Meeting of the North Atlantic Council at Turnberry, UK, 7–8 June 1990."
North Atlantic Treaty Organization. *Handbook on the Phased Armaments Programming System (PAPS)*. Vol. 1: PAPS Framework and Procedures, AAP-20. Brussels: NATO International Staff, February 1989.
– "Interlocking Institutions: The Conference on Security and Cooperation in Europe (CSCE)." *Basic Fact Sheet* 6. Brussels: NATO Office of Information and Press, September 1993.
– "London Declaration on a Transformed North Atlantic Alliance, 5–6 July 1990." Brussels: NATO Office of Information and Press, July 1990.
– "NATO Code of Conduct in Defence Trade." *Working Paper* AC/254(NDT)WP/2. Brussels, NATO, 2 December 1991.
– "NATO's New Force Structures." *Basic Fact Sheet* 5. Brussels: NATO Office of Information and Press, September 1993.
– Note by Belgian NADREP for circulation to all other NADREPs, regarding "Key Issues" paper of the Defence Trade study group, AC/259(NDT)D/4, 23 September 1991. Brussels: NATO, 11 November 1991.
– "Statement on the Resolution of Problems Concerning the CFE Treaty." *NATO Review* 39 (June 1991): 27.
– Chairman, Expert Team on Defence Trade Statistics. *Defence Trade Statistics: Expert Team*, ED(91)176. Brussels: NATO, 6 December 1991.
– Defence Procurement Policy Officer. "Issues Relating to the Development of a Code of Conduct in Defence Trade," DS/DCPS(91)108. Brussels, 2 December 1991.
– Director, Economics Directorate. "Expert Team on the Improvement of Statistics on Defence Trade Among Alliance Members." ED/(91) 119. Brussels, 25 September 1991.
Nye, Joseph S. Jr. "The Contribution of Strategic Studies: Future Challenges." *Adelphi Paper* 235. London: International Institute for Strategic Studies, Spring 1989, 20–34.

Nye, Joseph S. Jr., and Sean M. Lynn-Jones. "International Security Studies: A Report of a Conference on the State of the Field." *International Security* 12 (Spring 1988): 5–27.

Olson, Mancur, and Richard Zeckhauser. "An Economic Theory of Alliances." *Review of Economics and Statistics* 48 (1965).

Ontario, Government of. Ministry of Industry, Trade and Technology. *Aerospace/Defence Directory.* Toronto, 1990.

OTA: see U.S. Congress, Office of Technology Assessment.

Owen, Seth. "Job Hunting: New Roles for America's Military." *Defense Media Review* 6 (September 1992): 6.

Pastor, Robert A. *Congress and the Making of U.S. Foreign Economic Policy, 1929–1976.* Berkeley: University of California Press 1980.

Peden, Murray. *Fall of an Arrow.* Toronto: Stoddart 1979.

Pentland, Charles C. "Europe 1992 and the Canadian Response." In *After the Cold War,* 125–44.

– "Integration, Interdependence and Institutions: Approaches to International Order." In *World Politics,* 173–96.

Pepall, Lynne M., and D. M. Shapiro. "The Military-Industrial Complex in Canada." *Canadian Public Policy* 15 (September 1989): 265–84.

Pinder, John. *European Community: The Building of a Union.* Oxford, U.K.: Oxford University Press 1991.

Pietrucha, Bill. "Contractors Cautiously Diversify Product Lines." *Defense News* (22 July 1991): 20.

Pipes, Richard. "The Soviet Union Adrift." *Adelphi Paper* 283. London: International Institute for Strategic Studies, December 1993, 70–87.

Pitts, Gordon. *Storming the Fortress: How Canadian Business Can Conquer Europe in 1992.* Toronto: HarperCollins 1990.

Polsky, Debra. "Continued Upswing in FMC Profits May Prove Elusive." *Defense News* (11 May 1992): 24.

– "Diversity, Profits Guide Firms' Guns-to-Butter Conversion." *Defense News* (3 February 1992): 12.

– "Hughes' Missile Reach to Soar If Bid for GD Unit Wins." *Defense News* (11 May 1992): 16.

– "U.S. Industry Decries 'Industrial Darwinism'." *Defense News* (14 October 1991): 4.

"Pork and Bases." *Globe and Mail* (4 June 1992): A18.

Preeg, Ernest H. "The U.S. Leadership Role in World Trade: Past, Present, and Future." *Washington Quarterly* 15 (Spring 1992): 81–91.

Procurement Policy: The Way We Do Business. Ottawa: Supply and Services Canada 1992.

Pugliese, David. "Base Closure Delays May Impair Canada Equipment Buys." *Defense News* (22 June 1992): 43.

– "Bombardier, Ontario Purchase de Havilland." *Defense News* (27 January 1992): 41.
– "Canada Reviews Last EH-101 Bid." *Defense News* (6 April 1992): 16.
– "Canada to Take Over Troubled Refit of Destroyers." *Defense News* (29 July 1991): 22.
– "Canada Unveils $1.8 Billion Procurement Program." *Defense News* (13 April 1992, 34.
– "Canadian Lawmakers Fret over Saudi Ship Buy." *Defense News* (28 September 1992): 3.
– "Canadian Shipbuilders Seek Help." *Defense News* (13 April 1992): 16.
– "Canadian Shipbuilding Industry Wants Return of Subsidy Program." *Defense News* (12 August 1991): 4.
– "Canadian Warriors Seek New Enemies." *Toronto Star* (16 October 1992): A19.
– "EC Blocks Merger of de Havilland." *Defense News* (14 October 1991): 12.
– "Paramax Insists Spin-Off by Unisys Will Have Little Impact on Business." *Defense News* (7 October 1991): 30–1.
Purver, Ron. "The Contemporary Armaments Trade." *CSIS Commentary* 33 (July 1993).
Ratner, Jonathan, and Celia Thomas. "The Defence Industrial Base and Foreign Supply of Defence Goods." *Defence Economics* 2 (1990): 57–68.
RCN in Transition (The), 1910–1985, edited by W.A.B. Douglas. Vancouver: University of British Columbia Press 1988.
Real Worlds of Canadian Politics (The): Cases in Process and Policy. Peterborough, Ont.: Broadview 1989.
Reconstituting America's Defense: The New U.S. National Security Strategy, edited by James J. Tritten and Paul N. Stockton. New York: Praeger 1992.
Regehr, Ernie. *Arms Canada: The Deadly Business of Military Exports*. Toronto: James Lorimer 1987.
Reilly, Lucy. "Dark Days Arrive at DARPA." *New Technology Week* 4 (30 April 1990): 1–5.
Rempel, Roy. "Canada's Troop Deployments in Germany: Twilight of a Forty-Year Presence?" in *Homeward Bound?*
Rhodes, Carolyn. "The Evolving Japanese-United States Relationship: Reprioritizing the Foreign Policy Agenda." Paper presented to the Queen's conference on "Japan, the United States and Canada: The Political Economy of System Change." Queen's University Centre for International Relations, Kingston, Ont., October 1990.
Richardson, J. David. "The Political Economy of Strategic Trade Policy." *International Organization* 44 (Winter 1990): 107–35.
Risse-Kappen, Thomas. "Did 'Peace Through Strength' End the Cold War? Lessons from INF." *International Security* 16 (Summer 1991): 162–88.
Rogers, Marc. "Europeans in the USA: Easing Traffic on the Two-Way Street." *Jane's Defence Weekly* (21 December 1991).

Rogov, Sergey. "International Security and the Collapse of the Soviet Union." *Washington Quarterly* 15 (Spring 1992): 15–28.
- "Military Reform: Now or Never." *European Security* 1 (Spring 1992): 5–12.
- "The Changing Defense Posture of the USSR." In *Homeward Bound?*, 113–31.

Rohmer, Richard. "Giving Quebecers the Facts." *Toronto Sun* (22 May 1992): 18.

Romain, Ken. "Deal Moves Bombardier into Aerospace Elite." *Globe and Mail* (24 January 1992): B1.

Ross, Elizabeth. "The Defense Industry of Connecticut." *Christian Science Monitor* (27 November 1992): 10–11.

Rubin, Barnett R. "The Fragmentation of Tajikistan." *Survival* 35 (Winter 1993–94): 71–91.

Rupp, Rainer. "Progress Towards a More United Europe, Likely Impact on Defence Industrial Development." Paper presented to the NATO Defence Economics Workshop, Brussels, 15–17 May 1991.

Russett, Bruce, and James S. Sutterlin. "The U.N. in a New World Order." *Foreign Affairs* 70 (Spring 1991): 69–83.

Ryan, David (Minister Counsellor [Commercial], Canadian Embassy, Washington]. "Defence Sales in the USA: Is There Still a Market?" Presentation to the *Financial Post* conference on "Canada's Defence Industry," 1991.

Sabin, Philip A.G. "British Strategic Priorities in the 1990s." *Adelphi Paper* 254. London: IISS/Brassey's, Winter 1990.

Sandor, R.G. (Director, International Defence Programs, Aerospace and Marine Division, EAITC). "Notes for a Speech" at the Defence Resources Management Course. Kingston, Ont., 31 October 1990.

Saunders, John. "Defence Jobs Under Fire." *Globe and Mail* (20 March 1993): B4.

Schmemann, Serge. "Russia and Its Nasty Neighborhood Brawls." *New York Times* (18 October 1992): 4:1, 3.

Schmidt, Peter. "The Evolution of European Security Structures: Master Plan or Trial and Error?" In *From Euphoria to Hysteria*, 145–66.

Schrempp, Jürgen E. "Security and Economy: A European Standpoint." Paper presented to the 31st Munich Conference on Security Policy. Munich, 5 February 1994.

Schumacher, Brian. Presentation to the *Financial Post* conference on "The Defence Industry."

Scott, Gavin J. "Canada's Defence Industrial Base: Can It Support the Requirements of the Defence White Paper 'Challenge and Commitment: A Defence Policy for Canada, June 1987'?" Paper for the National Defence College of Canada. Kingston, Ont., April 1988.

Selected Problems in Formulating Foreign Economic Policy, edited by Denis Stairs and Gilbert R. Winham. Royal Commission on the Economic Union and Development Prospects for Canada. Toronto: University of Toronto Press 1985.

Shadwick, Martin. "Focus on Defence Industries in Ottawa." *Canadian Defence Quarterly* 20 (October 1990): S1–S18.

Shape of the New Europe (The), edited by Gregory F. Treverton. New York: Council on Foreign Relations Press 1992.

Shaw, E.K. *There Never Was an Arrow.* Toronto: Steel Rail 1979.

Shea, Jamie. "NATO's Eastern Dimension: New Roles for the Alliance in Securing the Peace in Europe." *Canadian Defence Quarterly* 22 (March 1993): 55–62.

Shehadi, Kamal S. "Ethnic Self-determination and the Break-up of States." *Adelphi Paper* 283. London: International Institute for Strategic Studies, December 1993.

Shevtsova, Lilia. "The August Coup and the Soviet Collapse." *Survival* 34 (Spring 1992): 5–18.

Silverberg, David. "Aspin Outlines Plan for Industrial Base." *Defense News* (17 February 1992): 42.

– "Atwood Rebuts Industry Concerns Over Buying Strategy." *Defense News* (4 May 1992): 12.

– "Compromise Defense Production Act May Face Presidential Veto." *Defense News* (15 October 1990): 72.

– "Defense Industry Breathes Relief." *Defense News* (16 November 1992): 31.

– "DoD Will Guard LTV Technology." *Defense News* (4 May 1992): 10.

– "EEC Import Plan Draws Rebuke From Carlucci." *Defense News* (12 September 1988): 1.

– "LTV Sale Stirs Little French Interest, Spurs DoD Probe." *Defense News* (11 May 1992): 8.

– "Proposed Defense Production Act Tightens Offset Parts." *Defense News* (28 May 1990).

Simon, Jeffrey. "Does Eastern Europe Belong in NATO?" *Orbis* 37 (Winter 1993): 21–35.

Simons, John (president and chief executive officer, Canadian Marconi Company). Presentation to the *Financial Post* conference on "Canada's Defence Industry," 1991.

Sims, Calvin. "For Weapons Makers, a Time to Deal." *New York Times* (17 January 1993): 3:1, 6.

Skibbie, Lawrence. Presentation to the *Financial Post* conference on "Canada's Defence Industry," 1991.

Snyder, Jack. "Nationalism and Instability in the Former Soviet Empire." *Arms Control: Contemporary Security Policy* 12 (December 1991): 6–16.

Sokolsky, Joel J. "After the 'Maritime Strategy': The United States Navy in the Post-Cold War Era." In *Can America Remain Committed?*, 163–88.

'Soviet Threat' Revisited (The), edited by S. Neil MacFarlane; *Martello Papers* 3. Kingston: Queen's University Centre for International Relations 1992.

Spero, Joan E. *The Politics of International Economic Relations*, 3d ed. New York: St. Martin's 1985.

Stein, Robert M., and Theodore A. Postol. "Patriot Experience in the Gulf War." *International Security* 17 (Summer 1992): 199–240.

Steinberg, James B. *The Transformation of the European Defense Industry: Emerging Trends and Prospects for Future U.S.-European Competition and Collaboration in Defense.* Rand Corporation report prepared for the Office of the Under-Secretary of Defense for Acquisition. Washington, D.C.: Department of Defense, April 1991.

Stewart, Greig. *Shutting Down the National Dream: A.V. Roe and the Tragedy of the Avro Arrow.* Toronto: McGraw-Hill Ryerson 1988.

Steyn, Julian J., and Thomas B. Meade. "Potential Impact of Arms Reduction on LWR Fuel Cycle." Paper presented to the U.S. Council for Energy Awareness, Fuel Cycle '92 Conference, Charleston, S.C., March 1992

Story, Jonathan. "La Communauté européenne et la défense de l'Europe." *Studia Diplomatica* 41, 3 (1988): 272–4.

Strategic Business Research Group. *Europe 1991: Your Business Opportunity.* Ottawa: Prospectus Investment & Trade Partners 1989.

Street, Simon. *Defence Bulletin*, Sector Review. London: Barclays de Zoete Wedd Research 1990.

Stuart, Douglas. "NATO's Future as a Pan-European Security Institution." *NATO Review* 4 (August 1993): 15–19.

Sturgeon, Ray. Presentation to the *Financial Post* conference on "The Canadian Defence Industry," 1992.

Stützle, Walther. "NATO Commander Galvin Looks at U.S. Troop Cuts in Europe, New Defence Priorities." *German Tribune* (31 January 1992): 5–6.

Sullivan, Mark (Director, Strategic Planning, McDonnell Douglas). Presentation to the conference on "Reconstitution: Force Structure and Industrial Strategy." John M. Olin Institute for Strategic Studies, Harvard University, Boston, 7–8 May 1992.

Taft IV, William H. "Prospects for a NATO Defense Trade Agreement." Paper prepared for the CSIS study on the "Atlantic Partnership: Building an Alliance Industrial Technology Base." Washington, 29 November 1990.

Technology and the Future of Europe: Global Competition and the Environment in the 1990s, edited by Christopher Freeman, Margaret Sharp, and William Walker. London: Pinter 1991.

Thain, Donald H. "The War Without Bullets." *Business Quarterly* 55 (Summer 1990): 13–19.

Thomas, Beth L. "The Environment for Expanding the North American Defence Industrial Base." In *Canada's Defence Industrial Base*, 220–37.

Thomas, R. "Canadian Annual Procurement Strategy." Speech to the Canadian Industrial Benefits Association, Ottawa, February 1990.

Tiersky, Ronald. "France in the New Europe." *Foreign Affairs* 71 (Spring 1992).

Todd, Dave. "On the Defensive: Canadian Defence Industry Faces Stiff Competition as U.S. Looks Inward." *Ottawa Citizen* (11 November 1992): A2.

Toward Political Union: Planning a Common Foreign and Security Policy in the European Community, edited by Reinhardt Rummel. Baden-Baden: Nomos Verlagsgesellschaft 1992.

Towards a Stronger Europe. Report by an independent study team established by Defence Ministers of the Nations of the Independent European Programme Group to Make Proposals to Improve the Competitiveness of Europe's Defence Equipment Industry, vols. 1 and 2. Brussels: IEPG 1986.

Transformation of an Alliance (The): The Decisions of NATO's Heads of State and Government. Brussels: NATO Office of Information and Press 1992.

Trebilcock, Michael J. *The Political Economy of Economic Adjustment: The Case of Declining Sectors,* Royal Commission on the Economic Union and Development Prospects for Canada, vol. 8. Toronto: University of Toronto Press 1986.

Treddenick, John M. "Regional Impacts of Defence Spending." In *Guns and Butter.*

– "The Defence Budget." In *Canada's International Security Policy* (forthcoming).

– "The Economic Significance of the Canadian Defence Industrial Base." In *Canada's Defence Industrial Base,* 15–48.

Tucker, Michael. *Canadian Foreign Policy: Contemporary Issues and Themes.* Toronto: McGraw-Hill Ryerson 1980.

Turenne Sjolander, Claire. "Managing International Trade: The United States, Trade Protection, and the GATT." Paper presented to the Annual Meeting of the Canadian Political Science Association, Kingston, Ont., June 1991.

"2-War Military Budget Goes to Congress." *International Herald Tribune* (8 February 1994): 5.

Tychonick, Rus. "Canada and the Arms Trade." *Strategic Datalink.* Toronto: Canadian Institute of Strategic Studies 1993.

United Kingdom, Foreign and Commonwealth Office. "Institutions of the European Community." *Background Brief* 1. Ottawa: British Information Services, February 1994.

United States Congress, Office of Technology Assessment, *Arming Our Allies: Cooperation and Competition in Defense Technology,* OTA-ISC-449. Washington: U.S. Government Printing Office, May 1990.

– *After the Cold War: Living with Lower Defence Spending,* OTA-ITE-524. Washington: U.S. Government Printing Office, 1992.

United States Government. *Budget of the U.S. Government, FY 1992.* Washington: U.S. Government Printing Office 1991.

– Department of Defense. *Critical Technologies Plan,* AD-A219300. Prepared for the Committees on Armed Services, United States Congress. Washington: U.S. Government Printing Office, 15 March 1990.

– Department of Defense. "Primer on Reconstitution Policy." Office of Strategic Competitiveness, Principal Deputy Under Secretary of Defense for Strategy and Resources. Draft copy, 1992.

- General Accounting Office. *European Initiatives: Implications for U.S. Defense Trade and Cooperation.* Report to the Chairman, Subcommittee on Investigations, Committee on Armed Services, House of Representatives, GAO/NSIAD-91-167 (April 1991).
- General Accounting Office, *NATO: A Changing Alliance Faces New Challenges,* GAO/NSIAD-92-252. Washington, D.C., July 1992.

U.S.-Canada Security Relationship: The Politics, Strategy, and Technology of Defense (The), edited by David G. Haglund and Joel J. Sokolsky. Boulder: Westview 1989.

van den Muyzenberg, Laurens, and Godfrey Spickernell. "Restructuring in the Defence Industry: A Survey of Acquisition Strategies in Europe and the U.S.A. in the Light of Possible Solutions to NATO Procurement Problems." H.B. Maynard Management Consultants [undated].

Van Evera, Stephen. "Primed for Peace: Europe After the Cold War." *International Security* 15 (Winter 1990/91): 7–57.

Van Steenburg, Robert. "An Analysis of Canadian-American Defence Economic Cooperation: The History and Current Issues." In *Canada's Defence Industrial Base,* 189–219.

Vastel, Michel. "L'armée des autres." *L'Actualité* (January 1993): 38–40.

Vernon, Raymond, and Debora L. Spar. *Beyond Globalism: Remaking American Foreign Economic Policy.* New York: Free Press 1989.

von Hippel, Frank. "Control and Disposition of Nuclear-Weapons Materials." Paper presented to the U.S. Council for Energy Awareness, Fuel Cycle '92 Conference, Charleston, S.C., March 1992.

Walker, William. "Defence." In *Technology and the Future of Europe.*

Walker, William, and Philip Gummett. "Britain and the European Armaments Market." *International Affairs* 65 (Summer 1989).

- "Nationalism, Internationalism and the European Defence Market." *Chaillot Papers* 9. Paris: Institute for Security Studies, Western European Union, September 1993.

Wall, P.H. "Defence and Industrial Policy in Western Industrialized Countries: The Case of Canada." Staff note no. 2, National Defence College, Centre for Studies in Defence Resources Management, Kingston, Ont., 1989.

- "The Economic Impact of Canadian Defence Expenditures, FY1989/90 Update." Report no. 21, Centre for Studies in Defence Resources Management, Kingston, Ont., Fall 1991.

Wallace, Helen. "What Europe for Which Europeans?" In *Shape of the New Europe,* 15–34.

Ward, John. "Critics of New Helicopters Like Them, but Price Tag Gives Them Ammunition." *Gazette* [Montreal] (11 March 1993): F3.

Watson, Laurie. "Building Frigates in Canada Costs the Country a Huge Premium." *Forum* 6 (October 1991): 14–15.

- "Quebec's Defence Industrial Base: Numbers Show Province Holding Its Own." *Forum* 7 (September 1992): 18.

Wegener, Henning. "The Management of Change: NATO's Anniversary Summit." *NATO Review* 37 (June 1989): 1–7.

Weiss, Thomas G., and Laura S. Hayes Holgate. "Opportunities and Obstacles for Collective Security After the Cold War." In *Building a New Global Order*, 258–83.

Werier, Val. "Helicopter Purchase Is Insane." *Winnipeg Free Press* (17 March 1993): A6.

"West's Arms Industry Faces Slump." *Manchester Guardian Weekly* (26 April 1992): 11.

What is European Security after the Cold War? Brussels: Philip Morris Institute for Public Policy Research 1993.

"What Kind of World and Whose Order?" *Peace and Security* 6 (Spring 1991).

White, Robert C. Jr. "NATO in the 1990s: The Burden-Sharing Debate." In *North American Perspectives on European Security*, 153–82.

Witt, Michael J. "Britain's General Electric May Buy Missile Division from British Aerospace." *Defense News* (24 February 1992): 40.

– "Plessey Runs Out of Room to Avoid Hostile Takeover." *Defense News* (7 August 1989): 1.

Wolfe, Robert. "The World in a Grain of Wheat: Farm Wars and European Security." In *From Euphoria to Hysteria*.

Woods, Peter E. "Defence Procurement Issues and Challenges." *Forum* 8 (December 1993): 10–11.

World Politics: Power, Interdependence and Dependence, edited by David G. Haglund and Michael K. Hawes. Toronto: Harcourt Brace Jovanovich, Canada 1990.

Wörner, Manfred (Secretary General of NATO). "Speech … to the Canadian Association of NATO Defense College Anciens." *Symposium Proceedings*. Ottawa: Canadian Association of NATO Defense College Anciens, October 1991.

Yates, Ivan. "Market Forces and the Defence Industries." *RUSI Journal* (Winter 1989): 59.

York, Geoffrey. "Copter Contract Casts Long Shadows." *Globe and Mail* (11 March 1993): A9.

– "Military Helicopters May Turn into Tory Campaign Issue." *Globe and Mail* (6 March 1993): A1.

– "Ottawa Lacks Defence Conversion Plan, Liberals Charge." *Globe and Mail* (27 March 1993): A8.

– "Rejecting the Peace Dividend." *Globe and Mail* (31 March 1992): A4–5.

– "Report Proposes New Process for Closing Military Bases." *Globe and Mail* (2 June 1992): A4.

– "Thousands of Jobs Placed at Risk, Liberals Charge." *Globe and Mail* (27 March 1993): A4.

Yost, William J. *Industrial Mobilization in Canada*. Ottawa: Conference of Defence Associations 1983.

Young, Christopher. "Campbell's Controversial Helicopters Deserve to Get the Chop." *Ottawa Citizen* (14 March 1993): B5.

Young, Thomas-Durell. "Reforming NATO's Command and Control Structures." *Arms Control: Contemporary Security Policy* 12 (December 1991): 27–43.

Your Way to the Government Market: Access to the Federal Procurement Database. Ottawa: Supply and Services Canada 1990.

Index